Transition from Military to Civilian Life

How to Plan a Bright Future <u>Now</u> for You and Your Family

Merle Dethlefsen

and

James D. Canfield

Foreword by James M. McCoy, CMSAF (Ret.)

Stackpole Books

Published by
STACKPOLE BOOKS
Cameron and Kelker Streets
P. O. Box 1831
Harrisburg, PA 17105

Illustrations by Jake Schuffert.

Printed in the U.S.A.

Library of Congress Cataloging in Publication Data

Dethlefsen, Merle
    Transition from military to civilian life.

    Bibliography: p.
    1. Retired military personnel—United States.
2. Retired military personnel—Life skill guides.
3. Retired military personnel—Employment. I. Canfield,
James D. II. Title.
UB357.D48 1984   355.1'14   84-10536
ISBN 0-8117-2190-6

Contents

Foreword

Those who serve in our country's armed forces do so because they believe that what they're doing is important. In the services, most young adults get valuable training and experience that simply cannot be obtained elsewhere. But even in the military such experience isn't free. Coping with the constant moves, family separations, and impossible requirements under the most unbelievable conditions, demands a full measure of dedication and responsibility.

Young military people accept these demands and build upon the experiences. As they advance within their service, their responsibilities increase constantly. Those nearing the end of a military career have faced and solved problems that are beyond comprehension—except to those who have "been there." Now they are senior in rank and experience, yet young enough in age to build a successful second career. After twenty or thirty years, they have the right answer to just about any situation—or know exactly where to get it.

Knowledge of how to obtain proper and timely support is every bit as important to military success as knowing one's own mission. In a profession requiring thousands of equally vital skills, every endeavor is a team effort. Each member of the team counts upon the others, and in turn is counted upon by them. So, even though a service career develops superbly capable leaders, it does so within a unique system—one in which even the maverick depends upon support from others—and gets it.

At retirement time, the entire system functions at its very best. The processing, physicals, parades, parties, movement of household goods, clearing of government quarters, and farewells all are accomplished with lightning speed. Then it's over.

What now for these fine, capable, and still young leaders? Where is the team? To whom do they turn? How should they have prepared? What can be done now? The system, as they knew it, is no longer in place. For many military retirees, they are now, for the first time, really on their own. It's a mighty lonesome feeling.

During more than thirty years' service, I was a witness to many sweeping changes in the armed forces. Among those was the development and constant improvement of retirement services. The retirement briefings and outprocessing procedures provided at each installation do the best they can to prepare the potential retiree for what lies ahead. Many join or continue to be a member of their respective service association to keep up on the latest developments that will affect them in the future. Additionally, through the retiree affairs offices and service newsletters the military retiree is kept informed of legislative matters and other changes.

Let there be no doubt, the services *do* take care of their own—while it's possible. But that is the official side of retirement. The personal side of the process cannot be delegated to anyone else. It cannot be handled by another member of "the team." Strangely, the personal side of retirement is generally the only problem. It's a problem no one wants to discuss.

In this book, Merle Dethlefsen and Dave Canfield go far beyond mere discussion. They help us separate what is really important from what only appears to be, and show us the importance of setting the appropriate priorities.

Reading this book is an excellent first step for anyone contemplating military retirement. As the authors show, their goals are to get the reader thinking in realistic terms, and to encourage further research and planning. They accomplish this and more. Using examples from conversations and interviews with active and retired military members and their families they start out by easing the mind of each of us who wonders, "Am I the only one having this problem?"

For a successful, comfortable move from military service into civilian life, some actions must be taken before others. The market is flooded with books describing how civilians should change careers, how they should plan their finances, or how they should pursue the right job. Parts of those books apply to military retirees. But none combine the unique nature of a military retirement and establishing oneself as a civilian.

The authors argue convincingly that a person completing military service should also be highly successful as a civilian. I share that belief. That success depends, as it always has, upon preparation. No one can do it better than those who will be reading this book.

James M. McCoy, CMSAF (Ret.)

Preface

If you are a career service person, this book is about you. We're going to talk about retiring from the military and your transition to civilian life. If you always thought you would just hang up your uniform one day and take it easy from there on—this book is for you. If you always thought you would just step right into a high-level job because of your "leadership" skills or "administrative and managerial expertise"—this book is for you.

Do you know anyone who really planned for military retirement? Few of us do. We have friends who said they "couldn't wait." But that isn't planning; that's anticipation. Most of us know families who, although they spent four years at their last duty station, still got caught in the last-minute rush on retirement day.

Transition to civilian life is a greater challenge than most of us dream. With little or no planning, it can be a real trauma for the service family. Those with goals within the military career, but not beyond, might never adjust to the change. This transition should be the start of a happy, contented, and well-earned period of your life. Proper planning and preparation can make it just that.

We began this book at our offices in Texas.* In an area with a large military population and huge corporations that thrive on defense contracts (and employ many former military people), we saw many of

_____

*Transition Management Institute, P.O. Box 8501, Fort Worth TX 76112.

the problems related to the military-to-civilian transition. Every day or so we met someone who was planning to retire from the military or had already done so. Those who were on a job search were just drifting, without any real plan.

We saw classic cases of the old "square peg in a round hole" adage. Military retirees, totally out of the fields for which they had trained, were bored and underpaid in jobs grabbed out of desperation. Just as frequently, we talked with executives whose companies were having a tough time locating certain skills and talents.

We often thought, if only we could get the two together—the talent and the need. Employers are hurting for medical technicians while experienced ones are coming out of the service and working on assembly lines.

We began work on special seminars designed just for military families, and we're pleased with the results. But we must be realistic— military families don't usually plan for civilian life.

This book evolved, you might say, to fill that void. We organized the key seminar points under one cover, and we hope at least to grab your attention.

This is not one of those "how-to" books that makes it all seem like a lark. Transition to civilian life after a full service career is not a lark. Don't let anyone tell you it is. But with proper planning, you can make it an event to look forward to rather than one to dread.

Unless you are phenomenally lucky, the success of your transition will be in direct proportion to your preparation. In that regard, this book is but one of many you should read. We believe you should read it first. Our goal is to get you thinking about the items discussed in this book. Once you do, you will recognize what individual action is needed. We got our fair share of advice from professionals as we compiled this material, and we hope it will help you get started.

When we sought help and advice from organizations such as the American Association of Retired Persons (AARP) and the International Society of Preretirement Planners (ISPP), their response was superb. Once we convinced service-related retiree organizations that we weren't competing (in truth, we recommend most of them), they also were of great assistance.

The basic difference between this book and others is that we discuss the human aspects of the transition. Most military retirees will tell you that the most significant adjustments were within themselves, and they felt very much alone at the time. Beyond a doubt, the most meaningful input came from military retirees and their families. You also should seek this advice at every opportunity.

Introduction

Military retirement is *not* retirement. It is a beginning of a new way of life and the end of another. It marks the completion of one career and the first day of a new one. It represents the greatest life-style change most of us will ever experience. It means planting some roots after decades of moving every two or three years. It may be the end of family separations. Old stresses are replaced by new ones. Everything changes. Military retirement is many things to those who experience it, but it's rarely *real* retirement.

Rather than think of it as retirement, with all the laid-back attitudes that word brings forth, we should consider retirement from military service as a mid-life career change. If, for the last half of our military careers, we would plan for a complete career switch on a precise date, it would probably go like clockwork. We would know precisely what we want to do and when we would begin doing it.

Military careers are excellent examples of the old carrot-and-stick approach to retention. There are many years between the retirement eligibility date and mandatory retirement. During that period, signifi-cant rewards for years of effort and dedication are just around the corner. No sooner does the military person reap one reward—for example, selection for a prestigious school—and another (perhaps a promotion) seems just within reach. This is perfectly sound management, but it has at least one negative effect: It is difficult for the active-duty person to decide the right time to become a civilian.

The classic question is asked routinely throughout the armed forces, with minor modifications: "Should I retire this year at age 39 and enter the business world or hold on for five more years and retire with a higher government check?" or, "Should I retire this year as a Lieutenant Commander or wait two years and hope for one more promotion?" The possibilities are endless and include many family considerations.

We submit that an even more classic question is: If you have no idea when you'll become a civilian, how can you be ready for it?

Once you know when you will leave active duty, you will also know how much time there is for preparation. Preparation for what? Leaving active duty? The services take care of that. You're processed out with the same efficiency you experienced when you joined. How about preparation for the new job? Well, that's certainly necessary. What *is* the new job? If you can't answer that, how can you prepare for it?

All these questions are part of a much larger one that only you can answer, but you must do it long before leaving the service: What am I going to be?

We believe that those who know what they are going to be and when they are going to make it happen have the transition battle half won. Imagine that you have both of those answers. Any new problems relating to resumes, salary, location, housing, or other requirements are easily addressed because you can be specific. You have narrowed the field, and you can concentrate upon it.

Once you decide upon a realistic job goal, you have some idea about where the jobs are; you know the salary range within which you should begin; you have some idea about what housing you should be able to afford; you can establish some contacts; you can scout out an area with military facilities; and above all, your transition preparation has direction.

Knowing when you will step out of uniform gives you another edge. Without a specific date, your best planning is only contingency planning—which is not what you want for this major event in your life. With a firm date in mind, your transition can now have organization.

Direction and organization. With them, you can begin civilian life with both feet on the ground. Without them, you might drift about until your future is decided for you by necessity.

After several months of conversations with military retirees and those in the process of becoming civilians, we decided to emphasize the human side of the transition. As we gathered information for seminars, we were constantly reminded that the major change is the internal, personal one—not the official one.

It's hard to find anyone nearing military retirement who will admit that he or she is concerned about a job or money. The truth is, just about everyone is concerned about those items. They combine with questions about medical care, benefits, financial planning, inflation, home purchasing, and many others to form a tremendous mental burden.

After the transition is complete—say in about five years—it is not at all hard to find someone who will tell you just how those decisions became a heavy load, caused family strains, and fostered unfamiliar self-doubts. Not only is this person willing to discuss the process and its psychological impact, but he or she is also anxious to pass the information on to help those who are facing the same challenge.

As you read on, you will recognize scenes and situations from your military career. Most of us didn't pay much attention to those who were retiring before us (we discuss that phenomenon also). But now that you are interested enough to start your planning, you might start feeling a touch of empathy for them.

This book touches upon many facets of the military retirement process. If, when you start feeling just a little nervous about it, you realize that your feelings are perfectly normal, we will have reached you. If you take it one step further and begin planning today, we will have accomplished exactly what we desired.

In several chapters we furnish condensed information that should help you decide if you need to pursue the item further or if you can check it off and move on down your list. We made no attempt to make these chapters into detailed references that would stand alone. That would take several shelves of books.

One of the most common needs retirees expressed was for a heart-to-heart talk with other military retirees before planning begins—a talk that has nothing to do with the official side of retirement but rather one that helps prepare the family for the personal aspects of transition to civilian life. They also suggested that we put our material under one cover, to be used as a starting point for personal preparation. We've done it, and we hope the "heart-to-heart" is there also.

One minor frustration: We emphasize that military retirement is not retirement, but that is what it's called. So, there are times when we just have to refer to it by that name. We've tried to make clear whether we are discussing military retirement or *real* retirement.

Start thinking about your transition to civilian life now. By the time you get there, you just might love every minute of it.

> Lose this day loitering; t'will be the same old story tomorrow, and the next more dilatory. . . . Each indecision brings its own delays and days are lost lamenting o'er lost days . . . What you can do or think you can, begin it—boldness has genius, power, and magic in it.
>
> —Goethe

2

The Military Member and the Transition

This chapter is about recognizing what is going to happen, identifying what you want to change, knowing what is beyond your control, and above all realizing that some of the most maddening concerns are normal. The secret, of course, is knowing about it in advance.

Face the Reality

You are going to retire. It doesn't happen only to the other guy. If each of us would just repeat, *"I'm* going to retire," every now and then, it would be a big step in the right direction.

Throughout active duty, we gear our lives to mission accomplishment. If we think about our own retirement, it's usually in a "what I'm going to do when I get out of this chicken outfit" thought, in the middle of another inspection preparation, field exercise, or Sunday alert. Serious consideration and planning come later, when retirement is just around the corner.

Retirement from the service is a major milestone. With reasonable planning it needn't be a traumatic one. Begin that planning within yourself. Recognize that you're going to have plenty of questions swimming around in your head, that the questions are normal, and that you won't have answers to them all right now. Realize that there are thousands in the same situation each year and that they have the same questions—plus some of their own. When doubts surface (and they will), it's important that you know you're in a normal situation, not one you've caused by some oversight or neglect. Once mentally prepared, you'll find it's much easier to look at other aspects of retirement, such as the spouse, the house, the car, finances, insurance, the job market, and the children's education.

At an annual conference of the International Society of Preretirement Planners (ISPP), we participated in discussions on the psychological stresses of retirement. Most participants, with no experience with the military, were astounded to discover that the same stresses and problems occur with military retirees as with civilian retirees. What's the difference between the two? For starters, about a twenty-five to thirty-year age difference. The cause? Twenty or more years of thinking "retirement" instead of "career change."

There aren't many 65-year-old servicemen or servicewomen. The scale for measuring "old" is different in the military than in civilian life. We can recall an OCS Lieutenant (a former NCO) we all called "Pappy." Lord, he was old! He was 28. But he also was only nine years from retirement. A civilian that near to retirement would be about 58—a thirty-year difference.

The catch comes when the military member starts thinking about retirement in the same terms as a civilian who's thirty years older. It happens all the time. Once he starts using the word retirement, it takes on negative terms. Think of the ways we use "retire" in our everyday language. We retire the colors (take them away). Troops are retired from action (pulled back). We retire stocks and bonds (pay them off). Industry retires outdated machinery (junks it). In baseball, the batter or side is retired (put out). Even our dictionary defines retired as: "1. Withdrawn or apart from the world; in seclusion, secluded. 2. . . . that has given up one's work, business, career, etc., esp. because of advanced age."

With a quarter of a century of that kind of thinking, you're bound to have some doubts. You're applying "retire" to *yourself*. Why should it take on a different meaning? It still means old, junk, out of action, go away, quit, withdraw, out, seclusion, and all the other similar terms. And with all that dedication in you, two of those words really grab you: old and quit.

You're neither old nor quitting. As a matter of fact, you're in a most enviable position. Get into the proper frame of mind and fully enjoy it. When thoughts like we just mentioned start gnawing at you, put them into perspective.

If you're going to have any control over this major mid-life transition, you've got to identify exactly what's happening. If you know it's coming, there's every reason to be prepared. Plenty happens during a major career change, especially when it's from the military to civilian life. You must (1) anticipate what's coming, (2) recognize it as normal, and (3) break the transition process into manageable pieces so that you can cope with each challenge as it surfaces.

The *Official* Process: No Big Deal

The first possibility for military retirement is upon completion of twenty years' service. There is some advantage to becoming a civilian then, without further delay. It's much easier to start over at 37 than at 47.

But it always seems there's a promotion just around the corner—if we wait "just a year or so" or, "Perhaps just one more overseas tour . . ."

When it comes to timing, there is no easy answer. Suppose there is no promotion in the near future, but there is a daughter in her junior year, so Dad decides he'll stay on for one more year. At the end of that year, a promotion might be appearing on the horizon. If he waits for the promotion, it might take another year. As a result of the promotion, he may have to serve a "lock in"—a mandatory year or so. What began as a one-year delay now becomes four or five. It is never an easy decision, but unless the service member is being forced out, it's one the individual must make.

How it all happens depends a great deal upon when it happens. In most cases, control of the time factor is available. Seize it! A vital key to successful transition is control. Getting control takes planning, anticipation, and lead time.

On a grand scale, official factors certainly are essential to transition planning. You might have to complete an overseas tour, a service commitment as a result of a school or promotion, or any of the numerous combinations the services offer in unlimited variety. Accept these requirements as given—start with them, if you desire—then get on with your planning, with *you* in the driver's seat.

It is not the grand scale that is likely to cause heartburn. The problem begins when small, routine official requirements take on much more importance than they deserve. It's most apparent when personal decisions are postponed until some trivial, mundane official form is signed. We've all seen it—so many times, in fact, that we may have accepted it as gospel at the time.

The most common example of trivia driving the transition train is when all plans are postponed until the retirement application is signed. It's as though the application includes permission to select a home, decide upon a career, write a resume, make some contacts, discuss it with the family, set a date, review finances, bone up on benefits, or read a few good books on the subject. Even more serious is the almost universal refusal to discuss retirement from the service until the payroll signature is in the little block by the X.

It doesn't stop on retirement day, however. Normally the services allow one year from that date for a final household goods move. This is a good program for many legitimate reasons. But it's amazing how many families leave service life with no idea what's next and use the mandatory movement day as the new deadline for home, job, schooling decisions, and so on.

Starting Now . . .

Research shows that at least 50 percent of military retirees decide when they will retire within six months of that date. Unfortunately, that is when many begin preparing for the transition.

The sooner you plan for transition to civilian life, the smoother it will go. Some of that planning should start years in advance. Some official actions can't take place until near retirement date, but there's no reason to wait until then to become informed.

The official process of military retirement is a series of important events. They must be accomplished, but each of them takes only a few minutes. With the exception of the Survivor Benefit Plan—which you should understand long before decision day—most retirement processing stops are checklist items, designed to ensure that you are properly processed and that the system works.

It is wrong to view the official and personal transition processes as equals. They aren't. So consider the transition to civilian life as a major, significant, personal experience. The official process is merely a series of brief events within the much larger personal one.

Anyone can deal with the official process. Everyone must, so there's no use pondering it. It's much easier than going into the service because the individual knows the system. And, everyone gets much more personal treatment when leaving the service than when joining it. It is over before you know it. You sign the papers, pick up some forms and a new ID card. . . .

But the personal side is much more complex. That's what we are addressing from here on, and it's what you should deal with, starting now.

The *Personal* Process: It *Is* a Big Deal

There are as many personal stories about the transition process as there are individuals who experience it. A person with grown (or

small) children has unique problems, as does a single person. But they
have many problems and solutions in common.

During our research we heard dozens of stories about the personal
retirement process—the one that goes on within the individual. This
process is the greatest challenge of all. In these conversations, we began
to anticipate what was next, and we were usually on target. Occasionally, we got a surprise. Every now and then, just by telling his own
story, a person would surprise himself with a new conclusion. But
there were more similarities than differences. This is important, since
(1) we see that we're not alone, and (2) we can learn from each other.

Rick was an Army Master Sergeant, with twenty-two years' service. Three months after his retirement, we talked with him about his
experiences between the time he'd made the decision and his final
month on active duty.

> As I look back, I can't believe it, but my early concerns about
> retiring centered on what others would think. I worried that
> I was letting my company down by leaving them at the peak
> of the training cycle. What would become of *my* troops? Maybe
> they really needed me . . .
>
> The commander gave me the same reenlistment lecture
> I got twenty years ago, but now the emphasis was on my
> experience, rather than on my youth and potential.
>
> My friends' reactions hurt most. I still haven't really sorted
> it out. Almost to the man, they said something like, "You
> don't want to do that—hang in there, at least until the E9 list
> comes out." Or, "I never thought I'd see the day when you'd
> quit." Every comment made me wonder if I'd done the right
> thing. In fact, as each day passed, I became more convinced
> I was screwing up royally.
>
> I owned a few acres in Tennessee, and I always thought
> about how great it would be to get back there, build a home,
> buy some horses, and do a little "light" farming. A friend
> reminded me that 44 is no age to start farming. As retirement
> neared, my confidence cracked, then crumbled a little every
> time I talked or thought about it.
>
> One young squad leader asked me, "Sarge, how many
> times have you been home since you joined?" I told him I
> figured about ten or twelve, counting emergency leaves. "Well,"
> he said, "don't you think there've been a lot of changes since
> you left? Most of your friends are probably gone. At least
> they've changed, for sure." I thought about that young buck's
> comments, believe me. From the mouths of babes . . .
>
> My wife, Becky, and I had talked some about retirement,

but until I announced the decision I had no idea how little we
had communicated. I got the feeling that, for the first time,
she realized I was serious. With the kids, it seemed like the
decision was a total surprise. In fact, I guess it was. They'd
heard old Dad talk about going back to the farm for years.
They'd heard it so much they didn't believe me.

I had this mental picture of the family together, sharing everything and enjoying life with no Christmas duty, midnight call-ups, or separations. It would be my only chance, I thought, because Susan, my daughter, was a junior in high school, and would be off to college, married, or working in a year or so. Eric was in the eighth grade. I knew he would love the farm. Wrong, again. Neither of the kids wanted to move.

Becky suggested I go to Tennessee for ten days or so to get a feel for what was needed. I wanted to save the leave time so that I'd get paid for it on retirement day. We'd been arguing about everything and it didn't seem worth it, so I went. That trip was a stroke of luck for me—a stroke of genius on Becky's part. She says she had no idea how it would turn out, but I'm not sure I believe that.

I beat around the old town for four days, visiting everyone and looking over my land. I located three of my high school friends. I was a little surprised at how quickly we ran out of things to say. We had just grown in different directions.

I returned from leave early. I'd made one decision. I couldn't go home to stay. I still love it, and I'll visit. But the old hometown and I just don't match up any more. I don't think I'm better than anyone there. No one is. We've just grown apart.

With that decision made, the whole family was relieved. But the relief was temporary. I had eighty-four days until I became a civilian. I had more questions than answers.

If there is a typical situation, this case touches upon it several times—a loving father and husband who wants the best for his family, and a dedicated soldier who wants the best for his outfit, all within one person.

In the above example, early planning and family discussion could have made the decisions much easier. But it is not just during the last days of active duty that timing is important. "Time" and "timing" are among the most critical elements in transition planning. They appear repeatedly throughout the process. The NCO in the above example managed the key decisions as most do—under pressure of time. He wanted perfect timing with regard to his career transition, the children's development, and his departure from his military outfit. Time worked against him as his retirement date neared and pressures compounded. He discovered his vision of life "back home" had become clouded by time. Everything had changed over the period he'd been gone.

The military is the epitome of teamwork. Every person has a specific mission, and each depends upon others. From the first day in uniform, a dedication to the "outfit," to superiors, and, in particular, to subordinates is developed. After a career in such an environment, it is natural to worry a little about the young troops and to feel guilty about leaving them.

The feeling of being indispensable doesn't affect only commanders and noncommissioned officers in leadership positions. In fact, it's equally common to staff jobs (for an extreme example, check anyone in a Washington staff position). But when it's time to ease out of the picture, it's also time to recall a rule everyone learns early in a service career: If your organization can't run without you, something's wrong.

Concern about what others think of your retirement would shock only someone who has never been around the military service. Perhaps it's a result of the dedication and teamwork we just mentioned. Some say it's just insecurity. Everyone is going to get out sooner or later. Those who are in control of their own situation are far ahead of the pack. There is no need to feel guilty about retirement from the service.

Attachment to the past—to a childhood home, for example—is perfectly natural. A visit (we recommend a long one) might reveal how much things have changed. Although little may have changed physically, memories of the old hometown frequently are distorted by youth and clouded by the passage of time. (Notice how much shorter the streets seem now and how much smaller the old neighborhood seems!)

Most home vistis during military service are accompanied by some pressures—emergency leaves for illnesses or funerals, a quick trip for a wedding or graduation, or a visit with grandparents on the way overseas.

It may be tough to be objective, but it pays to visit the old hometown for the sole purpose of sizing it up for the future. There's a place for nostalgia and sentiment, and perhaps those factors will play an important role in some retirement decisions. Nothing's wrong with a strong attachment to the home of your ancestors and childhood. But plenty is wrong with allowing it to overpower judgment about jobs, friends, climate, social activities, real estate, and the myriad other "hard-core" details of pre-retirement planning.

Sooner or later, childhood friends, with whom we once had everything in common, realize that "everything" was twelve years in a small school in a tightly knit community. Except for an occasional encounter, most military retirees haven't experienced anything in common with their schoolmates for over a quarter of a century. After a brief conversation with these friends, we sometimes find the silence deafening. Unrealistic expectations that it will be just like old times will almost certainly be disappointing.

The day arrives when idle chatter about the transition becomes

serious conversation. Then it's time for everyone in the family to contribute to the decision. No more assuming that what is good for the
service member is good for the entire family. Military families are
renowned for their remarkable ability to adjust to new situations, but
that trait is born of necessity. Most aspects of the transition move are
within the control of the person leaving the service, and the entire
family deserves the best.

Many military retirees take short leaves just to plan their transition.
At the time, it may seem wise to save leave time and collect the pay.
But the end result may be, as the old saying goes, "penny wise and
pound foolish." The time spent checking out a tentative home, job, or
other facet of the civilian world will almost surely pay greater dividends
than the few dollars saved by not taking leave. It's worth it.

Adjusting Your Life-style

For some, the life-style change outweighs all other considerations.

We talked with Paul, a Navy Commander, at a local restaurant,
as he was in his final week of active duty. He and his wife, Sharon,
were getting ready for civilian life. He was relaxed and (this is unusual)
ready to unload about his retirement concerns.

> You know why I went to that Kiwanis meeting today? That's
> been my only contact with the civilian community. I've be-
> longed for three years, and those guys are my friends. I hate
> to leave them. It's been refreshing, in a way, to have friends
> who aren't the same people I work with, socialize with, and
> spend the rest of my time with. I stopped by to say goodbye.
> After the luncheon, I had an hour before I met you, and I've
> spent it thinking about friends. It seems to me most of us are
> in a bad spot in the "friends" department.
>
> I once read that most of our friends are job-related. I
> remember thinking about the Navy. Whoever wrote that ar-
> ticle sure didn't understand the service, I thought. When you
> share the way we do, you make a lot of friends. And they are
> friends for life. I know that is true. But it's no consolation,
> because they won't be where we are. As a matter of fact, they
> say you're lucky if you're in touch with five friends two years
> after you retire. Five! After the hundreds of great people we've
> met. Of course, in no other occupation would you find your
> friends almost everywhere in the world . . .
>
> In the service, the people you work with are your neigh-
> bors. Your social life centers upon the same people. You
> depend upon one another and know each other better than a

civilian would know a fellow worker or neighbor in a lifetime. Religious functions, sports, picnics, work, good news, bad news, kids' accomplishments, and a thousand other things are shared. It's like a big family.

Just compare arrival at a new station to moving into your average civilian community. When a new service family moves in, someone from the outfit has already been getting things set up for them. They're met, and the move is made as pleasant as possible. Their coworkers and neighbors want them to like it. They want the new family to feel at home. In two days, the wife has friends, the husband has friends, and the kids (who were heartbroken to leave their old friends) have blended right in. Cooking's no problem while you're moving. The neighbors take care of that. Need a car? No sweat—someone will lend you one.

When you move into a modern civilian community, there's a shock waiting for you. If anyone comes by to say hello, you had better appreciate it because that may be the only visitor you will have. It isn't like in the Navy when you move into a vacancy, and everyone is waiting for you. The civilian community's been getting along just fine without you, and your arrival makes little or no difference. The fact is, they don't need you and really feel they have no need to care about you.

As far as I know, none of the neighbors work where I'll be working. My coworkers don't even know each others' families. So we're breaking into several societies at once: work, home, church, school, friends, and of course the all-inclusive one—civilian life. We will handle it, but it is hard to figure where we fit in.

Where's the Structure? What Is the Structure?

Structure—or lack of it—is one of the most common concerns expressed by those in the transition process. Not necessarily the stereotype structure—procedures, discipline, uniforms and uniformity—but structure in more subtle and diverse senses.

Hardly anyone is surprised by changes at retirement. Everyone expects change far beyond the mere disappearance of the military chain of command. Even the old "company towns" can't compare to the structure of military life. In those towns, the company owned the houses, the company store, and perhaps a saloon or some other businesses. The workers were paid, then turned a good part of their money back to the company through rent and grocery bills.

Compare that to an average military installation where the family obtains medical and dental care, legal services, transportation arrangements, recreational activities, housing (including maintenance), utilities, shopping, religious activities, and educational opportunities. In short, it's a complete social structure.

Military service in itself is not secure. At times it is downright hair-raising. But it's made much more tolerable by the security families feel as part of a tightly knit, closed society. Without the camaraderie, military life could be unbearable.

Now, at transition time, all that will be left behind. If the house is wrong, there's no blaming the Navy, the base housing officer, or the engineers. A new home usually represents most of the family's savings plus a big debt. Before settling on it, the family must consider the climate, location, family, job market, and general quality of life in the new area. If they start in plenty of time, they can actually have fun making the selection despite some guaranteed heated discussions.

Deciding where to settle and what home to buy is a major beginning. But there are other bridges to cross. Becoming part of the new community (communities) must now be a main goal. That battle is half-won on retirement day if the family recognizes what is required. The problem is less overwhelming once it's broken into workable pieces:

1. Making new friends.
2. Joining a local religious organization, if desired.
3. Identifying and becoming involved in appropriate community activities. (CAUTION! Don't overdo it.)
4. Meeting neighbors and establishing a degree of mutual trust with them.
5. Settling in on the job with coworkers, management, and other business contacts.

After years in an environment where there is a regulation for everything, the person who is about to leave the military finds there's no rule book for the personal side of the process.

We liked the examples above because in them we can see a little of our own situation and also conclude that each of us has different considerations, despite all that we have in common. One family we talked to was most concerned with the process of selecting where they would live. The other had no problem selecting their home—at least that decision was behind them. They believed their greatest challenge was ahead—becoming a real part of the civilian community.

Even with the unique twists in individual cases, planning and preparation solve most of the problems. The secret is knowing what to plan for, what preparation is required, and where to turn for help. First, we'll identify the symptoms, then we'll work on the cure.

Go Ahead—Ask the New Questions!

Don't be surprised when you find yourself trying to sort out answers to questions like:

Where will I fit in?

Certainly this has not been a burning issue in the past. You always got that squeamish feeling as you walked into new assignments, but that was over in a day or so—and each time you experienced it, you knew it wouldn't last. It was something like a touch of stage fright or getting keyed up before a game: If it had any effect at all, it was positive.

The military job title, the rank, and the organization's name give a clear picture of where an individual *and family* fit into the overall scheme. But the various aspects of civilian life just aren't as closely intertwined as in the service. For example, your position at XYZ Corporation doesn't directly determine which home you'll live in, as it well might in the service. And neighbors won't be neighbors just because they hold similar jobs for the same company.

What am I qualified to do?

For the serviceperson, moving into a new job usually is a pleasure. Qualified by training and experience, each person moves through a highly structured system that provides increasing responsibility. If the job is unique, the services rely upon old "OJT" (on-the-job training).

But no one would dare contact an employer with an offer that says, Let me know if you want anything done . . . I'm ready for OJT. It's time to get specific. Somewhere there's the perfect matchup of a need and your abilities. The real challenge is spotting that need and—perhaps more difficult—clearly identifying one's abilities.

More questions, all related, but still all separate:

Will my experience suffice or do I need some schooling?

Where do I get it?

How do I know what schooling I need when I don't know what my job will be?

Where can I locate a prestige job—at least one that won't seem like a "flunky" job to me (the Colonel, the Chief, the Sergeant Major, etc.)?

How can I settle on a job when I don't know where I'll live?

How about what I like to do—where does that fit in?

Should I start with salary considerations, or should I put them last?

Which comes first?

These questions, among many others, seem to be everywhere when you make the retirement decision. Most center on concern about the immediate future. Some stress comes from the family's concern—or what appears to be their concern—about the transition into a completely civilian world. Whether or not there's good reason for the worries, they're very real to the retiree, and they seem to compound as time flies by.

The Retirement Syndrome: Is It Real or Imagined?

We're talking about what some call Retirement Shock and what others call Retirement Syndrome. We prefer "syndrome" because Webster's definition refers to "a set of characteristics regarded as identifying a certain type, condition, etc." There are as many combinations as there are retirees. What nearly destroyed your old buddy George might not even concern you. Then again, you might flip out over a retirement problem that didn't bother George at all. If you think in terms of "shock," you expect it to hit you all at once. Don't think that way; there won't be one big shock. Instead, expect a barrage of small ones.

Management experts recommend breaking a major problem into smaller, more manageable pieces. The very nature of transition to civilian life is such that dozens of small problems combine to the point where they take on the appearance of one large one: retirement. What is it specifically about retirement that causes the anxiety? The key is recognizing the pieces and anticipating their arrival.

When and how do the first pangs of the syndrome hit? They vary in form, timing, and severity. Without a little help, you may not recognize the symptoms when they first appear, but they're easy to spot as one looks back.

It's also a little difficult to isolate what stress, mood changes, lack of concentration, sudden shifts in temperament, and other symptoms normally associated with those in the military retirement age group are caused by the old Mid-Life Crisis (MLC). It's entirely possible some of those characteristics would have emerged whether or not the individual was becoming a civilian.

You probably know someone who can argue convincingly that

there's no such thing as a MLC, and you probably also know someone who can "prove" the opposite. Even the experts disagree on whether or not it is a specific, identifiable crisis. Call it a crisis, a phase, or whatever you choose, but most experts and laymen alike agree that around age 40, most persons back off and take a good look at themselves.

For those who are introspective, a period of self-analysis is not unusual. For those who are not, this period can easily become a crisis. Many military personnel fit this category. Volumes are written on self-analysis, and some of us need all the help we can get. Others of us do it so naturally we don't even recognize it. Each may ask the questions in a slightly different way, but the essence is the same.

Daniel Levinson, a leading authority on adult psychosocial development, reported the following in a study:

> The Mid-Life Transition, which lasts from roughly 40 to 45, provides a bridge from early to middle adulthood.
>
> The start of the Mid-Life Transition brings a new set of developmental tasks. Now the life structure itself comes into question and cannot be taken for granted. It becomes important to ask: "What have I done with my life? What do I really get from and give to my wife, children, friends, work, community—and self? What is it I truly want for myself and others? What are my real values and how are they reflected in my life? What are my greatest talents and how am I using— or wasting— them? What have I done with my early dreams and what do I want with them now? Can I live in a way that best combines my current desires, values, talents, and aspirations?"
>
> For the great majority—about 80 percent of our subjects—this period evokes tumultuous struggles within the self and with the external world. Their Mid-Life Transition is a time of moderate or severe crisis. They question virtually every aspect of their lives and are horrified by what they find. They cannot go on as before, but it will take several years to form a new path or to modify the old one.

In the middle of all that, you're changing careers, moving across the country, upsetting the family routine, saying goodbye to friends, going into debt for a new home, and coping with the two rebellious teenagers the statistics say most of us have at transition time. We've finally arrived—and it's no longer in the early stages. We're right in the middle of the Retirement Syndrome.

How do you break your transition timing into workable pieces?

When should you expect the real crunch points? We view the process as happening in four major blocks, or phases: Foundation, Preparation, Adjustment, and Contentment. Most of the action with regard to transition to civilian life comes in the Preparation and Adjustment phases, which cover the period between the date you are committed to retire and the day you complete the transition. Ideally, more would happen in the Foundation phase, making the next two phases much smoother. The Contentment phase is where we want to be when the transition is complete. We hope this phase covers more time than the others combined.

The Foundation Phase

The *Foundation Phase* includes nearly your entire life up to the point at which you decide to retire. We all recognize the importance of the early developmental years, parents, home life, education, religion, and so on, upon the total person. The part of the foundation period we'll concentrate on is active duty, especially the last ten years or so prior to retirement. We'll be talking about "foundation" in a somewhat different sense—that is, building a foundation for the big switch to civilian life.

Success or failure at transition time is, in great measure, a direct reflection of the Foundation Phase. At about the ten-year point in most military careers, things seem to be working out very well indeed. At least that is the case with those who decide to remain on active duty. If the outlook wasn't good, few would remain for ten more years.

As you enter the Foundation Phase at about ten years into your military career, you're at a critical point. You've become a part of the "machine." All the early training is paying off. Back in basic you were totally lost, but the training was perfect for its purpose. At the end of that brief indoctrination, you'd become a soldier, sailor, marine, or airman. The training never stopped, and by now you've accumulated some of the greatest training ever—experience. You speak the language (and understand it!) and you know the system and are comfortable with it. The knowledge that you're halfway to retirement is great comfort to you and the family.

There's the trap—"halfway to retirement." What does it really mean? Halfway to age 40? Halfway to achieving life's goals? The trap is in the mind-set we develop by using the term *retirement* and thinking "retirement" when almost none of us mean "retirement." So where are you as you enter the Foundation Phase? You're halfway to a complete, major career and life-style change. You're in the strange but real position where you're well established in one career but must start thinking about the next one.

For ten years you've become more and more dependent upon the "system." That makes it all the tougher to unplug without any preparation. During the Foundation Phase, the psychological dependence becomes almost total, and this works against you later on at transition time.

Just as the Foundation Phase is the ideal time to get your act together, it's also the time when you're most vulnerable to the tendency not to think about life after the service. By the time you hit the Foundation Phase you've had several efficiency ratings, been promoted several times, picked up a row or so of ribbons, and supervised a lot of subordinates (most of whom, you're convinced, loved you—because they said so at your farewell.)

The "Invincible Man" and Transition to Civilian Life

It's right about here that the "invincible man" myth starts taking hold. The efficiency or fitness reports are generally good, and the resultant promotions are visible measures of success. The problem starts about the time one starts believing, "I can handle anything in the service; therefore I'm ready for anything in civilian life." First, no one can handle *everything* in the service. Second, success in the service doesn't mean success in civilian life. Third and most important, anyone who really believes that all those efficiency scores (and many of the comments) are dead accurate will be among those shocked most when it's time to transfer military talents to the civilian market. Be tough with yourself; realize it is necessary to prepare and that it should start here, in the Foundation Phase of your career.

Certainly, there are many similarities between civilian and military careers. There are differences also. Mid-level managers or business executives will tell you they have the same problems as military leaders.

For example, the civilian manager faces problems of incompetent workers, disgruntled low-level employees, compliance with equal opportunity laws, and competent employees who feel stifled by the system and pressure from superiors to produce more with less. Sounds exactly like the military. The difference is that both the military and civilian managers also solve their problems *in the context of their own systems.*

A perfect solution in the military probably won't come close to working in a union cannery. The reverse is certainly true. Ask today's military leaders, who are trying to reemphasize "leadership" after a

"He's been upset ever since he found out his office didn't collapse when he retired."

decade of trying to "manage" the armed forces like a business. Within that leadership is plenty of management, but it's markedly different from that in business. Failure to realize this fundamental difference is a major source of disappointment for military retirees.

Confidence is essential to a successful military career. About half-way through that career, confidence gets into high gear. The self-concept grows: "I can do anything!" And the system rewards that attitude with promotions and awards. One feeds upon the other, building to a frenzy—good report! promotion! good school! good report! great assignment! promotion!—until it ends abruptly at retirement. No wonder it's so tough to get anyone's attention about retirement planning ten years in advance. The system's working as it should. Except for one thing: It is *not* a goal of the system to prepare anyone for civilian life, for a good job, to get rich, or to be happy after retirement day.

So, back here, about ten years before retirement eligibility, the groundwork is laid for a successful military career and a disastrous transition to the next half of your life. Don't let it happen. There are a lot of positive steps you can take. The toughest of all is deciding what to be after the military. Those who know can keep it in mind throughout their military career. It's an easier decision for those with specific hard skills. For the combat arms guy or the generalist it gets sticky, and it's a lot tougher to answer the question, "What am I going to be?" Think for a moment what a difference it might make just to have the answer to that question.

Setting Your Goals

Service life is so all-encompassing that there is a great tendency to treat the end of it as the end of life itself. Ask an active-duty friend about his or her goals. Chances are you'll hear, "I'd like to make Colonel before I retire," or, "If I can make it to E9 by the time I'm 42, I'll feel I've done well." Suppose both succeed, then retire. They have a right to be proud, and their military retirement checks will reflect their grade. Now what?

If one sets a goal, achieves it at 40 or 45, then steps into an entirely new environment with no further goals or direction, the accomplishment becomes hollow. There is an irresistible urge to live in the past, which soon wears thin with everyone except those in the same boat. Most of us need goals, and stepping into civilian life with none is asking for trouble.

Set some specific goals—particularly answering the question, "What am I going to be?"—and shoot for them as early as possible while you're on active duty. You can orient a job search if you know what you want to do. Deciding where you want to live becomes much easier if you know what you're going to do for a living. Doing it backwards might be troublesome later. If you pick a spot just because you like it, what about your life's work? Once you've moved, will you be able to pursue that work in the location you've chosen? If not, you have a tough and expensive relocation decision on the horizon.

Most obvious of all is the fact that you must select your career field before you can prepare for it. Once you determine your goal, you can slant education, off-duty activity, preference statements, and perhaps even duty assignments in that direction. There's absolutely nothing wrong with that, so long as "it doesn't interfere with the mission."

Go Ahead—Think *About It!*

As you ease toward what you think might be your last tour, you must think more and more about retirement. It takes on much greater importance when you consider your final military assignment. Ideally, the final assignment will allow you to establish some contacts, buy a home and get settled, brush up on specific skills you'll need, and make a smooth transition into your new career. That's ideal. But few of us luck into that situation. Some choose not to. For example, take the family that wants to retire in Missouri but has a chance for a three-year tour in Hawaii. They'll probably take it. And there's not always a military installation near the second career and new home location. Even if there is, the old "needs of the service" come into play, and an assignment there might be out of the question.

Do You Really Want a "Gangplank Retirement?"

One of the hazards of the situations we've just mentioned is the "gangplank retirement"—going from overseas directly into retirement. Think of the impact, the worry, and the heavy psychological and financial burden of such a retirement upon someone with no home and no idea where to settle. A proper job search is practically out of the question under these conditions. We believe gangplank retirements should be avoided if possible. There are, of course, cases where families would rather go through one difficult move from overseas to retirement rather than settle at a duty station only to move to retirement in about a year. In these situations, preparation is doubly important because the service will bring the family home from overseas and deposit them at their selected retirement location—and say goodbye.

The Final Duty Station: Make the Best of It

If you've got an idea when you're going to retire, the last tour of duty (about three years) should be a busy one. The more you've prepared, the better off you are; but now you must get with it. You've spent a little idle time thinking about what you'd like to do after retirement. Now is the time to read every current book on job changing, mid-life career changes, financial planning, and everything else we talk about in this book. If you're planning to turn a hobby into a source of income, you should experiment with it now while there's still time for a change. Determine where you want to settle, then start scouting out the job market.

Start Your Research

Assume nothing. If you're planning on working for the petroleum company back home, learn something about the petroleum business. You can't count on your "administrative and managerial expertise," because they're going to ask you what you know about the petroleum industry, specifically about the area in which you plan to work.

Do the Paperwork

If you haven't already started your worksheets, do it now. Compare locations. Compare jobs. Compute net worth. Review your insurance. *Rehearse* (see chapter 13). List your post-retirement goals. Take a hard look at your qualifications and shortcomings.

Sign Your Retirement—and You're Out of the Foundation Phase

If, at the end of the Foundation Phase, you have your retirement plans pretty straight, you're in a small minority. Those who have planned and prepared know exactly what they must accomplish between now and retirement day. It'll be a busy time, but the advance preparation will pay off for life.

The Preparation Phase

The *Preparation Phase* begins when you commit yourself to retire. In most cases, this is the date you sign the retirement application. There are a few exceptions where the service member decides, plans, uses the time wisely, then applies and sticks with his plan. At least half decide on a retirement date within six months of that date. For the remainder of this chapter, consider the Preparation Phase as the period between the day you're committed to retire and the day you become a civilian.

The Foundation Phase doesn't fade into the past. It's gone, as if a switch was thrown, at the moment you sign your retirement application. You've committed yourself. And now you're into what we call the Preparation Phase. For the few who are committed to a retirement date *before* signing—and stick with it—we'll grant that the actual signing isn't the magic moment. But it is a definable point that applies to most persons.

Retirement's real psychological impact first grabs you during the Preparation Phase (normally about six months before the big day). Time starts flying faster and faster, with requirements and unsolved problems multiplying. The prime cause for this pressure? Putting it off until "later." Most of us try to cram three or four years' worth of planning into these last six months. It can't be properly done.

The Future Arrives

You have decided to retire. Everything we've been talking about is happening—or will soon happen—to you. If you've prepared, you've got most of it under control. It's important that those physical items are out of the way because there's something else demanding your immediate attention.

Now to the Mental Machinery

All the way through your career, you built your self-image. You had to. You needed confidence to inspire confidence. When someone else retired, you wished them well, but in the back of your mind you couldn't understand them "quitting." The ones who were forced out were easier to handle. You just thought, "Too bad. Nice guy. But it's 'survival of the fittest' and I'm still one of them." Serious talk about retirement just wasn't "in." Now you've got to talk about it.

You've planned a positive picture of yourself throughout your career. You've never "quit," always been a "take-charge type," and certainly had "unlimited potential." Now you start feeling like you're quitting, you're not really in charge, and you've reached your full potential.

You rely upon each other almost totally in the military. Now you start getting feelings that you're letting someone down. Is it your troops? The boss? Your family? All of them? It strikes right to the heart when you begin to realize you're being phased out. The "In" box isn't as full as it once was. Your responsibilities are being reduced. You're told there's no need for you to attend the briefing. Someone's eyeing your desk. Well-meaning subordinates ask if they should "hold" certain items until later. Your friends pull away from you, and you feel it. It's hard to define, but there's a change. Ask any retiree. Maybe it *is* "all in the mind," but it doesn't matter. To you, it's real.

Procrastination: It Won't Work

One negative effect of all this is the tendency to postpone everything that can be postponed. You know it's coming, but you see no need to tackle it now. In the past, when you didn't know where you'd live, someone decided for you. Now it's almost as if some power is holding you back in the hope that someone will come to your rescue. That someone has to be you.

Consciously, you're willing to postpone those tough decisions; subconsciously, you're aware you have to make them. That awareness gnaws at you, as it does when you put forth only enough effort to get by rather than give a project your best shot. The gnawing is a little deeper now because this—your transition to civilian life—is probably the most important personal and family move you've made.

You start feeling a little guilty—then a lot guilty. It's always been "mission first," but now you need to concentrate on yourself and your family. If you're fortunate enough to have a boss who'll cut you some slack during this period, count your blessings. We haven't located any scientific study on this point, but we'll bet that such bosses are in the minority—at least our interviews leaned that way.

The Mind Rules the Body, So . . .

About now, you start developing all sorts of physical "ailments." You've been tough all those years, and you aren't going to give in now. So you try to weather the storm of headaches, stomachaches, chest pains, lethargy, and irritability. Retirees remember these symptoms, but most of them never associated them with retirement. We hope this brief mention might key you to it. (Just because it may be retirement-related doesn't mean you shouldn't see the doctor.)

The Retirement Physical: Make It Count

Related to physical symptoms is the retirement physical itself. It adds just a touch of its own guilt. We talk about physicals elsewhere and make the point that it's in your best interests to get a VA disability evaluation. So, after all the years of gutting it out, biting the bullet, and avoiding the medics as if they had the plague, you find yourself sitting in the dispensary whining to the doctor about fifteen-year-old strains and other sundry ailments you've denied for years. (Air crewmen are masters at this. They love flying and would try to hide an amputation to stay in the air. But on retirement physical day, they can recite every symptom from twenty years of aviation medicine training lectures!) But the act of switching from acting healthy to pointing out all your ailments takes its toll on your ego.

Rejection Shock: It Is Not Terminal

With the physical comes the feeling that maybe you really aren't the "fightin' fool" you've been portraying all those years. Now, in the Preparation Phase, you have more to do than ever. You're tired and irritable with a thousand things to do and even more to think through. And you'd swear everyone above you has declared, "We want to get all we can out of him before he abandons ship." Pride slips in and you work even harder, not wanting to leave on a bad note. All those projects you wanted to see through—you realize there isn't time to complete them all.

Through all the years and jobs you've managed to separate your work and your home life. Now you find you're mixing the two. At work, you worry about the move, the children's schools, the new job, and money. When you get home, all those duty projects stay on your mind. You'd swear the children saved their problems to spring on you during this final six months. After years of planning for all sorts of contingencies, you realize that one more surprise—a big car repair bill, a medical emergency, or anything that takes your limited time—could be a personal disaster.

You've always tried to be realistic about problems. Oh, when you left home for combat, you faked the stiff upper lip and cried later, in private. Confidence inspires confidence. You believe it with duty, and you believe it at home. You and your spouse shored each other up through problems and strains most civilians could never begin to comprehend. As you did you never quite let each other know how much you were concerned. Now, when you need each other most, the problems seem almost impossible to discuss. Discuss? You can't even identify them.

The struggle with your self-image continues. You come up with all sorts of protective devices, most of them about as effective as whistling in the dark. One of the most common is the old "it can't happen to me" attitude. We all have it at some time or another. It doesn't protect us, but it helps us keep our sanity. Without it, we'd never have climbed into that first hot rod, never have jumped from a perfectly sound airplane, never have flown one, and probably never have left home. And certainly, without it, we'd have gone mad in combat.

Here at the Preparation Phase, everything combines: the dependence upon the system and the realization that the plug is about to be pulled, impending separation from friends and familiar surroundings; the "invincible man" reports; a proven record of success—in one career; the physical; being "phased out," while the workload seems to double; not enough time . . . where did it all go? Everything's cool, you convince yourself, "It can't happen to me."

What happened to the invincible man? How about the record of success? Where do you turn? How do you keep up the image? What will the family think now? Are you still steady as a rock? Should you try to keep that image? Can you? You wonder, "What's wrong with me? I have a lot of ability . . . Why won't they listen?"

For now, suffice it to say, nothing happened to the invincible man—you're still the same person with the same capabilities. You're just looking at yourself from a different angle. Probably the greatest shock to most military retirees comes with job rejections. We have chapters on the job-hunting process, but in this chapter we're concentrating upon the retirement process and what goes on in your head. But we can't miss the opportunity to stress (as we do constantly): If you have a job and a home to go to and have your personal affairs in order before you enter this phase, you'll be a different person, and your family will be eternally grateful. With it all done, a mid-life career change is still tough. It seems there should be a period of training, a month or so to adjust, or at least some way to ease into this new life. If there is to be one, you've got to create it.

Time to Move on

The big day comes. It can be anything from just not going to work, to a simple ceremony, to a parade. It's amazing how many just want to ease out. After all's said and done, the ultimate measure of "tough" might be that last national anthem in uniform. As a retiring soldier once said, "Anyone who can handle that with dry eyes should be shot for treason." But no matter how you go out, at the end of the day it's over.

The Adjustment Phase

The *Adjustment Phase* begins the day you pick up the gray identification card of a retiree, and it ends when you are no longer adjusting to civilian life but are a full-fledged civilian. For some, sadly, that day never comes. They live in a world of "ex"—ex-soldier, ex-general, ex-frogman.

Now That You Are a Civilian

On the first day after your retirement from the service, even if you've done everything right, you'll start one of the major adjustments

of your life. The Adjustment Phase begins in full force. No basic training, no drill sergeant, and no transition period. One day you're in, the
next day you're out. Out. Period.

The job transition, if it goes well, can smooth a lot of rough spots
at home. But there are adjustments the entire family must make, and
they have little to do with the job. They start as you (the family) start
realizing you have some role adjustments to cope with.

Is There Any Organization Out Here?

As our friend mentioned earlier, the structure is gone. In the service, everything is based upon rank and precedence. Income was sec-
ondary although related to rank, but housing, jobs, family status (though
most of us tried to avoid it with the children, it was always there), and
just about everything else tied into our position in the military society.
And the organization! We knew just where to go to accomplish just
about anything. If there were problems, we knew how to solve them
and who was in charge. In civilian life, the military rank and status
don't matter any more. There seems to be a structure, but it's almost
impossible to figure out. Status still depends upon how you fit into the
society, but you have to know the rules. Try drawing an organizational
chart of a civilian community.

You start feeling it after about a month as a civilian. Until now,
it's been like a month's leave, and you've enjoyed it. But the years of
conditioning to the military system seem to tell you, "Orders are on
the way, time to move on." There aren't any orders. No one's telling
you anything. There's no "outfit," no chain of command, and no one
waiting with open arms for you to save the organization. As a matter
of fact, a month after you're gone the service has filled the hole, and
your old comrades are getting on with running the show. Your name
may be mentioned now and then.

The familiar signs and symbols are gone. It was easy to measure
a person's success in the service. Out here, visible signs if there are
any, aren't so easy to read. Your ego takes another blow as you realize
the civilians don't really care about your former status. Out here, you'll
be measured by a different yardstick; as far as they're concerned,
you're the "new guy." It's tough on the confidence, this business of
adapting to civilian life. Sure, you've lived "on the economy" before;
maybe even owned a house or two, but your life still centered on the
military world. About now you start realizing the vast differences between the two worlds.

A Little Old-Fashioned Resentment

Now, as you're trying your utmost to establish yourself in a new environment, your friends and neighbors have more than a little trouble accepting the fact that you're retired. You're only in your forties, the prime years. Your neighbors are busting their tails to stay ahead of inflation. The economy is in a mess, and the guy on TV says part of the problem is the high cost of military retirement! Half the civilians still think you pay no income taxes. They remember PX prices like those during the "Big One—WWII," and the commissary is considered a taxpayer's expense (though we know it isn't). The same guys who laughed at anyone who "re-upped" a few years back now tell you, "I could have retired last year," and you detect a slight touch of resentment.

In the End, It All Comes Home

An elderly friend recently told us retirement is "twice as much husband and half as much money." Well, the part about the husband seems like a good deal . . . or is it? It's nice, but remember, your wife is also going through a transition. She might have been a civilian all along, but she was still part of the military community. You know that, but it's sure easy to forget. She's trying to maintain her sanity without her friends, the system, the exchanges, the commissaries, the familiar surroundings, and the social structure.

If you don't go straight into some new work routine, you'll be around the house as much—more if your wife has a job—as she is. If she doesn't run you out, you might find yourself showing her better ways to run the house. You know all those ways of getting things done in a military manner—quick, precise, and always ready for inspection. Just what she needs after running the show with precision during all those years.

But having a new "expert" around the house is only part of the load your wife has to bear. It's the rare person who can cut off most of his past and not miss part of it. When you start missing the service, friends, the routine, moving, or any part of your former life, she sees it first. She knows your moods and has spent a lot of time coping with them. Now, without realizing it, you're expecting her to take the place of all those people you used to deal with each day. Since you have no one else to straighten out, you decide to tighten things up around the old castle. Bad move.

If you want to do something constructive, why not finish those chores? Have you considered the possibility that you're taking your time with them because you really don't have anything better to do? That makes them seem more important, even though you used to take care of them *and* work eighteen hours a day. Or, maybe you just haven't "felt up to finishing them," probably because you're feeling low about the entire transition process, particularly the job picture.

Your wife saw all that coming before you recognized it. Now her day is shot listening to you complaining and coming up with excuses for being smack in the middle of her daily routine. The nightly routine isn't much better. Worry and the feelings that you've got to get your act together don't do much for your love life. Again, your ego takes a hit.

It's easy to imagine how this home situation hits the children as hard as the adults. They wonder what happened to your confidence, why you don't have a job, and where they fit into this new life. The familiar landmarks aren't there for them, either. They don't like some of the belt tightening and can see it might have some far-reaching effects—on college tuition, for example.

When you think of all this, don't think it can't happen to you. It will happen to you to some degree. We want it to be an absolute minimum, so plan for it; you'll find there's plenty you can do to ease the pain.

Handling the Challenge

Slipping through a mid-life career change without a hitch is just about unheard-of. No matter how you plan and organize, there will be a surprise or two. Remember all those trips you took over the years in the service. Each member of the family had individual responsibilities. One of yours was loading the car. The first few times, you had everything loaded just right, and then someone came along with another suitcase or a weird-shaped item (hobby horse, beach chair). You unloaded and reorganized and found to your amazement that it all fit. After a couple of those experiences, you beat the system—you left room for a large suitcase. The space was always filled at the last minute with a "surprise" item. You never knew what it would be, but by organization you were ready for the unknown.

What strategy should you adopt for your transition? First, determine your answer to the question, "What am I going to be?" Once you can answer that, you have direction. Your thinking and efforts will point toward a specific goal, and every action you take will get you a little closer to it.

Only you can determine your tactics for your situation. The whole idea is to have every identifiable item taken care of so that the unexpected ones won't cause major crises. Just like loading the car.

Later we're going to discuss in detail more tangible items like finances, benefits, insurance, and the job search. Our research and interviews have convinced us there are some tactical moves that can help just about everyone. But cut down on the mental stress and everything else runs twice as smoothly.

The "Grocery List": Things to Do Today

1. Above all, learn about the career transition phenomenon. Think about it, and research it. Pick up a book on the subject now and then, read it, and note any item you need to square away. Not all the books are good. If you find one that isn't, or if it doesn't fit the situation, don't try to make it fit. Just keep educating yourself.
2. The most important move you can make is to start early. Develop some long-term goals far beyond a military rank or position. Start planning to achieve those goals. The earlier you start, the easier your transition will be. Throughout this chapter we used phases as reference points. You should do everything in your power to move as much as possible back in the phasing so that it's done as early as possible. It's a lot easier to make a simple change—in a will, for example—than to start from zero in the middle of a career change. Do it. Now.
3. Develop some roles outside the military community. It's unbelievable how few do this. When the cord is cut on retirement day, you're going to need something familiar—besides the family—to turn toward. Do not let the severance from the service represent severance from everything you know. Don't let it *be* all you know. Join some local organizations; get active in school and other community matters. It'll give you some continuity; it'll be your only recent "civilian" experience; you'll have some contacts; and it could possibly get you a good start toward your next career.
4. Develop as many "civilian" skills as you can before the pressure is on. This critical move is much easier, as we keep repeating, if you know what you're going to be. And please remember, military expertise does not necessarily transfer directly to civilian expertise. The training and experience are valuable and will be a great help. But gear your skills to what you want to be, not to what you are now.
5. Take time. Write down your skills, goals, and requirements (that will be a revelation—we guarantee it). Work on whittling away at

your requirements. Identify intermediate objectives, and accomplish them as you go. Assess exactly where you are and where you need to go in every area we discuss in this book.

6. Start your reconnaissance (can't avoid the military lingo—it fits) as early as possible, and make it detailed. Apply it to work, housing, community, and every other aspect of your transition. Never try "winging it" or going cold turkey. With the best of planning and preparation, you'll have enough "winging" to do.

7. Keep the entire family involved and informed. It's easy to withdraw into yourself, particularly when you've spent a career keeping your worries to yourself, not worrying the family. You need the family now. If you're too stubborn to admit that, realize the family needs you—more than ever. You can be a big help to each other.

Early in this chapter, we said we wanted to talk a little about the Retirement Syndrome. This syndrome consists of all the thoughts and stresses we've discussed and a lot of others that fit only specific cases. You be the judge as to whether or not you think there is such a thing as a Retirement Syndrome. Call it what you want; there are a lot of symptoms that occur in most of us at the time of a major change. Changing from military to civilian life combines many major changes. If you plan to keep your thoughts straight during the process, remember: Those things happening to you are the same ones that happen to thousands each year. You recognize them, and therefore you're just a step ahead of the game.

You're planning for the next third of your life—or longer. Treat it with some respect, and plan properly. Seek counsel when you need it. Take courses, and keep a handle on exactly where you are in the planning process.

The Contentment Phase

The *Contentment Phase* is really a goal. We wrote this book to help you achieve this goal. We look at it as a phase since we hope it'll take up the major part of your postmilitary life. A friend calls this the "be something else" phase. Once you are something else, you've got the transition whipped. Oh sure, you're still authorized to get all choked up at a parade and to remember the days in uniform. No one is prouder and few are more dedicated than military retirees. Rightly so. But the past is past, and it's time to look to the future.

3

The Family and the Transition

Early in your planning you must recognize the importance of the effect of your transition to civilian life upon your spouse. Success or failure in this department can, and sometimes does, mean success or failure of "marriage after the military."

We're going to talk about wives here and use *she* to refer to them. We hope the reasoning is clear to you and that no one will get up-tight about the choice. The number of women retiring from the services is increasing in direct proportion to the number reaching eligibility. Consequently, the number of husbands of military retirees is increasing. They have many of the same problems we'll talk about here plus some of their own. But by far, most of those retiring today—those who started twenty or more years ago—are males. As hundreds of other writers have noted, using "he or she" every sentence or so just doesn't make smooth writing. So, in general, we're going to speak of the service wife.

Sharing a Career—Sharing Retirement

Military retirement is sort of a "yours, mine, and ours" thing. You can get so wrapped up in your career change and all it entails that you fail to notice that someone else is going through all your agonies and some of her own.

Through the service years, just about everything at home is geared to the military career. Many accept that fact without appreciating it. The moves, the separations, the long hours, career highs and lows, field duty, combat, increasing responsibility—all weigh heavily upon the service member. But a huge share of that burden is borne by the service wife.

Hundreds of articles have been written about the military wife. There have been a few factual books and a lot of fictitious ones. No one has really captured the typical wife, and chances are they won't. It's doubtful there is such a person. But, despite their individuality, service wives have a lot in common with each other. This similarity is a result of that essential ingredient of service life: the "school of hard knocks"—experience.

Some of the crises a military wife handles routinely would totally panic a major portion of the population. It takes her years to become an expert on the system, just as it does the service member.

Now she can move across the world on a month's notice (or less) and become a leader in the new military community the week after she arrives. She keeps the family together—physically and spiritually—while her spouse traipses around fulfilling military responsibilities. Today, more often than not she has a career of her own. She juggles her responsibilities to support his career as well as her own, combined social obligations, the children, the house, the church, and the community with a skill that would impress P. T. Barnum. Somewhere in there she finds time to be wife and lover.

The greatest miracle of all is that service wives keep their sanity, despite the stresses heaped upon them. They manage, individually and as a group, under conditions unimagined by most. At first, it's just coping. Coping with holidays without husband and father. Coping with giving up the job to move to the Philippines. Then she gradually adjusts from coping to planning. It's a big step, but chances are she never recognizes it when it happens.

It could be argued that planning is just a way of coping. Maybe, but it's a better way. Most of the planning is in her head. It is nothing formal, but she seems ready for anything! After a few years of service life, she knows exactly what she'll do if orders to the Philippines come

. . . in the middle of the school year . . . when she just settled into a new house.

She knows exactly how to handle just about any crisis because she's been functioning within a system for twenty years or more. She knows what to expect and can take surprises in stride. Now, while you're in the planning stages, consider your military retirement—your transition to civilian life—from her point of view. Remember it throughout the process because you, the one who loves her most, are about to drop another problem in her lap: You are becoming a civilian. In doing so, you're taking away the system she knows so well, and you're forcing her to play by different rules.

Occasionally, military jobs force a person into several sectors of society and require participation in activities other than military ones. Generally, however, the service member lives a sheltered life within the military system (a fact, incidentally, which is denied by most while on active duty). Work, worship, recreation, and social functions usually center around the same people. In other occupations, each category might well include totally different individuals. In the military profession, however, it's the normal situation for "duty" and "off-duty" to involve those who share the same profession and work within the same system.

To a greater degree than her husband's, the military wife's lifestyle overlaps into other parts of society. Whether she lives on an installation or in the civilian community, her civilian job, her participation in civic activities, her involvement in school and religious groups, and of course her ties to the military community all have a great impact upon her outlook. She is more likely than the husband to have civilian friends; she is, after all, a civilian. It's a pretty safe bet she's better prepared for the transition to civilian life. But, at the same time, she's been part of a military system for a long time.

Consider what the coming change to civilian life will do to (or for) your wife. Most of us think we do that automatically; subconsciously we consider her in everything we do. Subconsciously isn't good enough. Surface it, and keep it surfaced. Address her part of the transition just as specifically as you do your own.

Making Retirement Decisions

As we discussed military retirement with service wives, some themes were repeated again and again. Occasionally someone would surface a one-of-a-kind situation, but most striking were repetitions of stories we'd heard before. Since this is the case, why don't military couples plan more carefully and avoid some of the problems altogether? You'll undoubtedly come to your own conclusions. We came to several, but one dominated them all. It didn't particularly please us—we've recently gone through the transition process—but it sure hit home. Try this on for size:·

Until now, your military career drove the family train. *What* you were (First Sergeant of Battery "B," Commander of 2d Regiment,), *when* you became it ("effective 2 Mar 1983") and *where* you did it ("report to. . .") were determined for you. A great deal of the *how* was decided by regulation. The *why* is easy: To accomplish the mission. Always the mission. Nothing left for much flexibility except the *who*. We know who. You.

A person can get into a real heavy psychological trip just by asking, "Who am I?" We will avoid that one, but we are confident with this observation: It would be difficult to deny that twenty or more years of having the what, when, where, why, and how determined for you must have a profound effect upon who you've become. And, you've become a part of the system. There's nothing wrong with that; it is a primary goal in most careers.

Through it all, if you were to continue your career you had little choice. Neither did your wife if you were to keep it all together. Everything was geared to the military, primarily because there was little option. What was best for the career (even if it only meant a choice between staying in or getting out) always dominated other considerations. Everyone in the family recognized that fact, and life just ran that way.

After retirement, the military will no longer determine the directions your life will take. But it will take a deliberate effort to remember that. And that brings us to the conclusion we mentioned earlier. It took a while to get here, but this is the basis for much of what follows in this chapter: *Most retirement decisions are based upon what is believed best for the military retiree in the immediate future.* Frequently, these decisions are shortsighted, aren't best for the retiree beyond about a year, and are made with little or no regard for the wife's desires, needs, abilities, or personality.

Note, however, this is not a cruel, deliberate, male chauvinistic deed designed to impose just one more hardship on the service wife. Most of us make these decisions with love and the best intentions but also with a degree of ignorance. It's equally important to note that the wife's agreement, or at least acquiescence, is usually part of the process. In capsule form, we're saying that although critical retirement decisions are made by both partners, they fail to consider adequately the wife's needs.

Several key words in the above should sound an alarm: "believed," "best for the. . . retiree," "immediate future," "shortsighted," "about a year," "little or no regard for . . . needs, abilities, . . . personality." Think about it.

Get Your Wife's Input

If ever there was a time for the military wife to make her feelings known, it's now, as final planning for civilian life begins. Military orders won't be dictating where the family goes, and when. You will need her support throughout this entire process, but right up front you need to know her honest views about each course you are considering. Without her input, you're almost sure to run into problems later.

You've never needed her support more. One of the best ways for her to express that support is to let you know her preferences, and the sooner the better.

For the military wives who read these words, please recognize that we've chosen to address the retiree in this book. It makes it a lot simpler and clearer. We hope you'll both consider our suggestions and divide the responsibility to suit your case. One brief exception now. We ask you; we plead with you (he won't, so we'll do it for him!): Be sure your preferences and needs are addressed during your husband's planning. The consequences of not doing so are great. If your desires match his and the location and life-style you settle upon matches the needs of both of you, you're in tall cotton. You owe it to yourself and to your family to discuss every angle and possibility. If you put it off, you'll have no one to blame but yourself.

The earlier you surface your preferences on where you want to live, how you want to live, financial arrangements and plans, career plans and desires, family considerations, and the other possible problems, the happier you'll be in the end. Sure, there will be some disagreement. The important thing is that you pinpoint the disagreement when you have time to resolve it. There's nothing to gain and plenty to lose by waiting until you've made that final government move to your country home, then announcing, "I always wanted to settle in a city, where we could. . ." Announce it now! If you want to pursue your career—or begin one—make it clear. If you want to live next door to your parents but dread surfacing that possibility, surface it anyhow and clear the air. When the two of you walk away from the retirement ceremony, you need to do it as one. He needs you more than ever, but he may not be able to tell you (he's supposed to be tough and confident). The effects of your decisions are lifelong. This is no time for a "wait and see how it turns out" attitude. If you make some really rotten decisions you can't expect orders to save the day. It'll be up to you. So please jump in with both feet, as early as possible, and make those choices—together.

And when she does, fellow military retiree, listen to her. She's helping you more than you'll realize for quite a while.

Determining Your Needs

"Believed best for the military retiree . . ."—there are all kinds of dangers with that. The most obvious is that what you *think* is best for you might not be. It happens all the time as a result of poor planning or no planning at all. If you've really thought about this retirement thing, you'll have a pretty fair idea what's good for you. And anyone who just walks out the main gate, planning to let the chips fall where they may, deserves just that. But does the family deserve it? Of course not.

Why do we think what's good for us is automatically best for our families? It had to be that way for years, and everyone cooperated. It would be more accurate if we said our families made the best of the situation. Certainly, each of us can recall at least once when what was best for the military member was disastrous for the rest of the family, but the service won out. The two of you will be living with your decisions for the rest of your lives. The service won't win or lose; it's out of the picture. The kids are a big part of your decision process, but they'll be moving on soon enough. The one who will be at your side at your mountain retreat—although she'd rather be running an antique shop in Des Moines—is the one we're talking about in this chapter. Think in terms of what's best for the two of you. Don't inflict another disaster upon her (and in turn, upon yourself) because you assume she'll be completely happy so long as you are. Maybe she can run the antique shop from your mountain retreat, or perhaps the two of you can pay for the retreat by working three or four days a week at the antique shop. Or maybe neither of you has any business in a mountain retreat or an antique shop. When do you want to hash all this out? After you've moved? No way. Communicate now, and keep up the dialogue throughout the process.

Think About the Long Haul

"Immediate future . . .," "shortsighted . . .," "about a year . . ."
This entire book is about looking beyond the immediate future. Usually, the trap springs when the service member takes the approach, "We'll settle wherever I get a job," and the job turns sour. That is only one of many ways it can occur. It happens, and often. If, in the process, the military wife is plunked down in the middle of the last place she wants for a home, the seeds are sown for big trouble.

Just as you start discussing the pending transition to civilian life as far in advance as possible, look at postmilitary life beyond the day of your military retirement. You can formalize it or just do it over a cool one some quiet evening. We suggest just a little formality—at least use a note pad and pencil. Weigh each selected alternative against the others. Each of us has unique questions to answer, for example:

"Will the house we want now be best for us in five years, after the kids are gone?"

"We love this location now, but is that because our friends are here? If so, will they be here in five years? Ten?"

"How will this area look twenty years from now? Will we like the climate then?"

"What if we plunge our savings into that old home, then need to move?

"How about emergency funds?"

The list could go on without end, but we're ending it there. You can see that an accurate answer to most questions about the future depends upon both marriage partners. The question is no longer, "What's the next step in my career?" with everyone following along. Now, at last, you can put other priorities first—if you choose to do so.

Sharing the Responsibility

These are cold, hard decisions the two of you should make together. It is so easy to believe it's your responsibility—and yours alone. We've talked with military retirees who stated, "I believed the military career was mine. The new career was going to be mine. Since I was the one making the big switch, all the decisions were my responsibility. I put my family through it, I believed I should shoulder the entire load and make it easy on them." Past tense, because they usually followed up with, "and I was wrong."

That assumption—that it's you alone who's going through the big change—is the worst one you can make. Not just from a point of view of home selection, financial planning, the new career, climate, and other solid, tangible angles. In fact, your wife may be going through the same psychological stresses as you, plus her own. Most important, she's almost surely suffering through some caused by the simple fact that you think you're the only one weathering the transition storm. As a result, in the grand tradition of military wives, she keeps you from coming apart at the seams while you appear to be the strong one. She soothes your ego—particularly if you're getting some job rejections—and boosts your morale. She runs the house, keeps up with her own outside job, and seems to be slipping right through the entire process. She keeps everything together, all the while listening to your bitching and bellyaching about how tough this process is on you. Never once do you get a clue—or take time to look for one—to indicate what she's going through. Don't wait for a clue; recognize it ahead of time. Think about your own situation. Go through this thing together; it's the only way.

The Military Identity

Think a little about how a military person is identified—by the job, rank, position, or title. You might be the Finance Officer or a platoon sergeant, a Staff NCO or a line officer, a clerk or a base commander. But everyone in the military society can immediately relate to you and determine with pinpoint accuracy where you fit into the scheme of things.

Most of us try not to let our military identity (temporary as it is) rub off on our families. Nothing's more obnoxious to us than the wife who remembers when "we were lieutenants" (unless she was in the service) or the kid who says, "Don't fool with me, buddy, my dad's the Colonel." Despite television and novels, real cases of that attitude are now pretty rare. (Most military kids stick with the old "my dad can whip your dad," just like in civilian life—much to the chagrin of dads worldwide.) We try to leave our problems at work, but even then we bring the "structure" into the home. It's probably natural, but we seem to do it in direct proportion to our seniority.

When we began military life, we found out right away where we fit into the organization—usually at the bottom. It didn't bother us because we expected a gradual process to the top. (Besides, as one General said, it's more fun at the bottom when you're young than at the top when you're old.) Our friends were in the same field of work and belonged to the same major organization. Our social life normally centered around those friends, with whom we had so much in common. If we lived on a military installation, our neighborhood was made up of others at the same level. With everyone making the same money, it was rarely a status topic. "Keeping up with the Joneses" just isn't a big game in the military neighborhood—one of the nice things about it.

On the other hand, if you or the Joneses move up, you move to a new neighborhood—again one determined by your position and filled with others at the same level. As you move up the ladder of success, your responsibilities increase rapidly. In a more subtle way, the family's responsibilities increase too. As you become a military leader, you and your family become leaders in the military community as well. Younger folks turn to the senior ones for advice and assistance and for an example. You can't avoid it. If you try to "just do your job"—and not be a part of the community, they'll use you as an example anyhow: a bad one. There's no such thing as just doing your job in service life. We all know it's a way of life, and it includes much more than primary duties. And it includes the entire family.

In the civilian community, there are also, as the song goes, "games people play." The service family has its role in that environment, too. The more senior the military member is, the more likely he will be involved in community affairs. By virtue of his position (commanders and key officers and NCOs invited to Rotary, Lions Club, etc.), his rank (which civilian business people can equate to dollars in half the time it takes the finance office), his influence (usually overestimated), or his visibility, the service member mixes with various levels of the civilian community. These roles come with the territory and may not give a true reflection of the individual. For example, consider the base commander near a large city who spends parts of three or four days a week at meetings, luncheons, dinners, cocktail parties, and other such functions. He's obligated to represent the service, the base, the outfit, and his troops, and so on, to the civilian community. He recognizes this as part of his duty and usually performs it well. Whether or not he likes it, he becomes part of it and gets used to it. So does his wife. Not only are they "movers and shakers" on the base, but they are in demand in the civilian community.

Now, yank that guy and his family out of that environment and plant them back on the farm where he's still "Sam and Ethel's oldest boy," and she's still "the Johnston girl from down the road." Whether they like it or love it, there's still some adjustment for both of them. A base commander can represent one end of the scale; the young person entering the service represents the other end. Most of us fit somewhere

on that scale. Each of us experience the adjustment in one way or
another.

Adjusting to a Civilian Identity: The Spouse

Since the sixties, it seems everyone has talked about roles, goals,
and self-identity. It isn't discussed a whole lot among those planning
their military retirement. It should be. Some adjustments apply only
to the one who's hanging up the uniform. But the spouse also has her
own adjustments, some directly resulting from your retirement and
relocation (or nonrelocation), some only remotely related to your transition, some that would occur whether or not you were leaving the
service. They're real, and they're almost everywhere she turns.

On the Job

While you're adjusting to your new job, it's much too easy to
forget that your wife is going through the same changes. If she is going
back to work after a long absence (or for the first time) the change is
even more dramatic for her. Her position in the pecking order is no
longer determined by the fact that you're the Sergeant Major or the
Colonel. In fact, the first time she tries that "Mrs. Colonel" routine—
deliberately or inadvertently—she'll get stung. Fortunately, there are
few who would do it on purpose. Those days are pretty much gone.
It happens today by accident—and not just to former military folks. It
may occur with anyone who has worked up the ladder of success in
one field, then decided to switch to a lower rung of another ladder.

About the time of the husband's military retirement, wives seem
increasingly interested in going to work. There are always exceptions,
but most we talked with believe this is a good time. The reasons vary.
Some want to cover the anticipated loss of income until "we get established." Ideally, there won't be a loss of income. But we're all
realistic enough to know it can happen, if only temporarily. But even
if income isn't the main reason, a lot of military wives feel the timing
is right when their husbands become civilians.

There is a good chance these women would feel the same about
going to work whether or not their husbands were in the process of
military retirement. In this one sense, we don't see much difference
between these women and those in the same age group from the civilian
sector.

The kids are grown, or nearly so, and she's still young. Her experience alone is priceless. But the fact that she has traveled around
the world, handled herself flawlessly in a wide variety of situations,

"I talked Alice into getting a job. It's part of my retirement plan."

knows firsthand what most know only from books and lectures, and can adjust overnight to new conditions must be translated into terms she can sell to a prospective employer. That employer wants to know, "How does that experience pay off for the Rocket Gizmo Company?" and "What do you know about Gizmos?"

If she has been dedicating all her time to her family or hasn't worked outside the home for other reasons, she faces the same difficulties in the job market as others her age. Chances are she has been out of the marketplace for some time, her job skills are a little rusty, and her job-hunting skills are undeveloped. If the family has been on the move (who hasn't?), and is now settling in a new community, she finds herself competing with lifelong residents who know their way around, have local references, and may have worked in the area for years.

Generally, most would agree that the woman who has been employed all along will have an easier time in the work force. The reasons are obvious, and we won't dwell upon them: recent experience, current in the field, current references, used to the routine, confident (big one), and psychologically geared to running the job and the home simultaneously.

So, if you're moving, your working wife needs to go through the entire routine—again. You think you've been through it with military transfers, but there's no comparison (as you're about to learn as a civilian).

If she decides to start working outside the home, she's surely about to take some psychological hits. She will hear "overqualified," "underqualified," "we'll let you know," "we just filled the position," and "call us in the fall" until she dreams about it. And she will gradually become aware that employers might also be saying, "I can get much more experience in much younger employees, at least with regard to experience in my business." That hurts too. Her confidence and pride begin to hurt as she tries to cope with the transition. She's suddenly the novice and it's mighty uncomfortable.

In the work force, she must adapt to the new conditions. If she has been employed all along, there's still the new boss, new location, new procedures, and probably a new structure. If she's entering the commercial sector for the first time, it's a whole bright new world— and she feels about as secure as she would in a jungle.

As with the military member, the spouse will make some attitude adjustments on the job. We say *will make*, because there really isn't any option short of losing the job. The boss may be ten (or twenty) years younger than she is. No one really cares about her former status in the military community—the status that took years of progress to achieve. In fact, most of her coworkers have no concept of military structure.

These adjustments are difficult for those who were really involved in the military way of life and who resist letting go. For others the change is a welcome one, but pitfalls remain. Even those who adapt easily (our bias says most service wives do), who were superb in the military community, and who are equally outstanding anywhere, must be on guard.

We interviewed a former Air Force wife—we'll call her Sue—who had been working in the ladies' department of a rather exclusive Texas department store. She was as happy as she'd ever been. The job was something she'd always wanted, in the town where she always wanted to live. This lady is unquestionably capable, intelligent, articulate, and confident. There's nothing pretentious about her. In fact, neither her coworkers nor her immediate supervisor knew that her husband was the former top dog at the nearby base.

One day the big boss came through the store and recognized Sue. They'd worked together on several community and charity projects and were social acquaintances from her days at the base. They greeted each other on a first-name basis. They asked about each other's families (by name). Then they grabbed a quick cup of coffee.

After that simple experience, the job was never the same for Sue. Her coworkers took the attitude you'd expect. After all, she was working at the bottom of the heap in an hourly job and was a close friend of the store manager's boss. One can only imagine how threatening and intimidating this fact was to her immediate supervisor, who wasn't exactly the most confident and secure person in the business. Eventually, Sue quietly left the job, simply because she wasn't happy there.

Sue's experience was a sad one indeed. We could say she's better off not working with people with such small minds and narrow outlooks. Some would say her situation was unavoidable. After all, what was she to do? She simply wanted to fit into a new environment. She certainly did her share. And one should not have to erase a past— particularly a proud one—just to fit into the present.

In Sue's case, she was not the problem. But there are cases where the former military wife self-inflicts this wound, just as the ex-Chief, ex-Colonel, ex-Sergeant Major, or ex-General does. It comes about when one lives in the past and constantly talks about "when we were in Paris . . .," "we liked Rome better than Madrid . . .," "I knew him when .. . ."

Why in the world are we discussing this here? Adapt the words to fit your situation; the point remains: After being part of a relatively closed society for a quarter of a century, a great deal of that society rubs off. When a couple steps out of it, they step into an adjustment process that goes far beyond moving off base.

The familiar measures and marks of success and position are gone. No longer can one drive down the street and figure just where everyone fits into the scheme of things by reading the name on the door. As a matter of fact, there aren't names on the doors. Even if there were, you still can't put everyone into the neat categories you are used to. How do you compare a vice president of a small outfit to a middle manager of a large corporation? You don't; at least not without a lot of other information you aren't likely to get. It's not that you care that much about the neighbors; it's just that you want to know where you fit in. It simply isn't as clean and crisp in the civilian world.

The search for identity is tough at any time. Begun during middle age, it is particularly difficult. With an abrupt change in life-style, such as the change from military to civilian life, it becomes more baffling. For many, the greatest changes are on the job. You need to make some major attitude adjustments, and so does your wife. Don't get paranoid about it, but look at it realistically. Recognize the fact that what was a big deal among your coworkers in the service can be a real "turnoff" in civilian life.

Starting Over

We think it's safe to say that most military wives are happy in that role. It is one of the most interesting life-styles on earth. But even though it seems it is time to move on, the well-adjusted service wife recognizes she's in for the biggest change of all.

One aspect of the dramatic change to civilian life drew divided comments from the wives we interviewed. Most believed that the best-adjusted service wives would make the transition easily, coping with it just as they had with dozens of other crises. But some believed those who completely adjusted to military life may have adjusted *so* well that they now could expect a rough transition to civilian life.

"After all," one lady said, "when you talk about all the tough spots we got through in the past, you're talking about incidents over twenty-five or so years. But the transition to civilian life is a switch from the entire twenty-five years. I happen to believe there is a difference. The switch at the end of a career represents turning away from what you've known most of your life."

That "turning away" causes a sense of loss for the spouse, just as for the service member. We interviewed Paula in a Washington, D.C., suburb. Her husband, Tony, had retired from the Navy two years earlier and was finishing his law degree work. She worked at a computer software firm in Virginia. Her story of adjustment was similar to others we'd heard.

I was totally happy with Navy life. We moved about every three years, and it was always an adventure—something we couldn't wait to try.

As Tony progressed in his career, I knew I was really contributing to that progress. We both knew it. I had no big problems with the system. As a matter of fact, I became part of it and I'm proud of that. I gained a lot of comfort and security from supporting Tony's career. During our earlier years, I'd cringe when some Chief's wife would talk about "our career." Time sure makes some changes. I contributed a lot to that career. Yes, I think it's fair to call it "our career."

Suddenly, when Tony retired, I realized there was no career for me to support. It was all in the past. There was a void; I felt just a little cheated. I guess it may have been subconscious, but I got great comfort from my role in that career, though I didn't really realize how much until the end. Isn't that always the way?

Over the years, I'd kept a job in spite of the moves. My job here isn't the greatest, but I enjoy it. I often wonder how much seniority and experience I'd have built if we hadn't moved so much. We needed my job, at least for the first couple of years after Tony's retirement. I was proud of that, but even it became a sore point. . .

There Tony was, going out every morning looking for a job. Sending out resumes by the dozens—rarely getting the courtesy of an acknowledgment. Calling all over the East Coast looking for a job. His self-esteem started slipping and, of course, I saw it first.

I would try to bolster his spirits, just as I had in the past. But here was the guy I supported all those years—and he couldn't even find a job that paid what mine pays. It was really tough on his ego. Now, I'm going to admit something to you. . . . It started wearing just a little on how I felt about him. I'm not sure I can describe it. It boiled down to the fact that I was feeling some insecurity from the fact I'd dedicated so much to his development, now we were sort of starting over.

There was no question about love. Don't read that into my words. It was just one of those complicated human relationship situations. His confidence was slipping. He knew I could see it. That made it worse. I was feeling the financial strain, and naturally I felt the emotional stress too. What happens in a case like that? You turn to the one you love most, and for some reason, you argue. . .

Does that make sense at all?

It does to us. Naturally, as with all transitions, this was just one small part of the picture. For each of us, the picture is a little different. But the more we know about and understand the possibilities, the better we can prepare for our own situation.

This is an excellent example of a phenomenon we encountered with most military retirees. That is, the solid belief (before retirement) that the best jobs are out there just waiting for the successful retiree. As we discussed this point, we found the spouse believed it even more than the service person. Consequently, we found the spouses we talked with had experienced greater letdowns than they, their husbands, or we anticipated. Some recovered quickly, others didn't. Surely, faith and confidence in each other is essential, particularly during the critical transition period. But kidding oneself can only lead to disappointment. Face facts. You *can* land a super job, but you'll have to hustle, and you need each other's support.

Whether or not your spouse is entering the job market when you are, she'll have a profound effect upon your transition to civilian life. Don't forget, however, you have as great an effect upon her transition, which she is making with you.

Plan together. Take time for each other. Talk about it. Most important—don't expect her support just because you're making a change. She's making one too. Hers is just as vital, to both of you. So start now to support each other.

4

Where *Is* Home?

Some Common Considerations: Some Unique Ones

Much of your future happiness depends upon your answer to the question, "Where will I live?" It's one that always seemed easy to answer because you were dealing in abstract, future possibilities. Now, it's time to look at the question realistically. As Coach George Allen said, "The future is now."

Selection of a home—including the location, the structure, and the finances involved—is one of the most important decisions of the transition process. The financial dangers are pretty well known to most of us. Other hazards are equally important, particularly in terms of our postmilitary happiness. Once again, we find that most literature is written for those who are *really* retiring, at about age 65 or older. There is plenty of valuable material there, but be careful not to jump at guidance written for someone twenty-five or thirty years older than you are. Throughout this book we emphasize: You've been thinking "retirement," but don't put yourself in the shoes of a bona fide retiree. You aren't. Retirement from the military, possibly at age 37, almost surely won't mean real retirement. You are in your peak years. Think that way, and consider advice in that light.

Suppose you have decided exactly where you'll live and have no intention of changing. The job outlook is bright, and the family is in complete agreement. This happens frequently when the retiring service member or spouse takes over the family business. Still, give serious consideration to how your home will fit your needs twenty years from now. Availability of medical facilities, shopping, and public transportation will be more important to you later. Since you know where you'll be living, maybe there are some changes you can make now that will pay off in the future. This is especially true if you know the town where you will live but haven't selected your home.

Your home selection criteria are different from those of most other retirees. Considerations not addressed in most retirement planning literature, such as availability of exchanges, military medical services, commissaries, and other individual benefits, are fundamental for the military retiree. Further, many service retiree couples are still in the child-rearing (indeed, in many cases, child-bearing) years. Settling down in the home you plan to keep for life requires you to look ahead about twenty years or so, at the same time considering family needs for the immediate future. And, of course, for the next few years where you live will be closely tied in with where you work.

So, ideally, the location and home should:

1. Be where you can take full advantage of military benefits.
2. Satisfy the needs of the family's growing children.
3. Be within reach of work.
4. Be suitable for your *real* retirement . . . and that's in addition to the factors that apply to everyone else. A tall order, for sure.

Uncle Sam pays for one move, within a year of military retirement, so moving costs aren't immediate concerns. That's a big help because the cost of a move is enough to keep quite a few Americans settled in places they'd rather not be. But moving expenses may take on added significance later since 70 percent of military retirees move at least once after leaving the service.

The decision on whether or not to move is answered for those who live in government housing, are stationed somewhere they dislike intensely, must move to take over a family business or for other family reasons, or are in the home they want in the perfect location for them. Families not fitting one of these categories must decide, "Should we move or stay put?" And it is rarely an easy decision.

The majority of military retirees who consider a move away from their final duty station aren't really sure where they want to settle. If you fit in this category, make an early start on your planning, and perhaps the pieces will slide into place as you build momentum. If you can't positively identify where you want to go, attack the problem from the negative side: Eliminate states, cities, or geographical areas where you definitely don't want to live. At least you'll narrow the field.

Climate

What will you look for if you know you're going to move? For one thing, you'll consider the climate. It's no coincidence that California, Florida, and Texas have far more military retirees than any other states. Employment opportunities (particularly "high tech" in Texas and California) and military facilities play a role in the selection of these states, but you can be sure the climate would draw young, active military retirees anyhow. They go there for the present and for their future years after real retirement.

Take time to check the climate where you plan to live. It's not uncommon to find families who moved to a state based on what they believed about the climate. To their dismay, they found the climate they expected was in another part of the state. In California, for example, the distance from the northern edge of the state to its southern tip is roughly the same as from Washington, D.C., to the southern tip of Florida. Everyone knows the differences—especially in winter—between Washington and Florida, and it is reasonable to expect about the same over the length of California. But even more extreme variations occur in much shorter distances, particularly in mountainous areas. In some states you can drive from freezing snow country to shirt-sleeve weather in less than an hour.

If there are health considerations, climate may be especially important. An early error in judgment can cost money later and add morale problems to an already difficult adjustment period. Avoid the perilous tendency to generalize. For example, most of us think of Arizona as warm and dry, with clean, clear air. Generally that's true. But compare the climates of Phoenix, Flagstaff, Yuma, and Tucson, and you might be surprised. If you plan a move to a particular city to escape pollution, fly there and try it. You might find all those people who went there for clean air are now polluting it.

Areas with a reputation for year-round warm, sunny days draw hordes of retirees. But many who love all four seasons say the monotony of the warm climate bears down on them after a few years,

Deciding where to locate.

especially around the winter holiday season. If you've visited the area as a tourist, you probably were there during the best season. How about the rest of the year? Delightfully warm, sunny vacation weather can become oppressive, stifling heat when you're working in it. Warm coastal areas also are hurricane prone. And how will you feel about all those tourists when you're no longer one of them?

"Bargains"

Who among us doesn't know someone who was stung on a real estate deal based entirely upon future development? Military families seem especially prone to this kind of hustle. If the family hasn't been to the location of the sale, they invariably know someone who has. So it seems they should be the toughest to con. Not so. In fact, the pitchmen usually use the experience and knowledge as part of their routine. Buying an undeveloped lot "just outside" of Tucson, Dallas, Fort Lauderdale, or Denver would seem like a good deal to anyone who's been there. But just outside can be desert, or mountain terrain without adequate roads, or swamp, or just too far out. But the pitchmen can make it look mighty appealing.

One of the standard routines is to capture a serviceperson about mid-career and offer a rare opportunity for some prime real estate—there's usually "only one or two corner lots left"—in a general area known to most military families as desirable. The plan calls for a new development, complete with swimming pool, park, recreation facilities, hospitals, and shopping facilities. But it's still out far enough so that you can get next to nature just by stepping outside your door. No matter that there's nothing there now. For a small monthly payment it can be all yours by the time you're eligible for retirement. If you decide you're going to live elsewhere, you'll be able to sell at a huge profit . . . enough to make a real difference in your retirement home purchase.

The number of families who enter into these deals with virtually no investigation is astonishing. Those who visit the area are much wiser but still are sometimes taken in by talk of the future. There's nothing wrong with planning for the future, but the planning must be realistic. Anyone who invests a large amount in real estate should at least take time to determine that it's a good buy. When you read about those who "made a killing in real estate" you can be sure they didn't do it by buying a bare lot on the other side of the country through a newspaper ad. If anyone makes a killing on these deals, it will be the person who placed the ad and sold the land to someone who didn't even investigate it.

The day of reckoning arrives when the unsuspecting buyer decides to move to the area or to sell the property. It might well be as barren as it was on the day of purchase. The promised development might have begun but failed simply because it had little appeal. Ordinances may prohibit some of the hoped-for development. Lack of water, particularly in the West, dashes plenty of development dreams. The cost of building a home there might just about double because of distances the builders must travel. You can probably think of other possibilities, maybe some experienced by friends.

All real estate deals aren't bad. But most good ones are made that way by careful shopping and selection, certainly not by merely answering a mail ad. If it's such a good deal, why must they go nationwide looking for buyers? Any local area of the country has someone just waiting to jump on a good real estate bargain. Is it logical that a lovely resort community would contact you in Michigan to offer you a choice piece of Florida at a great price? Many of the world's most competent business leaders are in Florida. If it's really such a hot property, they'll be waiting in line.

Quality of Life

If you are going to move, the question of "to where?" is probably best answered by a look at, for want of a better term, "quality of life" (overused during the last decade, but it fits). For most of us, quality of life depends a great deal upon what we get for our money.

We interviewed a military retiree who had bought a home in a Virginia suburb of Washington, D.C., during the early seventies. It turned out to be an outstanding investment. He was on active duty then, and once he transferred out of Washington, he had no intention of returning. He'd spent some time at Fort Carson, Colorado, and decided upon the Colorado Springs area as his retirement home. A scouting trip to Colorado Springs changed his mind. Although he still loved the area, he realized the cost of real estate there was now more than he wanted to bear. Both he and his wife were from South Dakota, and they decided to return there . . . not exactly to their home town, but to the region—within reach of both sets of parents and old friends, but not right in their laps. But the quality of life was their deciding point.

"We looked at homes in the Colorado Springs area and considered what we'd get for around $80,000. It amounted to a rather small house on a small lot and not much more. But up in South Dakota, we could custom-build our home for that, on a real nice lot. And we'd be a lot more at home there, too." Based upon that consideration—less worry, less expense—their decision was made. They sold their home in Virginia and built a new one in South Dakota.

The bottom line here amounts to a caution: Don't rush into buying just because you would like to live "in Arizona." Do the necessary fine-tuning, call for help, and start early enough to put it all together. Once you know exactly where you want to settle, many of the remaining challenges will become much less intimidating.

The Human Element

Secure in the knowledge you've decided upon your preferred area, you'll start toying with other considerations—ones that are hard to nail down. If you want to put them under one heading, call them "human factors." They complicate life and at the same time make it worth living. Children, grandchildren, parents, home, and friends fit this category. The stage of life at which most retire from military service is also the point where these human factors are most complicated. If they aren't more complicated than before, at least some changes are taking place.

At the time of retirement-home selection, most military retirees consider moving to be near their parents. After years of absence, a sense of responsibility toward aging parents—the retiree's and the spouse's—must be balanced against other considerations. And how about the children? In a typical situation, one is starting college near home, a married son just moved out West, and a daughter is expecting her second child in September.

If your parents live in Vermont, your spouse's live in Florida, you're now stationed in Kentucky (where one of your kids is starting college), your oldest son's in Nevada, and your pregnant daughter— mother of your only grandchild—is married to a Washington businessman, you've got some tough thinking to do. This is especially true if you'd really prefer to live in the mountains around Boone, North Carolina!

Children

This dilemma is actually common for military retirees. The solution is always easier when it is someone else's problem. But now, or in the near future, it is your problem, and you must think it out. For a start, consider this no-nonsense advice from Action for Independent Maturity, a division of the American Association of Retired Persons: "Don't make the common mistake of moving just to be near the children. You may find that your children's friends aren't your friends and that their way of living isn't your way." Well put.

There are myriad reasons you should not try chasing your children all over the country. Remember, they are young adults in the same modern, highly mobile society from which most military retirees are planning to settle down. What happens if you move based upon your children, then they move in a couple of years? Who is to say they want parents next door, anyhow? That thought might hurt a little, but we want them to be independent, don't we? If there's a real emergency, or if you've just got to visit, the capability is there. At most, consider the children's location as one of many factors—and one that may be temporary.

Parents

Being caught between generations, as military retirees usually are, requires a look in both directions—from perspectives of both parent and child. Parents tug at a different heartstring. You feel you owe them, and you may. As they grow older, they quite naturally want time with their children, and vice versa. You've been traveling most of your adult life and probably haven't had much time for parents. Now, the choice is yours; you want what's right for everyone. Think about what's right in this case. Do you want to be next to your parents constantly? How about your spouse's parents? How do they feel about it? Why? Do you want to be near so that you'll be handy in case of an illness or death? Couldn't you get there in a real emergency?

With careful planning, you can work out what to do in case of an emergency involving parents. Shake the tendency to avoid talking about crises, and face the reality that they probably will occur. This realistic planning lowers the "worry level" so that you can make sound, rational decisions.

Recent figures show an increase in "extended family" households. The reason for this phenomenon is primarily economic. Not since the Depression in the thirties have so many young adults returned home and so many families doubled up with parents. Economy is an angle that's hard to ignore, and you'll be looking at it as you plan to return to civilian life. But if living with parents is one of your options, don't overlook the lack of independence such an arrangement imposes upon you—and on your parents. There is no question that there are stresses involved in this type of arrangement.

Military Friends

When a military family faces a decision on whether or not to move, military friends—with whom they have moved all over the world— take on added importance. They have watched each others' children grow and shared the heartbreak and joy of dozens of departures, separations, and returns. There is no use trying to tell the children that they'll adjust fine without their friends. They have been through it all before. No matter how well they adjusted in the past, they know that it's tougher every time.

Without realizing the depth of her statement, an Air Force wife hit upon something we all know but just haven't put into the proper words. She said, "You know, in the service everyone is your friend until he proves otherwise. In the civilian world, he's otherwise until he proves he's your friend." She said it just right. We put a great value on friends, possibly because we need each other. But we also say goodbye to our dearest friends as regularly as most civilians mow their lawns. It never gets easier.

Retirement from the service isn't just another move to another base where old friends already live and where more will be arriving soon. No more, "If we don't catch you on Okinawa, we'll see you at Quantico." It's different, and the entire family recognizes it. You're stepping off the merry-go-round, and most of your present friends are still on it. Hold it! Present friends? Exactly. How about all your dear friends from over the years who've retired ahead of you? Where are they now? How long has it been since you've heard from them? Could you contact them now? If you're still in touch with more than three or four, you're truly the exception to the rule.

Why didn't we keep in touch with those old, dear friends? We were slaving away holding the service together, working on our own careers, and raising our own families. We had worries enough. We tried to keep in touch during the holiday season, but before long the address was lost or the card was returned with no forwarding address. We still think of them, even though we've lost touch.

Now, you need to look at the same hard fact as you become the military retiree. Your friends will still be on that merry-go-round. Your relationship will change, for a variety of reasons. Your list of common interests will dwindle rapidly. After a year or two, you'll find the same subjects that interest you today have become boring with a capital B. Promotion lists, who is the new Sergeant Major, who was selected for command, or how they reorganized the maintenance operation (again) just won't be high on your list. Several military retirees told us they consider their top item of advice: Do not retire at your final duty station because all your active-duty friends are there. They will be moving on.

Childhood Friends

When we consider old friends, we can't overlook those with whom we grew up. The pull toward the childhood home is also a strong one, but it is no different for a career military person than for a civilian who left after graduation and never returned. There is great appeal to the idea of settling in among old friends, catching up on the last twenty years or so, and picking up where you left off. But throughout those years, each of those friends has been growing in separate directions, in unique ways. It was natural to have everything in common when life consisted of five classes a day and a ball game a week. How about now? How many old friends are even there now? How has the town changed?

Consider Your Alternatives, and Weigh Them Carefully

When you leave the service, you get one last "free" move: Make the best of it. Now is the time to start thinking about it. Actually, finances may not be your main consideration. Suppose buying in one location costs $10,000 more than in another? It's a lot of money (especially with interest figured in), but if it means the difference between complete contentment and a life of discontent, isn't it worth considering?

Spend valuable time with your spouse talking about location. Are there family considerations or problems or potential problems you need to think about now? How about those friends? Will they still be a major consideration five years from now or will they have moved on? What type of housing do you want now? Do you really want the large lawn and home to care for? Are there any health considerations? Looking ahead twenty years or so, wouldn't a single-story dwelling be a little easier for both of you? Will you have access to your military benefits?

Answer the above questions and the ones you add. Start early enough so that you don't have to rush into a deal right at retirement time. Travel to the area. Remember the top three considerations in home selection: (1) location, (2) location, and (3) location. Be just a little selfish; think of yourself for once, and select as though you plan to spend the rest of your life there. You may.

5

Buying Your Home

For most of us, a home is our biggest expense. Certainly it is the most expensive single item we're likely to purchase, and as an investment it is normally one of the most productive.

Military life doesn't always lend itself to home ownership. Frequent moves, undesirable locations, availability of government housing, quality of off-base housing, and the future of the area (especially communities near installations that may be closed on a Congressional whim) are all major factors that may postpone or prevent home purchase.

The possibility of a move every two or three years just about rules out ownership for some until service life is over. Generally, advisors recommend against home ownership if you aren't going to keep the home at least three years. For those on the move, base housing seems ideal. In exchange for the government quarters allowance, the military family gets a decent place to live without the worry of utility bills, major maintenance, and insurance. In most cases, if the stove, refrigerator, or furnace goes on the blink, the installation engineers take care of it. The proximity of base housing to work, particularly for those in "critical jobs," is worth something in itself. Access to exchanges, medical facilities, theaters, and other base facilities makes on-base housing worthwhile to many families.

From a financial standpoint, some would argue that living in base housing or renting is always a losing deal. Not necessarily. Buying and selling a house every couple of years also can be a losing deal. Living in government housing or renting may well have been your best choice in the past, so don't fret about it. But don't go along just for the ride either; be sure you've got a plan. Most important, realize that government housing won't be available when you step out of uniform, so you've got to do something. For example, those living in government housing should save and invest the difference between their costs and costs for equivalent housing in the civilian community. Likewise, those who rent are actually making payments for someone else. They should be saving toward the day when they will purchase their own home and make the payments for themselves.

One of the ironies of military life is the fact that the huge old homes on installations are reserved for the senior folks—the ones with no (or few) children at home. Over in another area (out of sight) are the young NCOs' and officers' families in much smaller homes. Of course, the reverse would be downright ridiculous. There is no way you'd want to start out in a mansion and work twenty-five years to be moved into a duplex. After years of waiting, everyone wants a well-deserved turn in the high-rent district. When your time comes, the furniture doesn't quite fill the huge home, but you "grow into it." When it is time to leave the service, it's just become comfortable. But now it is time to buy a home, and you may be planning to spend the rest of your life there.

Match Your Home to Your Needs

Unless you are really hung up on image, don't base your housing requirement on what you've become accustomed to (or were anticipating) in that big set of government quarters. If you have owned a five-bedroom home when the kids were home, don't feel it's a come-down to buy a smaller house after they're gone. It makes sense. If you want money for your future and to enjoy life more today, don't put it ALL into payments, taxes, utilities, upkeep, and insurance for a home that's five times larger than you need.

Once you determine what is appropriate for you, don't allow tales of others' successes or failures to deter you. Someone who bought a home in 1971 in the Virginia suburbs of Washington, D.C., will rush to tell the tale of how he doubled his money in 1978. The guy who lost his shirt when Fort Wolters, Texas, closed after the Vietnam war, or when his home sat empty for a year before it sold won't be so eager to speak up. There's no point in dwelling on the past. Those who own homes may stay put or repeat the process in a new location. Many leave active duty having never owned a home or having sold theirs years ago. Before jumping into the housing market, it is healthy for all of us to review the basics, particularly in today's very dynamic housing market.

Hire a Lawyer

Sometime during the process of buying a home you'll think about hiring a lawyer. Do it. In some areas, only a lawyer can draw up the real estate contract. However in most, a real estate broker can do it, but he represents the seller. Who will represent you? It may be cheaper at the time not to have a lawyer, but it could cost you in the long run. You'll find the lawyer's fee is money well spent.

What Can You Afford?

When you start shopping for a mortgage, you'll wonder what you can afford. If you aren't yet settled in a civilian job and you need a home (say, for instance, you're in government quarters and must move by retirement day), you've just stumbled onto another example of the wisdom of locating your next job while you're still employed. Why is the job so important? Generally, lenders will consider a mortgage up to around two and a half times the borrower's (your) annual income. After debts are considered they may make some minor adjustments, but this figure is in the ballpark. Another approach is to consider the monthly house payment, which should not exceed 25 percent of your monthly gross pay. Many authorities suggest that long-term debts, including taxes, mortgage payments, and homeowner's insurance, should not exceed 33 percent of your salary. Apply these rules to a $1,400 military retirement. Then try it with that $1,400 retirement income plus pay from a good job; you'll quickly see the difference for you and your family.

The higher the down payment, the less you'll have to borrow. There is a tendency to jump the gun here and put together the largest down payment possible, using every available dollar. This can be a major error.

If you plan to sell the home in a few years, you will probably be ahead if you do not make a large down payment. Remember, your profit will be based on what you have in the house. If you put $20,000 down on a $60,000 home and sell it for $80,000, your $20,000 profit represents a 100 percent gain. But if you put $10,000 down and sold the same home for the same amount, your gain would be 200 percent. In addition, with the large down payment, you limit the number of persons who can assume your mortgage should you decide to sell.

Plan to take full advantage of your investment. Remember, interest on a home loan is tax-deductible. This can amount to quite a savings with no effort at all. Also, if you don't put all your cash into the down payment, you can invest it elsewhere. Combine the return on that investment with the tax break you get on your interest payment, and you may gain considerably.

Some home buyers prefer the peace of mind of owing as little as possible. Financially, this doesn't always make sense, but *you* judge the price of your own peace of mind. If you have definite plans to remain in the home after retirement, you *may* want to pay it off before you retire permanently.

Take a little time and study the mortgage tables in detail. Two items will leap out at you: (1) The longer the term of the mortgage, the higher the interest cost (by thousands of dollars), and (2) when you consider twenty-, twenty-five-, or thirty-year mortgages (for example), the difference in the amount of monthly payment is surprisingly small. You can probably stop smoking and with the money saved cut five or ten years off your mortgage (at the same time adding five or ten years to your life!). When you do that, of course, you are also cutting the same amount off your tax break. But, if you time your mortgage so that it will be paid off when you *really* retire, you'll probably also slip into a lower tax bracket at the same time. The result usually balances well; the lower your tax bracket, the lower the tax break for mortgage interest.

Types of Mortgages

In today's economy the pure and simple fixed-rate mortgage is about impossible to locate. Now the potential home owner is baffled by variable rates, rollovers, and other confusing ways of buying. In appendix 1 are descriptions of some of the methods commonly in use.

Sources for Mortgages

No matter what type of mortgage you get, your loan will probably fall into one of three primary categories:

1. **Veterans Administration (VA) Guaranteed Loan.** This loan is also commonly called a GI loan. It's one of the VA benefits, but it may be a tough one to collect. The VA loan is popular because of the low down payment; some homeowners have bought homes on VA loans with no down payment at all. Unfortunately, not all lending institutions are willing to give VA loans. Their main objections are VA interest-rate restrictions and the bureaucracy. As with other government programs, the paperwork and delays are drawbacks. For the borrower, this is one of the most appealing methods of securing a loan, but the catch remains: You must locate a willing lender.

2. **Federal Housing Administration (FHA) loans.** Much like the VA loan, the FHA loan is characterized by the paperwork and detail you'd expect in a government program. Any adult citizen may apply for a FHA loan. It also requires a lower down payment than a conventional mortgage. Although the basic cost of a FHA loan is low, there are some costs that can creep up on you, particularly at time of settlement.

3. **Conventional loan.** This loan, which is the most common, is a deal between you, as borrower, and the lender. Since the lender is taking the full risk, the interest rate will probably be higher than if the loan were backed by VA or FHA. For the same reason, you should expect to make a larger down payment.

Sooner or later, most military retirees own their own home. While on active duty, many prefer government quarters. But the day arrives when government housing is no longer a possibility. Then the choice is clear: You either pay for someone else's home or pay for your own. Most choose the latter. With all aspects of transition planning, preparation is the key to success. Since the home is usually our largest purchase, this preparation is doubly important. For contentment with your civilian home, start paying for it early with planning, research, and savings. The return will make it all worthwhile.

6

Start Early and Be Prepared

Start Early

A social scientist said that the best way to measure "class" is to look at how far in advance one plans. The further ahead, the higher the class. It sounds a little strange at first, but that rule could be applied to anyone. It certainly applies to those in military service.

Very few quality troops stay in the military for the active-duty pay. Even fewer of those now ready to become civilians did so; the pay scale when they started out was much lower, even with inflation considered. Odds are you remember those lean early years and don't need to be reminded.

Why, then, did we stay? Duty, honor, and country—sure! But we also had dreams, aspirations, and goals. And those who could plan ahead saw military retirement as a reasonable return on a heavy investment. Although it's getting expensive for the government, the retirement system is probably the best incentive for keeping quality people in the armed forces. At least it was for those who are reading this—those who planned ahead when it was decision time. Now we're proud that we planned, and that our advanced planning shows some class. But why should our planning stop when we leave the service? It doesn't. It can't!

We spent twenty, thirty, or more years in psychological preparation for retirement, but are we prepared to *really* retire at an age somewhere between 37 and 55? In the civilian world, these are the peak earning years! They're also the most rewarding and enjoyable years (once the tuition and orthodontics are paid).

So, when we become civilians, is it really retirement? Wouldn't we be better off if we thought of it as a transition, or perhaps, to use a currently overworked term, a passage? Officially, we may be stuck with the word *retirement*. After all, who can imagine a "transition parade" or a "passage ceremony?" But we must stop thinking of the end of a military career as retirement. Few are ready to stop work at the comparatively young age at which one ends a military career.

Why is it that we'll spend six months planning a vacation and little or no time planning for the next third of our lives? Dozens of cliches come to mind—the ones about each generation failing to learn from their elders. If those who are "getting out" would only talk and listen to those who've traveled the road just ahead of them, they would avoid most of the pitfalls. For example, if you're thinking of just taking it easy, talk with someone who retired ten or twenty years ago. You might discover it really isn't such a great idea.

According to a recent Harris Poll, the most common retirement advice to the young is *prepare early*. This is twice as important when we're talking about military retirement and the concurrent career change.

Perhaps as a result of half a lifetime in a world of detailed planning and deadlines, or from a tendency to organize based upon critical points, we tie our transition to civilian life to the military processing schedule. You've seen it happen. An example might help.

Sam announces he's going to hang up his uniform for good. He's immediately hit with all the standard questions, including, of course, the top three:

1. Who will you work for?
2. What will you do?
3. Where will you do it?

Suppose the earliest Sam can submit his retirement request is 1 March, six months before the desired date. Odds are that his answer to question 1 will be something like, "I'm really not sure, but I'll have six months to work on it. I've got a lot of contacts in Washington"

(Texas, California, high places, aviation, computers—take your choice) "and I'm going to work on them. I'm working up a resume they won't be able to resist."

Question 2—What will you do? is a simple, but tough question. It's obvious Sam hasn't seriously considered translating his military skills into civilian terms. Count on him to look back on his experience and cite the fact that he's an experienced manager and administrator. After decades of government work, everyone becomes, has become, or thinks of himself as an administrator of sorts. So, to question 2, Sam might say, "I'm not sure exactly what I'll do, but I'm used to doing just about anything that needs to be done—and doing it well, I might add. My record proves it. As long as I have a responsible job with decent pay and a chance to move up, we'll be happy." Who wouldn't be?

To question 3, Where will you live?, there are several variations of the same theme. In a moment of wisdom and compassion, the government decided to allow up to a year after separation before the last government-paid move. This wise decision has saved many a heartache but is too frequently used as a crutch, immediately following the answer to question 1 (Who're you going to work for?). For example, to answer 1, Sam adds, "Can't tell yet where we'll be living. But we're not worried about it. We've got a year to decide."

The problem here is that Sam (and thousands just like him) is already late. His planning is based upon dates that are solely for government administration, and have nothing to do with personal planning for a career transition. If Sam waits until he has requested release from active duty to start his transition planning, he has created a crisis at the worst possible time. He is not sure what he wants to do, for whom, or where, and the road is going to be a mighty rocky one.

When you leave the military you won't retire, despite the fact that you've been thinking "retirement" for years. Avoid becoming one of the unprepared veterans by planning and organizing your transition to civilian life.

Within the next week, set aside the time to draft a resume. Use any format, even a straight narrative on yellow paper. Don't worry about all the possible formats; you'll decide upon one later. Just sit down and write about yourself. Give it your best effort. Once you're done, evaluate it (be super-critical). Then have some friends, preferably civilian friends, look it over. Once you complete your first critical analysis, you will almost certainly decide not to use that first resume. The purpose of writing it is not to write a resume for a job search. But

"What are you going to do when you retire, Elmo?"

once you complete it, you'll agree that writing it is a valuable starting exercise.

You probably noticed that sizing up your own accomplishments and qualifications is a tough job. Without a doubt, some of your proudest accomplishments don't translate into civilian terms.

Perhaps you can spot several gaps in your qualifications. For example, you might feel that you need some computer training, or that you could take that one more course to get fully certified.

You might develop the feeling that you're "overspecialized" or "overgeneralized." When there's nothing else to grasp, interviewers sometimes use these handles to get you out the door. It's a safe bet that you're neither; but at this early stage, if you feel your draft resume leans one way or the other, go ahead and think about the correction. You've got time.

A day or so after writing it, you may realize that your resume reads like an obituary. It tells, in almost checklist form, what you did in the past. This is the most common problem, but you've spotted it early.

If you really gave this first draft a serious try, you probably can identify a few separate analyses you need to make and several lists you want to work on. Super. Now is the time, not a month before you become a civilian.

There are dozens of other benefits that can come from this exercise. Everyone who does it points out a new one. The resume itself is *not* the sole route to a satisfying new career. But the time taken to write one will be some of the most valuable time you can spend. Why? It gets you started!

How early should you draft a resume? Now. If you have a year of military service remaining and haven't done it, you're running late. If you have ten years until you become a civilian, why not write it now as if you were planning to start your job search tomorrow? Armed with the results of your effort and your remaining time in the service, you can make vital adjustments on your life's course. Five years ahead of time is about right. It's important to remember that this is the resume that starts your planning process. Don't get bogged down in making it pretty. It won't be the one you use. That one will be far superior because you'll have the benefits of an early start, several revisions, and time to do it right.

The toughest part of the process is objective self-analysis. Coming out of a successful military career, it's easy to be so impressed with yourself that you lose sight of the goal—a new career. Conversely, if you look only at shortcomings, it can have a devastating effect on your confidence and effectiveness. So strike a balance. Remember, you must be tough now or later you'll wish you had. But—and this is critical—be tough in both positive and negative areas. Recognize your strengths and plan to exploit them. Isolate and face up to your weaknesses, then do something about them.

Self-evaluation is a constant process, and it takes on new dimensions when it is time for a career change. Some forms of this evaluation process take months, even years. On the other hand, there will be a need for some quick, on-the-spot judgments. The latter are difficult to predict and will be dictated by the situation (an interview not going as you'd like, for example). But the evaluations and analyses you need to start on now are the ones you can identify. These include a hard, continuing, cold look at yourself; your goals; your desired field of work; where you want to live; and possibly most important, your attitude toward the transition in general and the items just mentioned in particular.

The key to the transition process is preparation—not a couple of phone calls before taking a short exploratory trip, or a month or so of scanning the Sunday want ads. Last-minute, panic-plagued decisions may haunt you for the rest of your life. Planning and research is necessary, and you have to do it. Read up on the subject of getting a job. As with most research, you will find that each book or article leads you to another. You will soon realize that there is help available and where it is. If you sort it out to fit your situation, you won't be stumbling around in the dark.

One of the fastest-growing employee benefits in industry is pre-retirement planning. Many corporations have programs for their employees, and the number is growing rapidly. It doesn't cost the company much, and it pays off tremendously. The employee leaves the company with confidence. He has his legal affairs in order; his estate is planned; he has attended seminars on psychological preparation for retirement; his finances are straight. He is prepared for most of the changes that come with retirement. The best advertisement for a company is a happy former employee. A prospective employee talking with such a former employee will get an outstanding impression of the company. When do the companies with these programs begin? *Ten years* before the individual retires!

If we had one wish (on retirement programs, of course), we'd see that the military started similar programs. The cost would be high, but the payoff would be fantastic because planning must be done while there's still time to put it into effect. There is one other, more significant reason: With industry, the retiree is a real retiree; with the military, we're actually talking about a mid-life career change. The need for the program is greater, and the people involved are twenty years younger than those in industry. But under the current scheme, if you start talking about pre-retirement planning in the military you might just as well talk about deserting. It isn't considered proper to talk about retirement.

No matter what program the services might adopt, there would be a problem of giving it the personal touch we'd all like to see. There are just too many people, scattered over the entire world, to allow a solid, reasonably standard program without unreasonable costs.

So head for the library. Start a file, noting anything you might use later. List your contacts or note the need to develop some contacts. List companies that specialize in your field and those that may appeal to you for other reasons. Get their annual reports. Who are the key people? Start a geographical file. Do you know exactly where you want to settle? What firms are there? You need a complete file, custom-made for your needs, and only you can develop it.

Although job-changing reference materials rapidly become out-dated and some are useless, most at least deserve a review. If you get one worthwhile tip, or one seed for an idea, the effort was worthwhile.

Soon after you start you'll begin to wonder whether to concentrate on the advertisements, contact a search firm, or take some other course of action. If you use only one approach, you limit your odds for success. Knowing a little about each, you can arrive at the best combination for you. The following chapters should help.

Prepare for Job Search Expenses

Now is as good a time as any to talk a little about money.

Those who start their pre-retirement planning early, as we all should, are aware that the very process of successful transition is going to involve some expenses. It's money well spent. If you are going straight to a job, it's the job you want, and it's where you want it, congratulations. But most of us should plan on expenses for the job hunt.

Some of the job-search literature implies that your results will be directly proportional to the money you spend. Other studies caution against spending on fake agencies and individuals claiming to have the solution to all your problems. We can best describe our view as this: Plan on postage costs, some travel, typing and printing fees, purchase of paper (and matching envelopes), and—this is a little tough to pin-point—costs of keeping yourself in circulation. (NOTE: Keep a record of all these expenses—most are tax-deductible.)

Stay in Circulation

There is no way you're going to launch a successful second career while living like a hermit. There will be unforseen expenses that must be paid at the time, such as luncheon appointments, memberships in civic organizations (a great way to maintain contacts in the community), and wardrobe items. More on that last item later; suffice it to say here that a majority of military folks are a little spoiled by wearing uniforms most of the time.

Keep Informed

There will be some expenses incurred just for getting informed about pre-retirement planning. Although you can save by using references from a library, there are some books and pamphlets you'll want to purchase to mark up or reread.

Take a Course

You might be one of the lucky ones who has a pre-retirement planning course available. Such a course will be valuable, particularly if it's through an educational institution. Many of these courses are designed for the person who is planning for the *big* retirement—not for the career change. Even those courses have value in that you come out of them knowing what needs to be done. And you are more fortunate than most students in the course because you still have time to do it!

There are a few courses designed for the military retiree. These are oriented on the job hunt and concentrate on the details of items discussed in this section. If you take one of these courses, you'll be much better off for the experience. Just be sure you know what the course covers before entering it so that you get what you want.

Invest in the Best

If you're applying for a position where a resume is appropriate, be assured that quality counts. Your first costs will be for paper and printing. If you go second-rate, it will look second-rate. Do it right. Get some help at the printer's or stationer's shop, and carefully select your paper and print style.

7

Search Firms and Employment Agencies

Executive Search Firms

Save a lot of energy and disappointment by learning exactly what executive search firms are and how they operate. As in any field, there are some shady operators here, but most well-known firms are on the level. Take time to check them out. For the rest of our discussion here, we'll talk about the "good" ones.

Executive search firms go by several names such as "headhunters" or "recruiters." They work for the employer, not the job-seeker. They are hired to find a person to fit a specific job, and their fees are usually based on the salary of that job. As a job-seeker, you need to keep this in mind if you decide to try a search firm: They don't owe you a thing; their loyalty is to the employer, and they're paid by him. For several reasons, this isn't all bad.

The headhunter with a good reputation becomes the employer's trusted advisor. To maintain that advantage, he's going to fill each position as perfectly as possible. If he misses the mark, his search firm may lose a valuable client, and *he* may be looking for a job. In the headhunting business, reputation is everything.

If reputation is so essential, it stands to reason that those who work for the better search firms are going to be carefully selected, and they are. Most are former executives themselves, who were hired away from their previous positions by their current bosses (brutal, isn't it?). They know the ropes, they're well educated, they're poised, and they're super salespeople. Real, honest-to-goodness headhunters are some of the slickest operators you'll ever meet. In this case "slick" is meant as a compliment (in a sort of "know your enemy" way). They have a mission, they know how to go about it, and they are trusted to deliver.

We know the headhunter is: (1) professional, (2) trusted by those who hire him, (3) "slick," (4) well educated, (5) experienced, (6) articulate, and (7) paid by employers. So wouldn't this headhunter also be just the person you want to get with? Not necessarily.

How They Function

Remember, we started off talking about *executive* search firms. Although there's an occasional exception, particularly in the cases of high technology specialists, headhunters still concentrate on executive positions. Why? Company executives normally draw the top pay. The headhunter, as we mentioned, is paid accordingly, usually a percentage based on the pay of the position filled. So if you're seeking and are qualified for an executive position, the headhunter may just be for you.

Since the method of operation for headhunters is to seek out a prospect, you have to let them know you're available. That isn't always as easy for a military person to accomplish as it is for a civilian. The reasons are important if we are to understand the big picture.

At first glance it appears that headhunters play dirty pool. Maybe so, but business is, by nature, competitive, and that competition includes getting the very best employees into the key jobs. A victory in this department is all the more sweet if the key position is filled by someone formerly with the competition. In fact, the competition is the happiest of hunting grounds for headhunter firms. In this case, the military certainly is not considered competition, nor is it a particularly appealing area for headhunting.

Headhunters will agree that the services are loaded with skill and talent. But they also believe that the same individuals who possess that skill and talent (1) have no feel for today's business world, (2) have no recent business experience, and (3) live in a different, isolated world. On the extremely rare occasion when a military member appears to be perfect for a position, timing and availability (of both the position and the individual) may become problems. (A person with eighteen years with one company may shift to another; no one with eighteen years in the military can be expected to leave that close to the magic twenty.) Whether or not we agree, if we are to win we must look at it from the headhunters' eyes. By doing so, we can help ourselves, and, if we're half as hot as we think we are, help the headhunter help us.

Despite their brilliance and finesse in the business world, most headhunters are uninformed about the military. They have no idea (1) what skills are available, (2) where the talent is, (3) the depth and breadth of the talent, or (4) how to match these skills with the civilian market. No one said headhunters are stupid. On the contrary, they don't waste time or motion; they see little to be gained by orienting on the armed forces when it's obvious the services will resist their efforts.

Let's face it—while in the military, we are conditioned to guard against anyone leaving. Remember how you reacted on those rare occasions when a civilian firm grabbed one of your most skilled troops just as he or she was about to take another hitch? Only recently have any job search, retirement planning, or career-change books appeared at the Post and Base Exchanges. A big part of military business is retention of a strong, youthful, and vigorous force. Nothing is wrong with that, either. But as we mentioned, no organization "retains" forever. Sooner or later, everyone is cut loose by choice or by the organization.

Still, the services want headhunters to leave their best and brightest alone. After years of expensive training and valuable experience, it's payoff time. The services want theirs. Headhunters, certainly not out of respect for this desire (are you kidding?), would just as soon do their shopping within the business world. After all, if they can fill a position with an executive with twenty years' experience in the same field of business, why should they bother to take a military person and start him at day one?

The headhunters' approach is reasonable, if we look at it from their point of view. For example, suppose a robotics company is seeking a purchasing agent. When the search starts, number one on the list is: Purchasing Agent; Number two, Robotics, then everything else. Unless the headhunter gets extremely desperate, he won't try the military. He probably won't even consider the military. He will try to fill the position from the same or a closely related industry. In one of our more memorable conversations with a search firm representative, we were asked this theoretical question: "If, during the WWII Allied drive in Europe a key general was lost, would the command have gone to Ford Motor Company for a replacement? Why should the reverse be true?" Point taken.

Some Mutual Respect Might Help

If a headhunter seeks you out, he might be of considerable assistance to you. He is already interested, or he wouldn't have contacted you. Keep in mind, though, that they submit several qualified candidates for each job, so you're never home free. But you have a contact, which can be worth its weight in gold.

If you happen to be called upon by a headhunter, treat him or her as you would a prospective employer. Headhunters are pros, and they can lull you into a false sense of security. (After all that military training, you wouldn't let that happen, would you?) They're looking for sharp people who are moving up in their organizations.

The good news for those in the military is that—as a side effect from the headhunters' almost total avoidance of the military—they are not in the least impressed with the Pentagonese double talkers. So the highly qualified professional from Camp Swampy will probably outshine the name dropper with the impressive title who counts paper clips in a tight, green, Pentagon basement cubicle (you know him, too?). Justice. At last. The question employers want answered, now and throughout the job search, is: What can you do for me?

Should You Contact Search Firms?

The big question now becomes: Should you contact executive search firms or not? Waiting for them to contact you is a waste of time. If, after thorough self-evaluation, you decide to go for an executive-level job (starting at, say, $35,000—and that's low), you've nothing to lose; contacting a search firm early in the job search may result in a pleasant surprise later.

Use of search firms can well be one of life's more humbling experiences. Don't despair; there's more (humility) to come. Since forewarned is forearmed, you should expect no more than 50 percent acknowledgment when you write to them. Responses will be in the form of postcards or form letters, advising you that, "should an opening arise . . ." Try about a hundred firms. Remember the odds. You could get lucky.

Employment Agencies

Employment agencies differ from executive search firms in several ways. Among the most important are method of operation, payment of fees, level of jobs handled, number of cases handled, and success rate.

Most employment agencies keep lists of job vacancies and job seekers in their area. If they can match the vacancy with the person, then everyone is happy. To become a part of this matching game, *you* must contact *them*. It's best if you do so in answer to a specific vacancy. You may also want to arrange an appointment with them, which is no problem.

How They Function

With most firms, you'll be asked to fill out an application that goes into considerable detail. You might avoid this requirement by attaching your resume and completing only the part of the application not covered by the resume. For executive-level positions, you usually won't be expected to complete the form, except for a signature. A caution here: Some employment agencies operate by rules similar to real estate firms. They'll ask you for exclusive handling. Don't give it, or you'll severely limit your future capability.

Employment agency fees may be paid by you or the employer, depending upon the situation. Generally, the employer pays for any position for which he advertised and for executive positions. You might pay if you've agreed to do so and you get the job. If you desire, you can list yourself as available only for fee-paid vacancies.

Although employment agencies sometimes handle positions in the $35,000-a-year-and-above category, most of their listings are below that level. Indeed, it's probably safe to say that in most cases their capability is below that level. (They don't know about most key executive positions because employers don't tell them.)

Should You Contact Employment Agencies?

Some job-search books write off employment agencies without giving credit for the possibilities they present. As you continue your research, you'll see what we mean. Count us in the minority, because we think employment agencies can help you. Of course, we are interested in a broad spectrum of qualifications and skills. We happen to believe that military people have an array of unique abilities and experience that needs to be matched up with the market. We're talking about all levels of skill and pay. The employment agencies just might have the ticket. Above all, don't ignore them.

Occasionally, an employment agency will specialize in a certain career field. The current hot items are computers and electronics. If you can locate one for your specific field, you're in luck.

But even with those agencies that are generalists and don't specialize in a narrow field, it pays to contact as many as possible in the area where you are concentrating your search. If nothing else, agencies should have a feel for the local market.

Even though we recommend contacting employment agencies, we have to face the fact that they have a pretty dismal placement record. Statistically, about any agency you contact will look grim. But know what you're up against and how they operate before starting a campaign. It would be foolish to skip a reputable agency simply because someone said the statistics weren't good. They have to score now and then, or they're gone.

To summarize, the best approach to employment agencies is:

1. Be sure it's a reputable firm. According to Richard Nelson Bolles in his classic *What Color Is Your Parachute?*, there are about 8,000 private employment or placement agencies in the United States. About 1,700 of them are members of the National Employment Association (2000 K St. NW, Suite 353, Washington, DC 20006), which maintains a set of standards by which its members should

abide. The others, although some are good, are more or less on their own.

2. List with those in the area where you plan to work. Go for fee-paid (by employer) jobs first. With these, realize your sales pitch must begin with the agency. Since the employer is paying the fee, the pressure is on the agency to satisfy him without wasting his time. Obviously, most of the screening is done at the agency. Don't overlook situations where the fee is negotiable. One of these might make a major difference unless you simply refuse to gamble any of your hard-earned cash on a job that might not work out.

3. Do not grant exclusive handling rights.

4. Don't expect much, but hope for the best. You've covered this job-search approach, now move on to others.

5. Follow up. Keep in touch.

8

Newspaper and Magazine Ads

It seems as though everyone looking for a job looks at the newspaper ads. Close your eyes and form a mental picture of someone sitting at home, planning a job search. It's a safe bet your picture will include two items—a cup of coffee and a newspaper. It's almost a tradition! But job hunting through newspaper ads is one of the toughest and most frustrating methods.

The Odds Are Not Good—But Don't Let That Stop You

As a result of the high number of persons using ads in their job search, success rates are extremely low. Many job-search experts advise against using ads at all. But you can say anything with statistics. If 100 persons apply for a job and one gets it, that's a 99 percent failure rate. But the person who got the job after answering four ads was 25 percent successful (or you could say 100 percent—he got the job!), and the company that placed the ad filled the position.

The best approach to the use of ads should be the same as with other techniques: Study the strengths and weaknesses of the method, and exploit every possible advantage. A lot of the pluses and minuses aren't apparent at first.

Look Beyond the Job Title

Well. in advance of your campaign, start screening ads. The best ones are in major newspapers and, of course, in the local papers from the area in which you plan to work. This latter source is frequently not explored. There's good material on other pages beyond the ads. You can get a feel for the community, the industry and business picture in the area, who's moving up, who's opening, who's closing, who's dying (don't laugh this one off—even if everyone moves up a notch to fill the void, there'll be an opening at the bottom), who's hiring, and who's firing.

That Language—Is It English?

Another advantage of becoming an expert on the ads is that you can't help but pick up some of the current jargon. Grab onto those buzzwords, and use them in correspondence (if they fit).

To those who love and cherish the beauty and clarity of the English language, the ad search is a maddening experience. It's true that you need to plow through some abbreviations, but most of the heavy abbreviating is done by individuals to save costs. A legitimate and worthwhile job ad will probably spell things out.

The ad may be spelled out in such detail that it's difficult to understand exactly what the job is. This is the opposite extreme from the abbreviations. For most former military persons, this situation is familiar, even though it is in a new setting. Look over some of your former job descriptions. Did you really do all that? Come on, now. Remember when replacement time came around and the person being replaced was asked to list the qualifications required for the job? He'd describe himself, then add all qualifications he didn't have but would like to. Then he'd add any that might enhance his image later although he didn't have the qualification while in the job. If a job now requires a person with at least an associate degree, most would assume it always did. So each time around, the job itself gets a little (or a lot) inflated.

Inflated job descriptions are bad enough in isolation, but couple them with the stilted, phony language used in the ads and you'll have one tough time breaking the code to answer the basic question: Just what are they looking for? We're familiar with the ads for a garbage man that ask for a sanitation engineer. A recent example was the New

"But the ad says, 'Sanitary Engineer!' "

York hotel ad for an access controller. To the rest of us, that's a doorman.

Beginning secretaries and middle-level executives are constantly embarrassed by applying for the wrong job because of a poorly worded ad. This problem is more prevalent in management and administrative areas than in those requiring hard skills. It's tough not to be clear if you are looking for a tool-and-die maker. But if you are looking for a person with strictly administrative skills, it's equally tough to be accurate. Not everyone tries.

All Isn't As It Appears

A newspaper ad looks innocent enough, but few ads are precisely what they appear to be. Not only is the wording frequently deceptive, but that may not be all that is not as it seems. The ultimate goal of the ad may be far from what meets the eye.

An ad may appear many times for one job. There are several legitimate ways this can happen. An employer might advertise in several newspapers or list the position through two or more agencies, each of which lists the job in a slightly different manner. That wouldn't be so tough to sort out if the job and the firm were clearly identified, but they usually aren't. In fact, most employment ads are appropriately named: blind ads.

Blind Ads

The blind ad is the one that looks appealing but doesn't tell who placed it or where the job is. Although the general location ("Washington area," "downtown Baltimore firm," "Midwest") is usually given, it is normally vague enough to discourage you from pinpointing the exact firm. Most blind ads look promising and ask that you reply to a box number.

Why won't they come right out and level with you? In the first place, if you are really the smart person they're looking for, your first move would be to bypass the personnel department specified in the ad (Good!). There are other legitimate reasons for blind ads. For example:

- Any discerning employer knows people will bypass application channels if details are known.
- The employer may not want it known that he's seeking a replacement.
- It is commonplace to receive over 100 applications for a job opening. In many cases, thousands pour in.

- The employer will turn down all but one of the applicants. A blind ad helps cut down on ill feelings resulting from rejection.

But there are also some not-so-clean reasons for blind ads. Simply stated, a lot of blind ads are fake.

Following through on the current hot item, computer technology, let's take an example. Suppose a placement firm in the Washington area is running low on qualified computer repair technicians. (In that area most businesses without some computer capability will definitely lose out, so demand is great.) The placement firm goes out with an appealing blind ad for computer repair technicians in or near the Washington area. Resumes pour in. No response is necessary by the placement firm. Good resumes are filed, and the weak ones are canned (usually by a secretary). The firm now has a feel for who is out there (and how hungry and eager they are) and can pass that information on. Meanwhile, the computer repair technician is out there in never-never land waiting for a reply—from a box.

Some Ads Gather Information

Not all ads are blind. Some of the more prominent ones are placed by reputable employers. The employer and the position to be filled are clearly identified. Although some companies will publish an ad, they may decide to fill the vacancy from within. Again, as a result, the company accumulates a pile of resumes and gets an idea of what talent is immediately available. With some analysis they just might learn a thing or two about the competition. For example, if there are five applicants from Murphy's Super Widget Factory, something's amiss at Murphy's. Better interview at least one of them.

Most Jobs Never Make the Ads

The simple fact is that most jobs don't get into the ads. They're filled from behind the scenes, from within the company, or by someone who knows someone. Higher-paying slots may be filled by a search firm. And what's to keep the personnel department from calling someone from that stack of resumes they accumulated six weeks ago with a blind ad?

It's apparent to the most casual observer of ad listings that the lower the pay, the more listings. Conversely, there will be a few clearcut, on-the-level ads for high-paying jobs.

One exception to all of this might be ads for a field in which there is a critical shortage. A recent example was the nurse shortage. With the ads from most major papers, a qualified nurse could just about pick her job. The reason for the shortage was that nurses were being paid about half what truck drivers were, and they left nursing in droves. The shortage was apparent.

A Short Checklist: What to Expect from Ads

When we use ads, we:

1. join the majority of job hunters;
2. can expect limited results;
3. can develop a feel for the market;
4. can keep up to date on the current jargon;
5. will have a tough time determining the exact nature of the job;
6. are seeing only a small fraction of available jobs;
7. are not seeing the best-paying jobs;
8. may be able to spot critical shortages and plan accordingly if qualified.

9

The Resume

Resumes are not used in military service. That fact alone should alert us that there is a new language to learn, new formats to master, and new procedures and channels to follow.

The misconception that the resume is the solution to all job-search problems abounds throughout the military services. Maybe that's because the first real resume most of us see is our own. It is almost always a sure loser, at least before about twenty revisions. Writing a good resume is an art. For many, it's a full-time business. There are a lot of ripoff artists in the field; before you pay a fortune for someone to write yours, research the subject and try it on your own.

As with the rough draft we mentioned in chapter 6, the *act* of writing the resume keeps you involved with every word. You know the answer to possible questions about each item and why you feel that item is important. You can get help writing your resume, but you must stay involved in the process from the start. Imagine your embarrassment when a prospective employer questions a resume item that was thrown in by someone else and which greatly distorts what you are trying to say.

Some Rules

There are a few rules for resumes:

It Must Be Neat

More than neat—it must be perfect. There should be no typing errors and no spelling mistakes. One of either can kill your chances.

"I asked for a resume, not a sequel to *Gone with the Wind!*"

It Must Be on Quality Paper

It should be on the best paper you can buy. Use at least 20-pound weight. If you decide to use other than plain white, choose something subtle such as off-white, ivory, or one of the parchments. Avoid trying to attract attention with garish colors. That kind of attention is the kind you attract when you wear a sports jacket to a formal. DO NOT make a photostat of it and expect it to work. If nothing else, it shows you don't care enough to go first class.

It Must Be Truthful

Emphasize a point, play it down, or leave something out. But do not lie. If you do, you will regret it.

It Must Be an Appropriate Length

If the resume is more than two pages, it is probably too long. If you can capture your qualifications on one page, do it. If you can't, use more. But many long resumes don't get read.

It Must Be Grammatically Correct

A minor error might escape the first screening, but it will be noticed by the person with authority to hire you. Along with grammar comes the pitfall of trying to be so brief that the resume reads like a telegram. The other extreme is going into too much detail. Make the point and then go to the next one.

It Must Avoid Gimmicks

Subtle techniques, such as type selection or paper choice, are not gimmicks in this sense. Some of the books that try to guarantee your resume will "get attention," "sell," or "stand out" resort to outlandish gimmicks. One, for example, has a homemaker listing her qualifications—based upon running the home—as transportation manager, budget director, long-range planner, and so forth. That gimmick could only serve to humiliate someone (in the unlikely case the resume passes the first screen). Homemakers do perform a variety of difficult functions. But to compare running a family budget with corporate budget direction is downright falsification and a waste of everyone's time. If she wrote an honest resume, her chances would be much better. How does she answer the question, With what organization did you perform these duties? That farfetched example is one to keep in mind as you write your resume.

It Should Indicate Educational Achievements in Clear Terms

Don't forget all that military training, some of which is worth a fortune.

It Should Reflect Experience in Terms Appropriate to the Company

It would be nice if what is most impressive in the military transferred directly to civilian life. It doesn't. Now it is time to speak the language of the company to which you are applying. It's also time to weed out what military jargon has crept into your resume. Impossible as it may seem, there are actually people out there who don't know the meaning of NCOIC, SAC, TAC, OSI, CNO, DOD, Brigade, Company, Squadron, or deuce-and-a-half. They aren't impressed, and they don't really care about ATTs, IGs, ARTEPs, Mass TACs, or two holers. The onus is on you to put your experience into "civilian."

It Must Give Appropriate Personal Data

This is one area upon which the experts disagree. There are many variations. These data consist of age, marital status, health, religion, sex, citizenship (if other than U.S.), and other items about yourself.

Equal opportunity laws forbid discrimination for reasons of age, race, creed, religion, color, or sex. But there are times when it may be useful for you to clarify or even emphasize one of these items. If your name could be mistaken for one of the opposite sex, naturally you should make it clear. If you are applying for a job that is closely tied with a religious faith, it makes sense to indicate yours. If you are in excellent health, say so, with no elaboration. If you are not, don't mention it.

Some experts say indicate your military rank; others recommend that you do not. As rank is one measure of success, and we're talking about career military people, there is no need to avoid it. Just say, "leaving Navy as a Master Chief Petty Officer" or "leaving Army as a Colonel."

Few civilians have the travel and international experience to compare with that of military members. This is a plus and should be mentioned along with your willingness to travel or relocate in the job for which you're applying. Include foreign language proficiency in the resume. But don't exaggerate your proficiency, especially if the language is required for the job.

The resume must give information necessary to get in touch with you: address, phone number, or specific instructions if you are applying through an intermediary.

It Must Be Current

A resume becomes outdated as quickly as a service record. When you change it, retype it and have it reprinted. No cutting and pasting.

Resume Styles

There are many resume formats, each of which serves a useful purpose. For the person leaving military service, we recommend you use one of the two most common: functional and chronological.

The functional resume lists your experience by function, such as personnel management, logistics, EDP, planning, and operations. It is particularly useful if there are gaps that you don't want to emphasize or if you are targeting a specific function. In the functional resume, you list your strongest field first and others in order of your strength or proficiency.

As the name implies, the chronological resume lists experience in chronological order, as it occurs. You reverse it, listing the most recent experience first. There should be no unexplained gaps. In the case of former career military personnel, it is common to have job gaps covered in the education portion of the resume. Don't worry about one or two months between tours.

10

The Interview

You Need a System

There are many ways to contact prospective employers. Some are original, some are freaky, some are standard, some are stupid, and some are brilliant. Among the least brilliant methods is stuffing resumes into envelopes, sending them to answer every ad you read, and waiting for employers to come knocking on your door. You must have a system.

Assuming you've done your research on *what* you want to do, *for whom,* and *where,* it's about time to hit the streets. Above all, make every event a learning experience, and don't think you know it all just because your resume is done (or you've made a decision not to use one). Keep the final objective—the job—in mind, but concentrate on the intermediate objective: getting the interview.

One of our favorite references on the transition process gives the impression that keeping records on your job search is a little silly. Well, no reference fits all needs, and on that one point, we disagree. Most say that records are critical to the process, and we agree with that. As a minimum, keep a 3 × 5-card file showing the following information:

Front of card:

1. Name and correct address of the firm.
2. Key personnel by name and position. Who would have the authority to hire you?
3. Name of the secretary of the person you are targeting.
4. Essential phone numbers within the organization.
5. Notes on company size, specialty, etc., that you may want for quick reference.

Back of card:

1. Dates of contact with firm, and method.
2. Follow-up action, date, method.
3. Notes for your personal reference (i.e., "Smith really doesn't do the hiring," "Brown is a miserable so-and-so," or anything you want to write down). Remember (here's a familiar military term): *Lessons Learned.* Any time you blow a chance, or do something that really has super results, jot it down.

Write a Letter

Resumes pour into companies at varying rates, with top rates in the thousands per day. Chances of weathering the initial screening process are slim. But even after that process is beaten, there are several screenings more before final considerations begin. Your thoughts must be toward getting around all that. One of the most straightforward approaches is also one of the most successful. Write a letter.

Rather than sending a resume, write a letter to the person in the organization who would have authority to hire you. This is where research will pay off. If you have difficulty pinpointing that individual, write to the vice president whose title reflects your general area of interest, or write to the CEO (Chief Executive Officer) of the firm. That person will probably refer the letter to the appropriate person for reply; then you at least have a contact. Address all correspondence to a person by name, never by just a title.

The greatest advantage of using a letter for initial contact is that you can tailor the letter to the situation. This is particularly true if you are answering an ad. If you are a supply specialist who has worked in personnel for the last four or five years and you are applying for a personnel-related job, the letter will allow you to emphasize that aspect of your background; a resume might stress personnel as a small part of your military career.

In writing the letter, gear it to the ad you're answering or to the job for which you are applying. If you are just applying for a job with a firm—not in response to any specific job opening—try to make your letter fit the industry.

There is nothing wrong with using a standard basic contact letter with minor modifications to fit each situation. Each letter, however, must be typed separately. Don't try to have a dozen or so run off, then just type in the name and address, the salutation, and the date. It won't work. And it certainly won't fit multiple situations. This touch of individuality points out the need for another strict rule: Keep a copy of everything you send out! You'll find it makes follow-up easier and helps avoid stupid mistakes when you get busy.

If you decide to send a resume, always send it with a cover letter. Never just fold a resume into an envelope and mail it. Good cover letters, specially tailored to the situation, generate good vibrations with employers. There's a risk that something in the resume will work against you; something that might result in you being screened out. But a brief (no more than one page) letter with your resume is far superior to just a resume. Think about using this technique as a follow-up to the initial letter rather than for initial contact.

Follow-Up!

How about the follow-up? When you write your initial letter, indicate that you will call on a certain date, normally about a week or two after you send your letter. Note the date you will contact the person again. Do exactly as you promise. A successful career transition takes time.

Selling Yourself

For many former military persons, the job search is also their first attempt at selling a product. The product is the individual job seeker. Throughout the process, keep your eye on your goal: getting the right job. The employer isn't really interested in your need for a job; he wants to know what you can do for his company. It is the answer to this question that you must think of as you write, and particularly as you call. If you're successful in getting a key person on the phone and all you can say is, "I'd like to come work for you. Will you interview me?" you're sunk. Think about what you will offer, and how you're going to appeal to the company. For most military people, this is like trying to communicate with another planet. But you've got to learn the language.

Learn to Think $$$$$

In the military your whole life has been event oriented. Everything is measured by training tests, inspection results, retention records, AWOL rate, deadlines, equipment maintenance, and above all, mission accomplishment. In civilian business life, everything is dollar oriented. There are different ways of expressing it, but that is the bottom line. Think that way when trying to sell yourself.

Think of the Secretary—Some Kindness Both Ways

We mentioned the secretary. If you think she's about the most important person in the world to you right now, you just may be right. The higher the level, the greater the importance of the secretary. Most executive secretaries actually run the office, and included in that operation is the careful screening of who gets through to the boss. The better ones are particularly expert at keeping unwanted callers and visitors out of the boss's hair.

One of the most common methods the secretary will employ to keep traffic away from the boss is referral to another department. No doubt about it, a lot of business callers start in the wrong office. But if she is to be effective at this, she must know her way around the company, right? So ask her for assistance.

When you call, it should be as you promised in your letter. You are then faced with the old challenge of slipping through the secretarial net. And it's a real challenge. You might start by stating, "Good morning, Miss X, this is Y. Mr. Z is expecting my call. Is he in?" (Obviously, you have already obtained her name before this call.) Now, it may get sticky. What do you do if she says the boss isn't in? Don't just say "OK" and hang up. Find out when he'll be back, then say you'll call back. If she just tells you that the boss won't talk to you, ask her about what other department you might call, names of key persons, and secretaries' names. Then try them, saying that you were referred there by (boss's name) office. Don't misrepresent yourself, just stick with it. Get any lead you can, and follow up.

After you have received help from a secretary, drop her a brief note, thanking her for taking time to help you. Don't overdo it, but she'll appreciate it and will remember you.

Don't Get Discouraged

As you do your pre-retirement planning, you will find all sorts of statistics about what you should expect. One of the most striking is the low response rate you should expect when you send out your resumes and job search letters. We're talking about favorable response—that which asks for more information, asks you to get in touch with a company representative, or offers an interview. The range we've seen has run from 2 percent to 8 percent, depending on the level of employment sought. The higher the pay, the lower the response rate. Let's be optimistic and say you should get about a 6 percent favorable response.

Of the 6 percent who responded favorably, you will probably get an interview from only half of them. Then, it's so obvious it's embarrassing to say it: Don't screw it up! Or at least, if you do, take notes!

An Interview!

You have been working on getting an interview. Finally, you get one. The mission now: Turn that interview into a job offer. This is a skill in itself.

The Dress Code

The next item is one you'd better get hard-core about whether you like it or not, at least if you are going for a middle management or higher job: dress. If there's any area where military retirees are more in the dark than civilians, it would have to be finances, but the general lack of knowledge about civilian clothing and appearance is really something to behold. This is one of the areas where we've got to get tough with ourselves, or we'll lose out. We just never worried—or cared—about the whole subject. We're not trying to pretty anyone up now, but try this on for size; see if you recognize a friend or two.

Most career military personnel (male) rarely buy their own clothes. Their shopping is done by their wives. They wear civilian clothing (suits) so infrequently that the suits are still "new" after several years. If a necktie still matches the suit, it's good enough. There is little need for good shoes; the shine on the uniform shoes is terrific. Most social functions involve others in the same boat, so there is little opportunity to measure just how one's wardrobe will fit the civilian business environment. The result is this: You feel and look sharp in uniform and can spot a flaw from a mile away, but you'll probably fail inspection in your new "uniform"—that of a civilian.

Show up for an interview in a ten-year-old polyester suit, wide tie (or narrow if the style changes again) and your military shoes, and you're going to lose out in the "first impression" department.

We said it before—the purpose of this chapter is to get you thinking about these things. Get a current book on the subject. Dress the part with a sharp, conservative look. Become an expert on your uniform now, just as you did before.

Know the Company

Before you go for an interview, scout the company from every possible angle. Check the wealth of information in the library, and get a copy of the company's annual report. Know what the interviewer's main interests are (VP for engineering, planning, etc.). Know what problems the company is facing. You have something positive to offer; think about how you'll present it.

Don't Stop Everything for One Interview

When you get an offer to call for an interview appointment, don't just drop everything else in your job search. Until you gain some interviewing experience, you must keep every wheel turning. If you are fortunate and have several offers brewing at the same time, you'll be dealing from a stronger position. Most likely, the first one or two won't work out. (This is one reason some counselors advise you to hold off on your prime target until you gain interview experience.)

It Isn't All New

Now for some similarities between civilian and military interviews—and some differences. When we first considered the following items, we wondered if they were appropriate for ex-military types. We concluded they are—as much or more so than for civilians. Most are second nature to military persons. A prospective employer will expect them to be second nature. But counting on second nature at a critical time doesn't always pay off. We hope you agree.

Punctuality is critical. You should arrive at the appointed place about five minutes before the scheduled interview. If you're going to do this, a reconnaissance will be required. Don't be early or late.

Appearance counts. It counts as much or more than anything else. All this time you thought appearance mattered only in the military. Before you open your mouth, you're sized up. You must look sharp, but not necessarily in the military sense. Appearance also includes your composure, posture, mannerisms, and speech style. Be prepared, and your confidence will soar. If you are confident and knowledgeable, your ability to carry on the necessary conversation will come naturally.

Before an interview, do everything possible to relax. Preparation is the key. Have your clothing ready. Don't leave home with the gasoline gauge leaning on empty. Have parking meter change. Get a good night's sleep. Allow plenty of preparation time.

Do not drink alcohol before a job interview! If you feel you need a stiff belt before the interview, take comfort in the fact many others feel the same way. But that doesn't mean you've got to do it. A job interview is one of life's most stressful situations. Everyone feels the strain. The person who feels no strain in a job interview is either dead or doesn't want the job—and won't get it. Do not drink alcohol before a job interview!

If the interview takes place, as many do, during lunch, and the interviewer offers you a drink, it's still best if you avoid it. You can say you're watching your weight, or you have a busy day ahead and you don't normally drink during the day, or whatever you can think of. If the interviewer wants to drink, no sweat—it gives you an edge. Caution: Don't say you can't drink because of doctor's orders. That indicates a physical ailment (or possible drinking problems) and might be a turnoff.

After it's all over— if you get the job—then get with your favorite partner and pop the cork. Cheers.

Don't allow yourself to be put into some sort of subordinate situation. This is tough for all of us, coming out of military board and interview experiences. When you begin your conversation, you can do much to set the tone of the interview. Be prepared to ask a question or two. Do not answer questions, "Yes, sir" or "No, ma'am." You can be courteous, but you also want to be as much in control as you can handle.

Remember the old high school speech class trick to help get over nervousness: Imagine the audience is sitting out there in their underwear. We'll go one better, and it's not imagining anything: *The person interviewing you is just as uncomfortable as you are.*

Few persons are comfortable conducting interviews, and fewer are adept at finding out what they really need to know during an interview. You'll probably feel all those silly, unrelated questions are an effort to put you at ease. In truth, they are probably being asked because the interviewer doesn't know what else to ask. It's a ridiculous situation. You've spent a lot of time preparing for this interview, and here you are answering some idiot question about the weather in Kentucky. And as you talk, the person across the desk is pondering what to ask next. You're just playing another of life's little games, and you can handle it. Do not be intimidated.

The Big Three

There are three questions you can count on being asked. They won't all ask them in the same way, but you'll get them.

1. Why do you want to work here?
2. What can you do for this company?
3. What will it cost us?

Count on a lot of smoke before those questions surface, but be ready for them. Rehearse your answers. Again. Again.

Do Not Volunteer

You must come across as confident and on the ball. If you are confident, one easy error is to give more than you're asked for. No sense wasting bullets you may need later. Do not offer a copy of your resume unless asked. And, although it's tempting, don't offer references unless requested to do so.

The whole package you are trying to achieve is one of poise and confidence; of a person who would bring certain skills to the company; of a person who will represent the company well; and of a person with potential to grow within the company.

Some New Situations

If you get out there and ask some of the veterans who've gone before you, they'll tell you a couple of other tales that you should keep in mind. You won't forget them when you hear them from the person who suffered through the experience. Of all we've heard, there are a couple we've heard enough to repeat.

First, there is a strong possibility you will be interviewed by a

person who is considerably younger than you. Under such circumstances, NCOs and Warrant Officers have a strong edge. After all,
they've been adapting to shavetails for years. Some of the old colonels
and captains just fall all over themselves in this situation. The more
arrogant ones even get so insulted they lose interest. There's not much
we can do to salvage them.

Next, some of the questions you're asked will really tempt you to
reach across the desk and do something drastic. Since you can't do

"Your resume says you worked in California, Texas, Japan, Florida, New York, Japan, Florida, New York, Alaska—how come you couldn't hold down a steady job?"

that, do the wise thing and prepare for them. Write down all the questions you can imagine you'll be asked, and then write down your answers. Rehearse them. Write down your main weaknesses. Rehearse an answer to questions that might zero in on them. Two of the most common (exact opposites of each other) are:

"Frankly, John, we are looking for someone with diverse experience and a broad background. I'm concerned that your twenty-nine years of Marine Corps service doesn't quite fit that mold."

"Frankly, John, we are looking for someone with a little more depth. I'm afraid that the vast diversity of your Marine Corps assignment—skipping from one job to another every year or so—doesn't quite fit that mold."

If you've considered answers to these questions and others, you'll jump right on them and come across like the professional you are and always have been.

Don't sacrifice that professionalism. There are times when the thing to do is just get up and thank the interviewer, and hit the road. Guard against any hot-tempered, hair-trigger reaction, but you are not there to be insulted or belittled. Use your judgment.

Negotiations During the Interview

After all the small talk is done, the interviewer will get to the nitty-gritty. Or maybe you'll be left cold and depart the office with a handshake and "We'll be in touch." If they do get in touch with you and ask you to return, they're interested. In extremely rare cases, you may just have done so well that the interviewer gets down to business during the initial interview. When either occurs, you'd better have your best arrows ready. Practice is over. This target is for the record.

Negotiating for Salary and Benefits

Salary

When the time comes to discuss salary, there is an old rule that holds true time and again: He who mentions an amount first, loses. That's really a good rule, and you can see how it works. If you say, "I was thinking about something in the range of $30,000," the interviewer then has something with which to work. He counters by acting amazed and telling you that $30,000 is "in excess of what the company would be willing to consider for the position."

On the other hand, if you can get the interviewer to say something like, "We are considering paying in the neighborhood of $30,000 to the holder of this job," you have the upper hand. Raise his offer about 10 percent and work from there.

Negotiating for our pay is something most of us dread. It's distasteful to us, but we've got to do it.

Any civilian who is changing careers will go for at least a 10 percent or 20 percent increase in pay. If you don't set that standard for yourself— as a minimum—you are selling yourself short. If you do set that minimum standard, sad to say, you will be in a minority of military retirees who do it.

It must be because we are accustomed to pay scales, knowing just what to expect, what our boss is paid, and what everyone else in the organization makes that our standards have become geared to that military pay scale. Why are so many new military retirees the only ones in the country who *plan* to take a pay cut when they change to a new job?

An Army colonel told us, "I'd be satisfied with about $18,000 a year." There is a lot wrong with that attitude. First of all, as a colonel, he's about a $60,000-a-year executive. Now imagine a $60,000 civilian executive telling an interviewer he'd be satisfied with about $18,000 a year. There are all sorts of possibilities, but almost surely he won't get the job. At least he won't get a job at the appropriate level. Neither will a First Sergeant who agrees to go to work for half of his pay or less. He won't get the *right* job.

Suppose he gets a job at the pay he was willing to take. It's almost a sure thing he will be employed at nowhere near his capability. His supervisors will be sweating him out because he's obviously as well or better qualified than they are and will soon show it. He's hired at well below the going rate, and he's resented, much like illegal immigrant workers—and about as welcome. His self-esteem will slide rapidly. Each year he's underemployed, he gets older, and his credentials for advancement become less convincing because most recent experience, particularly the current job, is what is weighed heaviest.

Pay Attention Now!

Another giant bugaboo about your military pay is the *employer* who tries to play games with it during the interview. It'll go something like this, "With what we're offering you [rock bottom—you can bet on it] and your military retirement pay, you'll have a real healthy income." Now, this just may be one of the times when you want to take a walk. Listen. Your military retirement is none of anyone's business! That is a return on an investment you made—a lot of tears, a lot of sweat, and in many cases, a lot of blood. It's like suggesting you take less pay because you already own your home.

If you had inherited a sum from an aunt or uncle, invested wisely, or been born rich . . . what would your reaction be to the employer who said, "With what we're offering you [same rock-bottom amount], plus your investments, plus the money you have in the bank, you'll have a real healthy income?" What's the difference? Only one. Within a few dollars one way or the other, your military retirement income is a matter of public record.

Military retirement income gives you a hedge—there's no doubt about it. If you need to job-hunt for a month or so longer, you still can make the mortgage payment. But don't let anyone throw it at you, and on the other hand, don't flaunt it. Consider it an investment that's paying off, and get on with your life.

"Perks"

As you consider a compensation package, don't forget the perquisites, or "perks," that may be available. We're all used to some fringe benefits, so this isn't all that strange for us. It's just that there are so many possibilities it's staggering. Among the more common are: stock options, medical insurance, matching investment programs, retirement plans (usually a big drawing card for state government employment), reimbursement of expenses, company car, company credit card, and tax assistance. You can use perks to boost your actual income, and you can use them to salvage a misstep in your negotiations— if you perceive it in time.

Suppose you're cornered (which happens, particularly during some early interviews). You say you think about $xxxxxx is appropriate for starting salary for the job. The interviewer lights up and, either by words or by expression, says "Great!" Whoops! If he's all that tickled with your numbers, they must be low. So, staying the cool dude you are, you lean back and say something like, "Of course, I'm referring to base salary. Naturally, I'd expect to participate in the company's stock option and insurance plan. And I'm sure you cover travel expenses for employees."

Turn it around if you need to. Once again cornered (this will happen less as you get experience and confidence), you misstep in the other direction. The interviewer reacts in such a way as to leave no doubt that you have overbid. You then lean back and say something like,

"Of course, I'm referring to the total package. I'd expect to participate in the company's. . . ."

The younger you are, the more appealing future opportunities with the company are. As most military retirees are at least in their forties, futures may have a little less appeal. But don't overlook some of the more short-term prospects, such as a salary review in six months or a year, particularly if you really like the company and aren't quite satisfied with the initial deal.

Every facet of transition to civilian life takes preparation. We've been harping since page one about doing your homework before the last minute. The transition to a new career is a big change in your life. It's every bit as big a change as the one you suffered the first day that drill instructor greeted you at the bus stop, and it can be even more traumatic.

By now, you know searching for and getting the right job is a tough job. It's probably one of the toughest you've ever tackled. But if you get your stuff together, and *if you start early,* you'll get the job. Consider the other parts of the retirement process—the ones we discuss in other chapters. Plan your job search. Now you're more prepared than the competition, and you and your family can look forward to the transition. And that's as it should be.

11

Your Net Worth

No matter when you become a civilian, there are going to be some life-style changes. That's sort of a catch-all term which includes work, play, income, dress, health, and just about any other facet of life. During the transition, changes in some areas will be more pronounced than in others and will vary depending upon the individual family involved. At the center of any life-style must be some financial planning. If the planning is to be the slightest bit successful, it must be directed at a goal.

Keep Your Goals in Sight

Throughout this book, we emphasize the importance of establishing sound goals that extend far beyond the military career. This is particularly important when considering financial objectives because so many other goals depend upon reaching a certain degree of financial independence. Owning a summer home takes money; simply maintaining today's life-style in the same home will take money—plenty more than it takes now, considering inflation.

Those who have sound financial goals surely recognize that their main consideration at military retirement time will be, "How do we maintain our momentum, and what changes are required to do so?"

Those who have not yet established solid objectives, or who planned only military life, face a different challenge. For them, the top question (once the goal is set) may well be, "How—and where—do we begin?"

Establishing and reaching financial goals must be viewed as a process. As with any process, there is a need to maintain a running total of how it's going and what changes are required. In other words, every now and then we must ask, "Where are we now?"

Figuring Your Net Worth

If you take a couple of hours and compute your net worth, you'll have a reasonable idea of where you are now and how you are doing as you work toward your financial goals. Chances are, you'll also learn that you're worth more than you thought. That usually has a very positive effect, even though most of us feel we should be worth even more at this stage in life.

Your net worth is the difference between what you own (assets) and what you owe (liabilities). There's nothing difficult about figuring it, once you overcome inertia and get started, taking one item at a time. The format you use isn't important. Use plain paper, if you desire, or any of hundreds of formats available in just about any financial planning publication. As in those publications, we also are furnishing a computation sheet. And we hasten to add, you will probably have an additional item or two. If so, add it. There are many possibilities.

Guard against overestimating the value of your possessions. Some financial authorities recommend that you estimate the value of an item, then cut that estimate in half. Several recommend even more drastic cuts, up to 75 percent of your estimate. Most important, remember that a net worth computation is based upon *current value* of assets. It also must reflect the current status of debts, or liabilities.

In the event you bought stock last year for $10,000 and it is now worth only $6,000, you must consider it based upon its current value: $6,000. Figure items such as automobiles based upon what they would bring if sold today. For example, if you owe $5,000 on your car and could sell it today for $6,000, consider it an asset worth the $1,000 difference. If you desire, you can just list the debt of $5,000 as a liability and the $6,000 resale value as an asset; the end result is the same.

Every now and then it pays to look at one's personal situation from a purely business point of view. Preparing a personal net worth statement is one such occasion. You are actually auditing your account,

"Guess what? My salary is finally catching up to my taxes, mortgage, and deductions."

determining precisely where you are, and obtaining a picture of your financial strengths and weaknesses. Based upon this knowledge, you can then organize for whatever action you deem appropriate. Your net worth statement will be of great help when you plan for civilian life, *real* retirement, college for the kids, insurance coverage, home purchase, or any other major financial decision. Even if you don't use it for any of these, do another one in a few years and compare them. Then you'll have a clear picture of how you've been doing.

Once the net worth statement is completed, another valuable benefit becomes apparent. You can see, just by reading it over, what steps you should take to increase your net worth. You can easily identify strengths and weaknesses (such as heavy installment debt, too much insurance, or not enough set aside for the future). It's all there in one statement.

Before beginning on the net worth computation, here are a few examples of what to list:

Assets: Cash, checking accounts, savings, stocks, bonds, mutual funds, real estate, personal property (furniture, jewelry, autos, etc.), art, collections, money due you from reliable individuals, life insurance cash values, savings bonds, business holdings, and any other asset you care to list.

Liabilities: Amount owed on home mortgage, automobile, personal loans, installment debts, charge accounts, bank loans, margin loans for stock, insurance loans, taxes, and any other liability you care to list.

PERSONAL NET WORTH

DATE _____

Assets

Liquid Assets	Dollar Amount:
Cash on Hand	_____
Checking Account Balance	_____
Savings Account Balance	_____
Life Insurance Cash Value	_____
U.S. Savings Bonds	_____
Money Due from Others	_____
Brokerage Accounts	_____
Total Liquid Assets:	_____

Real Estate   Current Market Value:

Residence   _____

Other Properties (list)   _____

Total Real Estate: _____

Personal Property   Current Market Value:

Household Furnishings   _____

Automobile(s)   _____

Jcwclry   _____

Collections   _____

Furs, Art, Antiques,
   or Other Special Items   _____

Misc. Personal Assets   _____

Total Personal Property: _____

Investments   Current Market Value:

Stocks

   Common   _____

   Preferred   _____

Bonds   _____

Government Securities   _____

Mutual Funds   _____

Real Estate Investments   _____

Total Investments: _____

Other   Current Market Value:

Business Interests   _____

IRA Savings   _____

Keogh Savings   _____

Total "Other":   _____

Total Assets: $_____

Liabilities

Loans   Amount:

Home Mortgage   _____

Other Mortgage (second
   home, investment real
   estate, etc.)   _____

Automobile Loans   _____

Insurance Loans   _____

Installment Loans   _____

Margin Accounts   _____

Total Loans Due: _____

Other Debts   Amount:

Charge Accounts   _____

Credit Cards   _____

Taxes Due   _____

Insurance Due   _____

Rent Due   _____

Other, individual debts   _____

Total "Other Debts":   _____

Total Liabilities: $_____

Total Assets minus Total Liabilities equals your net worth.

12

The Survivor Benefit Plan

You Can Take It with You—For a Price

Although it is a major benefit, most active-duty families haven't tried to comprehend the Survivor Benefit Plan (SBP). In the past, official publications and briefings only hurt the SBP program because of the "fog factor." After trying to comprehend SBP most of us simply put it out of our minds. If we had fewer than twenty years' service, it didn't apply. If we had over twenty, it would be there automatically if we died on active duty. The references on the subject appeared to have been written by someone trying to impress us with a mastery of SBP, English, and the current federal buzzwords. Briefers, partly because of lack of depth on the subject, hesitated to stray from the lousy reference material. We use the past tense here because there has been a change. As interest in SBP increases, written material about it is becoming increasingly readable. Everyone should read and understand it. What is it all worth to you? Plenty!

As soon as you are eligible for military retirement (twenty years' service) you're automatically covered by SBP while on active duty.

On active duty, SBP is based on what your retirement pay would be on that date if you were retired. Your dependents receive 55 percent of that amount.

At the time of retirement from active duty, everyone is a SBP participant to the maximum extent possible (computed on full retirement pay) unless written instructions to the contrary are submitted by the service member at least thirty days prior to retirement. The choice may be for less than maximum coverage, or for none at all. In such cases, the spouse is notified of the decision by official letter from the appropriate Service Secretary.

Start with SBP, Then Plan the Rest

Why learn about SBP while you're still on active duty? Because this is a MAJOR item of your estate planning. Once you're familiar with SBP, you may choose it over life insurance options, investing the life insurance money elsewhere. Conversely you may decide against SBP. It's important to you and your family that the choice be a thoroughly considered one.

How Much SBP Do You Want?

SBP is free while you are on active duty, but you pay for it after retirement. The computation of SBP after retirement has always appeared to be much more complicated than it is. We believe the problem in the past has been that too many examples were used. If you see twenty examples and only one applies to you, the process gets confusing. So we're going to the opposite end of the spectrum and give only the basic formula. Understand about where you stand, and fine-tune the pennies later.

1. Begin with your retirement pay (gross): $xxxx.xx

2. Cost for the first $300 is 2.5%, or: $7.50

3. Cost for the remainder (item #1 minus $300) is 10% of that remainder: xxx.xx

4. Add 2 and 3, and you have your cost: $_____

5. Your beneficiaries will receive 55% of your retirement pay.

"I don't care if he *is* your dependent and lone survivor . . . he's not eligible!"

You Don't Have to Take Maximum Coverage

One of the most common complaints about the computation method is that it begins with a "base amount" from retirement pay, rather than the desired amount to be paid. Most military retirees with whom we discussed SBP said they would rather begin with a question like, "What will it cost if I want my widow to get $800 per month?" Of course the answer to that question can be computed, but discussions and computations normally begin with the base amount.

In the above example, the calculation is based upon maximum

coverage, using full retirement as the base amount. You may use a lesser amount by using the same formula but inserting the desired amount as item number 1.

If your retirement exceeds $300, the minimum you may use as base amount is $300. If your retirement pay is less than $300, use the actual retirement as your base.

Sergeant Anderson will retire with a retirement of $1,056 per month. He decides that he will use $900 of that as his base amount rather than the full retirement. His calculations go like this:

Base amount:		$900
Cost of first $300 at 2.5%	=	$7.50
Cost of remaining $600 at 10%	=	60.00
Total cost to Sergeant Anderson:		$67.50

How much will Mrs. Anderson receive each month? Just multiply the base amount by 55 percent. In this case she will receive, $900 × 55 percent, or $495 per month. NOTE: For a comparison, had Sergeant Anderson selected maximum coverage, his wife would have received $582 ($1,056 × 55 percent).

A Quick, Relatively Clean Look at SBP

In the examples above, we've used straight situations with the sponsor electing coverage for his wife alone. There are, of course, other combinations. We'll mention them here along with some other frequently asked questions about SBP. Rather than long explanations, we're going to give you a brief list with hopes that your questions will be answered:

1. The cost of SBP is tax-exempt (federal). It is subtracted from your gross retirement pay before taxes are taken out.
2. SBP annuity payments are taxed as normal income by the federal government. For example, at the end of each year your spouse will receive a W2 form from the government for the amount she received through SBP. State laws vary, usually giving some tax break on SBP annuities.
3. The entire SBP is indexed to retirement pay increases. If retirement pay goes up 10 percent, the entire program goes up 10 percent. The deduction from your monthly check, the amount of annuity, and the amount of annuity paid to those who are already drawing SBP payments, all rise 10 percent.

4. We just referred to it briefly in 3 above. Any time there is an increase in retirement pay, widows or other beneficiaries receive the same percentage as a raise. This is a big consideration. If you had died ten years ago (and were covered by SBP) your spouse would now be receiving about 250 percent of the monthly payment she received immediately after your death. Remember this one.

5. You may elect coverage for your spouse and children. In this case if your spouse does not survive you, payment is made equally to children under 18 (22 if in school). The cost of including children is small and is a factor of the child's age. On the average, costs are about 0.5 percent of the base amount.

6. You may elect the "children only" coverage. The system is the same as above, with payments going to eligible children upon your death and until they reach age 18 (22 if in school). There is no age limit if the child is incapacitated. The rate is computed using a factor determined by using your age and the age of your youngest child.

7. If you have no spouse or children at the time of your retirement, you may elect SBP coverage for anyone you designate, much as you designate a beneficiary on an insurance policy. This option, however, is dependent upon age (yours and the beneficiaries) and costs more than the options for spouse and children. The charge is 10 percent of your entire retirement pay plus 5 percent for each five years the beneficiary is younger than you. This can cost up to a 40 percent maximum of your retired pay. This option is the "Insurable Interest Option." We are not so keen on this option. If you are considering it, check other insurance possibilities.

8. If you have no dependents when you retire you may enroll later. If you get married or a child becomes dependent upon you, you have one year to apply for SBP.

9. The greatest hangup with the SBP program is the so-called "Social Security offset." This has caused many to decline SBP. In an oversimplified form it amounts to this: Once the spouse is eligible (normally at age 62) for widow's Social Security survivor payment, SBP is "offset" (replaced) by Social Security, up to a maximum of 40 percent of the SBP. Full Social Security is paid; it is the SBP that's offset.

10. As a minimum, consider SBP and make your decision one of the cornerstones of your retirement planning. Until you know your degree of participation in SBP, the proper course for your other investment and insurance decisions is only a guess.

Dependency and Indemnity Compensation (DIC)

No discussion of SBP would be complete without mention of a separate but closely related program: Dependency and Indemnity Compensation, commonly referred to as DIC.

DIC is Veterans Administration payment (monthly) to beneficiaries when the service member dies while on active duty. It is also paid after retirement if death is a result of a service-connected disability. This is yet another of many excellent reasons for the VA disability evaluation at the time of retirement from active duty.

If the spouse or children are eligible for DIC, the monthly SBP will be reduced by the amount of the DIC payment. DIC payments are tax-free, whereas SBP is taxed when paid. So the tax-free DIC payment is advantageous.

DIC payments are based upon the grade of the service member. As with most programs the rates are adjusted periodically.

Suppose a former serviceman dies of service-related causes after paying for full SBP coverage for several years. Once the VA awards his spouse DIC, the amount the husband paid for the portion of SBP that is now replaced by DIC payment is refunded to the widow. This is a hard combination to beat anywhere.

An example of the DIC/SBP combination (approximate figures): A service member, using $2,000 as SBP base amount, dies of a service-connected disability five years after retirement. The widow's original SBP authorization of $1,100 is replaced by a tax-free DIC payment of $500 and the remaining SBP, $600. The total she receives is the same ($1,100 in this example) with some notable changes—$500 is now tax-free. Her husband paid for $1,100 SBP coverage over the five-year period prior to his death. She is receiving only $600 from SBP. She will receive a refund of the amount her husband paid for the $500 SBP she is not receiving.

A Decision You Must Live With

Once the decision is made there is no turning back. With few exceptions (mentioned above), your decision at retirement time is permanent. Think it over; you don't get another chance.

13

Rehearsing for the Big Switch

When we suggest an actual rehearsal for civilian life, we're usually asked questions like, "Isn't that just a little silly? After all, we are dealing with adults here," or, "I can figure it all out on paper, so why go through that drill?"

The idea of rehearsing for the inevitable, particularly when the rehearsal is added to an already cramped schedule, may not seem worthwhile. In fact, of the vast number of possible retirement preparation actions, a rehearsal might be most valuable of all.

Many changes occur immediately after military retirement. It is sad when military families are surprised by routine events as they enter civilian life. It's even more disturbing to see their plans and hopes turn into major disappointments simply because they weren't prepared for events they knew were about to happen.

Rehearsing for the transition doesn't have to be a huge project. Even if you just "test the water" before entering it, there's always something to gain. We call it rehearsal because we believe the closer you come to a complete "dress rehearsal" the fewer surprises you'll encounter and the happier you'll be in the postmilitary years. Just how detailed you want to get is up to you, but give some thought to the following.

For the moment, look at military retirement as if you were actually retiring with no additional income and no job-related requirements. In almost every case, this won't be the situation. But it's a fine place to start because by doing so, you eventually separate the necessities from the "nice to have" items.

If you retired today, where would it be? Have you lived there? If not, have you visited, particularly during the least desirable season? How expensive will it be to live there year round?

We discuss "home" in other chapters, and that reinforces what we say here: Don't move somewhere just because you *think* you'll like it!

There are many ways to investigate the area you choose for a postmilitary home. Pursue every one of them. Send for material on the area. Get the opinions of others who live there. Locate someone who lived there in the past and moved away. Why did they move? Find out how the area meets your needs for (1) family preferences and needs, (2) recreation, (3) medical care, (4) climate, (5) expenses, and (6) military facilities.

Above all, visit the area as much as possible and at different times of the year. Get to know everything you can about local facilities, governments, taxes, transportation, and any unique characteristics of the area.

The real estate angle may be the most important one of all for you. Can you find and afford the type of home you want? How easily will you be able to resell it if you decide to move elsewhere?

The ultimate rehearsal for living in any location, is, of course, to live there. Next best is to check it out so thoroughly there is little you don't know about it.

Consider What You Will Do

It's almost a certainty that a military retiree will get another job upon leaving the service. So it's not yet time for pondering all that free time that comes with "true" retirement. That "golden years" free time won't be there for at least twenty years—if then. But there is a definite need to consider use of time as a civilian. Military duty days can be anywhere from eight to twenty-four hours. You can easily be gone from home for six months or a year (longer, in the worst situation). After

You wouldn't plan your retirement like this, would you?

military retirement, what will you do with those hours? You'll probably fill part of them with a new job and devote the rest to your family or some other personal pastime. What job? What pastime?

Do not view your situation as retiring *from* the service. Instead, look at it as retiring *to* something. (You fill in the "something.")

Rehearsing for what you want to be after the service may not be easy for everyone. In the case of someone who intends to teach college, teaching a night course or two would provide an excellent opportunity to check it out as a career. Many other jobs can be experienced while still on active duty. Some are the same in civilian life as in the service. In some cases though, the actual experience is beyond reach until after military service is over.

In instances where there is no parallel between service and civilian careers, how do you rehearse for the civilian job? As a minimum, you study it with regard to time required, how it will influence your choice of a home, what it pays, and how the family feels about it. Above all, is it what you want to do? If not, change now. Remember, retire *to* something. You should be able to look forward to it, and to look forward to it you must be able to identify it.

Rehearse for Your New Financial Status: Can You Do It?

"Your military retirement is all you need to get by."

You've heard it before and you'll hear it again. Do yourself a favor—don't believe it. You can survive on your retirement. You'll be able to make the house payment and cover most of the fixed expenses. When you think of it, that is a fantastic edge.

We agree with the experts who maintain that any sound financial program must begin with a computation of net worth. It's the old assets versus liabilities routine, and we've already discussed it. For anyone about to retire from the military, there's a much greater financial eye opener. Live for a month or two on your retirement pay.

The next time someone tells you that he didn't have to sacrifice a thing in retirement (we'll say after twenty years), ask, "How in the world did you manage to save your quarters allowance, your subsistance, and half of your base pay while you were on active duty?" If he didn't give up anything, that means he was living on half his base pay— the same as after retirement. Not likely.

Starting next month, take all your pay above your anticipated retirement and put it out of reach (in a savings account, for example). Then, using only what you'll have after retirement, try to make ends meet. Use the following for planning your rehearsal.

YOUR REHEARSAL MONEY—HOW MUCH WILL THERE BE?

Your military retirement pay is 2.5 percent of your current base pay for each year of service. The most familiar examples are 50 percent at twenty years' service and 75 percent at thirty years' service (75 percent is maximum). There are some rare exceptions (e.g., an E8 retiring as a captain or major). If you fit into one of the special situations, you'll know it, and you should use those figures. For the majority, we'll use anticipated base pay at time of retirement.

Active Duty Base Pay at Retirement $_____

Years SVC × 2.5% (years × 0.025):   _____

Gross Retirement Pay: _____

Now from this "gross retirement pay" figure, subtract the cost of your SBP coverage. (NOTE: This is before taxes.)

SBP Cost: _____

Your Taxable Retirement Pay Will Be: _____

Now, for a look at how much you'll need, and how much you'll have, fill in the following blanks to the best of your ability. Add your answers, and subtract Total from the Taxable Retirement Pay, above.

a. House payment or rent.   _____

b. Electricity bill.   _____

c. Water and sewer bill.   _____

d. Gas bill.   _____

e. Telephone bill.   _____

f. Gasoline bill.   _____

g. Car payment.   _____

h. Auto insurance.   _____

i. Homeowner's insurance.   _____

j. Allotments in force which you
   intend to continue.   _____

k. Taxes (all of them).   _____

l. Any other fixed expenses
you're aware of (i.e., college, clothing,
entertainment).   _____

Total   _____

This simple computation causes you to think in real terms, some-thing you probably wouldn't do until nearly retirement time, or later. Now, using these figures, live on your retirement pay for a couple of months. If you do it, you'll be in a distinct minority. Be honest with yourself, and make it count.

Of the prospective retirees who have completed a financial re-hearsal, the most common problem was the "special case." The car broke down, a house full of company stayed for ten days, or a family emergency required a long trip. These same crises will continue to occur after retirement, so you might as well include them as you prac tice. You probably won't want to disrupt Christmas or vacation plans with a rehearsal; go ahead and pick a couple of "off months" if it doesn't mean a major delay. But once you've come through it, re-member that there are several periods of the year in which you will experience greater financial stress.

Those living in government housing must do just a little extra figuring. Remember that on retirement day you will no longer be housed by Uncle Sam. With that change comes a mortgage (or rent), utilities, taxes, upkeep, and insurance. Use averages, but be sure to include these items in your rehearsal. If you just give this procedure a fair try, you'll be amazed at how much confidence you gain. You can now plan in real figures, not something dreamed up. You have an idea of what you need, and more important, what you have.

If we were talking about the "Big R"—*real* retirement, say at age 65 or 70, there would be an urgent need for more detailed rehearsal, but we aren't. Eighty-nine percent of military retirees go into other jobs, and 86 percent have families to support. We are talking about a major milestone—transition to a new career. In order to plan for it you need a definite starting point. You are at that point when you have determined your net worth and rehearsed living on your anticipated retirement pay for a month or two.

14

Social Security, Military Retirement, and Inflation

Benefits of Social Security

Social Security is one of the most valuable benefits available to American workers and their families. Computing Social Security benefits is, to put it gently, not simple. The first half of most Social Security references, whether prepared by the government or by private companies, helps you figure out if you're eligible for Social Security. For our purposes here, we'll make it simple: If you are on active duty you're covered. Coverage is based upon calendar quarters in which you contributed. If you have forty quarters, you're "fully covered," which means some benefits are assured at age 65 or if you are disabled.

It's important to look at the positive side of Social Security. Many consider the retirement check the only benefit Social Security provides. Mention Social Security, and visions of elderly citizens struggling for survival on their "pension checks" come to mind. A cursory review of possible benefits versus costs will reveal a surprising amount of coverage.

First, Social Security is not just a program for the elderly, providing old-age benefits. It does this, but also much more.

Second, Social Security is not just a pension plan for "the needy." For many it is the only source of income after the working years have ended. It also provides income to those who aren't "needy" after their careers are over.

Third, most of those who receive Social Security retirement benefits receive much more than they paid in.

Fourth, Social Security actually pays four types of benefits: Disability Insurance, Survivors' Insurance, Retirement Insurance, and Medicare. Most families know little about the first two—disability and survivors' insurance—and are only a little better acquainted with Retirement Insurance and Medicare.

Disability

The disability benefit guarantees a monthly income if the insured is unable to work because of an illness or other disability.

After a five-month waiting period, a severely disabled person may draw Social Security benefits just as though he or she had reached retirement age (65). The disabling condition must be expected to last at least twelve months or to result in death. Military disability payments are not offset by these Social Security payments.

In addition to payments to the disabled person, payments may be made to that person's dependents. Payments usually are made to:

1. Spouse at age 62.
2. Spouse at any age if a child under 16 is in his or her care.
3. The insured's children under 16.
4. The insured's children over 16 who were disabled prior to reaching that age.

Survivors' Insurance

Social Security provides valuable benefits to family members after the death of an insured person. These benefits, which are really life insurance protection, are paid without regard to age of the insured, and include:

1. Payment to the widow or widower at age 65 (or 60 if reduced benefits are elected).
2. Payment to the widow or widower at any age if that person is caring for the insured's child who is under 18 or disabled and entitled to benefits.

3. Payment to a disabled spouse.
4. Payment to unmarried childred under 18—or those over 18 who became disabled prior to reaching that age.
5. Payment to dependent parents over age 62 ("dependent" is defined as receiving over 50 percent support from the insured).
6. Payment to a divorced, unremarried spouse who was married to the insured for at least ten years. This spouse must be at least 60 years of age or have the insured's child under age 16 in his or her care.

Retirement Benefits

The amount of your monthly Social Security retirement check depends upon your average earnings during your working life. Those who reach 62 in 1984 or later—just about everyone reading this—must use a complex indexing method to determine average earnings.

The purpose of "indexing" is to bring earlier wages up to the value of current levels. For example, $7,200 earned in 1951 equaled $36,000

"I see retirement in your future."

in 1983 dollars. Each year, the Social Security Administration issues a new set of indexing figures based upon current levels.

It is impossible to calculate future benefits in dollar amounts (without knowing the index figures), but you can estimate the purchasing power of your Social Security retirement by using this year's figures. First, request a Statement of Earnings from your Social Security Administration. (Write, or get a form from your local Social Security Office. The address is: Social Security Administration, P.O. Box 57, Baltimore, MD 21203. Be sure to include your full name and Social Security number). Then, with that information and current index figures, also available from the Social Security Administration, you can get an idea of your Social Security status.

Most military persons do not contribute the maximum amount to the program; therefore, they're unlikely to receive the maximum from it. However, most also have twenty or twenty-five years remaining in the work force. High income during those years will increase Social Security benefits accordingly. This is doubly important because the years of lowest income (at least five) are excluded from the averaging process.

Retirement at Age 65

The *basic benefit* is referred to throughout any discussion of Social Security, and it is the benchmark from which most adjustments are made. Once you reach 65, you are entitled to your full basic benefit. This merely refers to the full benefit to which you are entitled, based upon what you have paid into Social Security. The fact that you're first entitled to the full basic benefit at 65 is the main advantage to waiting until then to retire.

Another advantage of working until 65 rather than retiring at, say, 62, is that you continue to pay into Social Security during those additional years, probably raising your average earnings. As a result there actually can be more than a 20 percent difference between retirement at an earlier age and at 65.

Retirement Before Age 65

At 62, the earliest anyone can draw Social Security retirement, the benefit is 80 percent of the basic benefit. Those retiring between 62 and 65 receive benefits on a graduated scale between 80 percent and 100 percent. For example, a person who retires halfway between the ·two—at age 63.5 years—receives 90 percent of the basic benefit.

If two persons, entitled to identical benefits and exactly the same age, retired under Social Security, one at age 62 and the other at 65, which would receive more benefits? On the average, the person who retired at 62 would be ahead until he or she reached an age between 74 and 77. So those who wait until 65 to draw Social Security are, in effect, gambling on their longevity. Many win, but others would rather have the reduced benefit for a longer period.

Retirement Between 65 and 70

There is a bonus for those who work beyond age 65. Those born in 1925 receive a 3.5 increase in their benefit for each year of work between age 65 and 70. The bonus will gradually increase until it reaches 8 percent for those born in 1943 or later.

Work during the years between ages 65 and 70 may also increase the basic benefit as a result of the additional years of payment into Social Security.

Dependent Benefits

In addition to your retirement check, other Social Security benefits may be paid to your family members.

These payments are based upon your basic (full) benefit whether or not you retired early or worked beyond age 65.

Dependent benefits may be paid to your:

1. Spouse if at least 62 years old.
2. Spouse at any age who is caring for your child who is under 16 or disabled and entitled to Social Security benefits.
3. Unmarried children under 18.
4. Unmarried child who became disabled before reaching age 22 and has remained disabled since.
5. Divorced spouse who (a) is at least 62, (b) is not remarried (unless remarriage took place after age 60), and (c) was married to you for at least ten years.

Medicare

Upon leaving active duty, most military retirees have at least twenty years before becoming eligible for Medicare. Nonetheless, Medicare is a major benefit and is part of Social Security.

When military retirees reach 65, eligiblity for the CHAMPUS medical program terminates, and Medicare eligibility begins. Those who pause now to learn how Medicare works will be prepared for it when they are 65.

Medicare consists of two parts: Part A, Hospital Insurance; and Part B, Medical Insurance.

Part A

Hospital Insurance is financed by your Social Security taxes (FICA).

Part A, as its name implies, is designed to pay for hospital care. The basic benefit is for the first 90 days of hospital care during an illness. If a longer period of hospitalization is required, each person has a "lifetime reserve" of an additional 60 days.

As with all medical costs, Medicare expenses are rising constantly. As a result, the amount paid by the individual also increases. Although any figures are highly perishable, we'll use the figures from the 1983 Congressional Amendments as an example. With them, you can get an idea of how Medicare works:

For hospital care
First 60 days: Patient pays $356 total; Medicare pays remainder.
60–90 days: Patients pays $89 per day; Medicare pays remainder.
Over 90 days (lifetime reserve = 60 days): Patient pays $178 per day; Medicare pays remainder.
For skilled nursing facility after release from hospital
First 20 days: Medicare pays.
20–100 days: Patient pays $44.50 per day; Medicare pays remainder.

Part B

Medical Insurance is not funded by Social Security taxes; rather those using it pay premiums. As of the 1983 amendment, the monthly premium was $14.60 for an individual and $29.20 for a couple. Any increase in this cost cannot exceed the percentage increase in Social Security cash benefits; therefore the relative cost should remain about constant.

Upon becoming eligible for Part A, Hospital Insurance, each person is automatically enrolled for Medical Insurance unless coverage is specifically rejected.

You pay the first $75 on doctor bills each year, then Part B pays 80 percent of the remainder. It also covers other medical expenses such as radiology, pathology, home health services, diagnostic tests, ambulance service, and many others.

Social Security—Past, Present, and Future

Financial planning for *real* retirement, about at age 65, requires careful consideration of Social Security benefits in combination with military retirement, other sources of income, and inflation. The importance of preparation is more apparent when we have a brief look at the Social Security system as it was, as it is, and as it surely must be in the future.

Military retirees are eligible for Social Security benefits, just as are other workers who pay into the program. It comes as a great surprise to many civilians when they discover that military personnel have been participants in the program since 1957.

The System Survives

During and after the 1980 election, hardly a day passed without a news item about problems with Social Security. Media coverage was almost universally pessimistic. Americans, already accustomed to media pessimism, now became accustomed to hearing about the impending collapse of the Social Security system.

But for once the bad news wasn't just media hype. This time it was for real. Senators and Congressmen told the American people Social Security was in big trouble, and without major fiscal surgery it could not survive.

Social Security consists of three major trust funds—one for disability benefits, one for pensions for retirees and their survivors, and a third for medical programs, commonly known as Medicare. Disability and retirement funds were paying out more than they collected. The medical fund, although solvent, faced almost certain disaster as medical costs continued to soar beyond all reason.

As is the case with most major crises, Congress came through in the end, and the system was "saved." At least, disaster was delayed for a few years. In this most recent situation, the solution was mainly in delayed or eliminated benefits or adjustments in the cost of living formula.

A Turning Point Ahead

It is not over yet. Most estimates indicate that within the lifetime of most of today's workers, the Social Security system will face another turning point—of a slightly different nature.

One of the greatest misconceptions about the Social Security system is reflected in the often-heard statement, "I've put all that money into Social Security for my retirement and . . ." The fallacy in that statement is that what we pay in is not earmarked for us. The money we, as wage earners, feed into Social Security supports *today's* retirees, disabled, and elderly, and their survivors. The idea is that when our turn comes, the workers then will finance the program, and each of us will have a turn at the benefits when we need them.

Carrying a fair share of the burden and being repaid on an equally fair scale is the American way. But, changes in the population of the United States have been phenomenal. One of those changes is reflected in population growth, but other events and trends are altering the makeup of the country and are reflected in Social Security programs. A "fair share" yesterday *was* fair. Today, it's still reasonable, but tomorrow it might just be intolerable.

Consider the fact that in 1945, thirty-five workers supported each person collecting Social Security benefits. By 1960 only five workers supported each retiree. The same load is now carried by three workers, and soon after the turn of the century only two workers will be supporting each person drawing benefits.

"The Graying of America"

The reasons for these changes are familiar, although some are more obvious than others. Basically, it boils down to what is now being called "the graying of America"—gradual aging of the population as a whole.

Families now tend to be smaller than they were in the late 1930s when Social Security got its start. Couples are delaying marriage until they are older and limiting the number of children they have—if any. Effective birth control is available and in use throughout the population. The obvious result of these changes is that there will be fewer young persons to step into tomorrow's work force and pay for Social Security. As they do, another significant change in the work force will occur: The "Baby Boom" generation—those born just after World War II— will reach retirement age.

Modern medicine, health care, nutrition, safety, equipment, and numerous other developments are adding years to life expectancy. Those added years will probably be spent in retirement. Further, the current trend toward early retirement results in (1) early loss of a contributor to Social Security, and probably (2) start of Social Security checks to that individual at the earliest possible date.

By the year 2000, one-third of the American population will be over 60. Of them, most will be over 65 and retired. Those between 60 and 65 will be *thinking* retirement and considering Social Security from the perspective of a retiree who wants his or her turn. This situation—markedly fewer workers supporting each Social Security beneficiary—surely will generate some feverish political debate. The next time around (and each successive time), the population will be just a little older, and political clout among the elderly will grow in direct proportion to the population of that group.

Between 1950 and 1981, wages (adjusted for inflation) rose 490 percent, but Social Security levies shot up an average of over 2,000 percent. Increasing payroll taxes to pay for Social Security is a distasteful solution, and there are already signs that the electorate won't stand for it. Each additional increase generates an uproar among the workers. If Congress then leans the other way and considers delaying, reducing, limiting, or cutting benefits, it then must cope with strong accusations of neglect by an increasingly powerful over-60 constituency. The battle lines will be drawn.

Be Prepared for Changes

Recent Social Security Amendments (Public Law 98-21), most of which we've included above, were brought about by a need to maintain Social Security's solvency. Generally, the changes are gradual, such as the increase in retirement age during the early part of the next century. Partly as a result of this gradual nature of change, and partly because it seems "far off," most military families don't think much about Social Security.

Some changes are not obvious to the majority of Americans since they affect only a relative few. Examples of these include cutting student benefits and limiting some payments to children under 16 versus the former 18 years of age. Increases in Medicare costs appear insignificant to young or middle-aged working couples, but to an elderly person on a fixed income it is a serious matter.

One change made by the Social Security Amendments of 1983 is drawing more protests than the others combined: Taxation of Social Security benefits. Starting in 1984, individuals whose adjusted gross income plus one-half of their Social Security benefit exceeds $25,000 ($32,000 for married couples) will be taxed. The uproar isn't so much about the tax as about the fact that this computation includes income from interest on tax-exempt bonds. Many elderly citizens have planned and saved for decades and now count on tax-exempt bonds for income. Defenders of the amendment argue that it's actually the Social Security income that's "adjusted," but it really doesn't matter, does it?

Your Military Retirement

Most employees are extremely interested in their company retirement. Management knows the importance of solid retirement plans if they are to attract and retain quality employees. Unions fight to improve retirement programs even if it means giving up more immediate pay raises. When sharp people negotiate for jobs, retirement plans are near the top of the critical "perks."

In today's economic and political environment, one must concentrate upon the future—planning, saving, reviewing options, and selecting the package that will provide the soundest future security.

Military retirement has always been a main attraction for retaining vigorous, youthful, and skilled people in the services. Many join for other reasons, and most who stay on active duty do so for many reasons. Patriotism is always on the list, which may also include travel, interesting work, excitement, challenge, training, and many other attractions. But without the retirement system, it's a safe bet that most would settle for a much shorter service hitch, then seek employment where they could secure the future for their families.

Ask any military group that is about halfway to retirement if they would stay on if their retirement was cut by half. Ask if they would consider staying on active duty if their retirement was taken away until some arbitrary age, say 60. It will soon become obvious that few of these dedicated individuals would stay on. Most of them have family considerations. No matter how exciting and challenging the career is, that family responsibility is there.

A System Under Attack

From a real-world, strictly financial point of view, military retirement pay is the drawing card for a military career versus a civilian one. For an E8 retiring at twenty-four years, it's worth about $300,000. For an 05 with twenty-eight years, it's worth about $600,000. It's a reasonable payoff for long, dedicated, and until recently, underpaid years. But as costs of financing military retirement climb, so do protests about those costs.

There is no money set aside for military retirement. It surfaces for a vote every year and is attacked each year as too costly. In fact, it now is more accurate to state that the system is under constant attack.

If this was the case with the retirement plan at Ford Motor Company, would the employees be interested in what was going on? We know they would. They'd follow the process daily. On the other hand, how interested are active-duty military personnel in what's happening with (to) their retirement? Aside from the service Chiefs and their staffers who are fighting the battle, it's practically impossible to locate anyone who is even conversant on the subject. Some retirees watch it closely, but any argument they present is considered self-serving.

Service families believe the services "take care of their own." That's usually true, but the decisions on military retirement pay aren't made by the services. And Congress doesn't get much feedback from apathetic service members who assume they'll be taken care of—at least as well as they would have been the year they joined. That assumption is incorrect.

Suppose you worked for a large company where you must work twenty years before you were "vested"—could draw any retirement. Then retirement pay increased in small amounts until you had thirty years with the company. As part of the company program, retirees' checks were adjusted according to the Consumer Price Index (CPI), thus protecting them from the ravages of inflation.

Continuing with this example, imagine that you went to work for the company at 18, just out of high school. After twenty-five years of dedicated service you took your retirement. A month later, you received a letter from the company advising that your CPI adjustments will be cut in half until you are 62! Nineteen years. Even at a moderate inflation rate, the purchasing power of your retirement check at age 62 will be worth only about half of what it was the day you retired. You kept your part of the bargain. Age wasn't a factor all those years; how could the company throw it in now?

There is not a retiree or employee alive who wouldn't scream like a banshee in this situation. It is hard to imagine anyone supporting or attempting such an action. Yet it's happening to military retirement, along with other equally devastating moves.

The Omnibus Budget Reconciliation Act of 1982 did to military retirees exactly what the example above demonstrates: It cut CPI raises in half for retirees under 62. The provision was for three years, but there is every indication it, or something similar, will become permanent.

The feelings of military retirees were summed up very neatly by Tidal W. McCoy, Assistant Secretary of the Air Force, in *U.S. News and World Report* in response to an article in that magazine about military retirement expenses:

Three facts to add to your January 9 report, "Behind New Furor Over Military Pensions": Military retirement now costs less than four-tenths of 1 percent of gross national product. Even that small figure will decrease in the next 25 years as the number of retirees associated with past periods of national crisis declines. It will also be reduced as GNP increases in real terms.

Two-thirds of military retirees are compensated below the poverty level for an urban family of four ($9,800). They find second jobs because they have to. Our retirees are in demand because they are quality people, highly motivated and well trained. More than three-quarters of retirees in a recent year had drawn hostile-fire pay—having been assigned where someone was actively trying to kill them. This alone makes military service fundamentally—and irrevocably—different from civilian employment. Compensation, including retirement, must reflect that fact.

That is our point of view. But he's on our side.

Where Does This Lead Us?

What does this talk of Social Security and military retirement have to do with pre-retirement planning? Everything.

It is essential that every military retiree be aware of the value of military retirement and of Social Security. No matter what you do after leaving the service, both of them will be a big part of your future. We've tried to emphasize (it's impossible to overemphasize) that both programs will be in for some major changes in the coming years.

Those who are approaching military retirement today are going to be hit with some immediate changes. Then, as the same group nears *real* retirement they will be in the first group affected by the recent Social Security age changes, at the precise time new problems may well surface with the entire Social Security program.

Their retirement pay will surely be worth less; their Social Security benefits will start at a higher age because of changes in the law; their income after retirement may well be taxed; their Medicare deductible will continue to rise; and their dollars will be worth less because of the prime nemesis of the retiree: inflation.

Inflation

Knowing how many dollars you'll have in the future isn't enough. That figure is meaningful only when it's adjusted for inflation, which we can only estimate. It is *buying power* of those dollars that really counts, and inflation reduces buying power (see Table A in appendix 2). Even at modest annual rates, the effects of inflation upon prices, retirement, wages, and purchasing power in general can be downright frightening.

We have grown up with inflation. There have been only two years since World War II without inflation, and most who are now approaching military retirement were born after World War II. In fact, in the near future there will be military retirees who were born in the fifties. For them in particular, inflation has been a way of life. But being familiar with it is not the same as preparing for its future impact. For the military family, accustomed to annual cost of living adjustments (COLA), the long-range impact of inflation can be dramatic.

During the 1970s the cost of living doubled. In the early 1980s we saw some of the worst inflation in United States history. At the close of 1980 the inflation rate was 12.6 percent. At the end of 1983, it was down to 3.3 percent. But, getting it down and keeping it there are quite different.

For someone twenty-five years from retirement, inflation usually doesn't seem like a major problem. In fact, it is probably Number One for most of the work force, military retirees included.

At an annual inflation rate of 5 percent, a 40-year-old who plans to work until age 65 will need $3.40 for each of today's dollars just to break even at retirement. And 5 percent is such a modest rate many financial charts don't even show it! At the 1980 rate mentioned above (12.6 percent) the same person at age 65 would need over $19 just to buy what $1 would when he or she was 40 (see Table B in appendix 2).

Look at it from a reverse angle. If the same 40-year-old put $20 in a drawer and took it out at age 65, how much would it be worth? In purchasing power, that $20 would buy about what $1 would when it was put in the drawer. You might say that $1 invested at the same rate, rather than squirrelled away in a drawer, would equal $20 in the same period. True. But its buying power would be unchanged.

Surely, annual inflation over the coming years won't average 12 percent. But we can be equally certain it will exceed 3.3 percent. There is only one way to gain on it, and that is to plan and invest so wisely that return on investment is higher than the inflation rate. Even without worrying (for now) about taxes, that is a tall order.

Conquering inflation requires that the problem be recognized and faced head-on. Military families are seasoned in this approach to other challenges but not with regard to inflation after military retirement.

As retirement programs become increasingly expensive, civilians are realizing that, more than ever, they must set aside more of their own funds for retirement. Few civilian retirement plans have built-in cost of living adjustments. Those that do usually compensate for only a fraction of the cost of living increase. Federal government and military retirees have fared much better in this regard and have maintained reasonable buying power with their annual Consumer Price Index adjustments. But, at least for the military, times are changing.

In today's environment, few would be willing to wager that future military retirement will bear much resemblance to the current system. At least monthly, national magazines propose military retirement cost cuts. In military newspapers, it's a weekly item. And in Congress, there is always a politician or two who thrives on attacking military retirees and the system under which they retired. As usual, there is a majority in Congress who appreciate the sacrifices of military personnel and their families, but that isn't news, so we hear less from them.

Consider Senator Paul Laxalt's February 1983 speech to the Nevada legislature, during which he said:

> We've got thousands of retired military people sitting out there making more money than people doing the job in the field. We can't have that. That's a horrid social situation and a worse economic situation so we have got to retilt this; we've got to stop being political prostitutes, and pandering [sic] all those people who we think are going to vote for us because we are doling out money to them.

According to Defense Department figures, of 1.4 million retirees and survivors, only 343 fall into the category mentioned, and they are all of four-star rank. If Senator Laxalt was that ill-informed, and made a speech demonstrating that lack of knowledge, we must wonder if he is the only one of our elected officials in that boat. Probably not. After he received a more accurate picture of the military retiree situation, Senator Laxalt issued a letter of apology to military retirees.

It would be comforting to believe that any future changes in the retirement system will protect those already retired and those approaching retirement. But with everyone looking for places to cut the budget, military retirement presents an easy target—a group that can be expected to accept whatever happens as another aspect of duty. By nature of our system, there's little those on active duty can do about it. Actions that are appropriate in civilian life are inappropriate in the military. This is as it should be. But it also leaves the armed forces in a bit of a bind when it comes to protecting their flanks from their own legislators.

The bottom line, then, boils down to this: A fixed income, or one that fails to keep pace with inflation, is eaten away by that inflation. Those who fail to compensate for this erosion will find themselves becoming poorer in direct proportion to the ever-compounding impact of inflation.

There really isn't much difference between military and civilian retirees in this regard. Both need to protect their future income or suffer the consequences. The military retiree will probably work as a civilian for another quarter of a century. With military retirement pay coming in during that period, it's an ideal time to invest wisely for the future. *The* ideal time, of course, begins with a person's working life and continues throughout it.

Inflation is without doubt the retiree's greatest foe. But it's also another of those items most of us choose to ignore until it's at our doorstep.

As we've discussed above, around the turn of the century Social Security will face another crisis as fewer workers take on an even heavier load. Military retirement is under constant attack, and some changes are sure to be made. If the past is to be used as an example, many of these changes will seem minor, but their long-range impact will be dramatic. Inflation is sure to continue, compounding the situation.

Throughout this book, almost every item relates in some way to inflation and its effect upon our future. The task of making up for its erosion of our buying power is up to each of us. No one is going to hand us a solution on a platter. Rather, no matter what course we choose, we must keep one consideration at the top of our list: inflation.

15

Life Insurance

Before going off on some investment tangent, each of us wants to be sure the family is taken care of. That is as it should be. Assuming you are in that majority with kids to feed, house, clothe, and educate, those priorities are right where you want them—up front. If you are just now getting serious about your financial planning, don't get bogged down trying to play the role of sophisticated investor. Concentrate instead on known requirements such as your home, college expenses, building a sound life insurance program, and determining what you should have in an emergency fund. You are entitled to CHAMPUS, so your health insurance requirements are a little different from the average civilian's. But you still need to give it your attention to be sure you can handle your share of the costs in an emergency (CHAMPUS doesn't pay it all).

Of all aspects of financial planning, life insurance is most directly related to your military retirement benefits, specifically the Survivor Benefit Plan (SBP). If you select full SBP coverage, you provide your beneficiary with 55 percent of your monthly retirement. That can be quite a security blanket, particularly since it is adjusted with cost of living raises. Check your SBP *first* when you review your life insurance program.

Despite our almost universal ignorance of life insurance and our overreliance upon "advisors" (really sales representatives), we generally agree that the earlier in life one purchases an insurance policy, the lower the premium will be. Most of us buy life insurance soon after

"**Here are two 'Get Well Quickly' cards, Dear. One's from your health insurance, and the other is from your life insurance company.**"

marriage and review our needs about the time the family starts growing. Satisfied with our coverage, we start the pay allotment (which may continue after military retirement) and forget about it. Insurance should not be forgotten! This is true for many reasons, but primarily because you may be throwing your money away. Insurance requirements change constantly, and getting the most for your money requires reevaluation with each change.

In recent years, the insurance picture has changed dramatically. Much of today's good insurance advice is exactly the opposite of what it was twenty years ago. If your current insurance is based upon some of that obsolete information, there is a good chance you are overinsured or that you can get the same coverage for much less.

The primary consideration, and the question you must ask yourself is, "What am I insuring?"

The answer normally is: You are insuring against the loss of your income at the time of your death.

Unless we plan to make our heirs rich, loss of income is sufficient basis for life insurance. We might consider insurance to pay off college tuition and the mortgage, but when you think of it, that really falls into the "loss of income" category.

Review your requirements if the children are nearly all grown and gone and your home is about paid off. You probably don't need as much coverage as you once did. There are several options available, and you should look into them.

Term Versus Ordinary Life

When that camp follower sold you that ordinary life policy back at Fort Sagebrush, he probably convinced you that ordinary life (whole life, straight life) was (1) the least expensive insurance, (2) a strong investment because of the cash/loan value, and (3) an excellent method of forced savings. That is not exactly correct. As most of the good insurance companies are now stating, term insurance is the least expensive form of life insurance.

One study of military personnel revealed that approximately 90 percent of the respondents held only ordinary life policies. The same study showed that the older the respondent, the less they held onto whole life policies and the more they used term (and the more they were aware their insurance programs were now obsolete). Chalk it up to experience.

The insurance sales representative is there to sell insurance and make a profit. We must never forget that. This is not to say they are all dishonest. On the contrary, most are hard-working and honest. They would be the first to argue, with validity, that they want satisfied customers. Traditionally, the best profit has been in ordinary life; obviously, that is what any salesperson would rather sell. But in today's highly competitive insurance market, many companies are finding greater profits in saving money for their policy holders. If they fail, an increasingly sophisticated public will simply go elsewhere. Everyone has been looking for ways to economize, and this has resulted in a change in approach. At least one major company no longer sells ordinary life policies, and they use that fact in their advertising. There is a message for all of us there.

Insurance seems to be the only business in the country where we are so eager to believe sales representatives without any research on our own. We lay out huge amounts of cash based upon their recommendation, and we buy their advice (actually a sales pitch) without question. They help their own case by making insurance sound so complicated that we are eager to accept anyone's advice. It is not all that complicated. Basic research and careful selection of an insurance company can clear the picture enough so that we can make proper decisions.

Consider the two main types of life insurance policies—term and ordinary life.

Term Insurance

Term, as we said above, is by far the cheaper of the two. It is pure risk insurance, which is to say you insure against a specific risk (in this case, your death). It serves that purpose and no other. Premiums increase about every five years depending upon the term of the policy. The two most common types of term are "level term" and "decreasing term."

Level Term

Level term insurance is so named because the amount of coverage and payment remains constant throughout the period of coverage. For example, a five-year, $20,000 level term policy would pay $20,000 at any time during the five-year period. At the end of that period, premium costs would rise by a small amount. Normally the shorter-term policies are less expensive in the long run.

Decreasing Term

Decreasing term insurance is so named because, although your premium remains the same throughout the life of the policy, the amount payable to your beneficiary decreases. For example, with a $20,000 policy, your family would receive the full $20,000 if you died during the first year or so, but after about five years they may receive about $15,000.

Decreasing term is frequently used to pay off mortgages or other debts that are decreasing at about the same rate. It is good for that purpose and it is the cheapest coverage you can buy.

Ordinary Life

Ordinary life (whole life, straight life) combines the appeal of life insurance and savings. As the premium for this insurance doesn't change, the price per dollar of coverage appears to remain constant as you grow older. Actually, it does not. Here's the way it really works:

During the early years of your ordinary life policy, not much of the premium goes into savings. As years go by, the amount of each payment directed to savings increases gradually. Remember, the savings part is your money that you can get anytime, by borrowing on it, cancelling the policy, or (in some cases) taking paid-up insurance for an amount significantly lower than your original policy. When you die, the company returns whatever savings you have accumulated, plus the difference required to reach the face value of the policy. So, actually you are paying a constant amount for decreasing insurance coverage.

"Aha!" you say, "How about the savings?" It is yours, but be certain of one thing: You could do much better with little effort by taking the same amount of coverage in term insurance and investing the difference. Now if you don't feel you can discipline yourself to do that and you'd rather have it accumulate at a low and slow rate, leave it in ordinary life. Knowing your insurance will be cancelled if you don't pay is a powerful incentive for saving. But really think it over and be sure of what you're doing. There are other forced saving methods (payroll deduction, direct deposit, etc., where you never see it) by which you can do much better.

Isn't the loan value of that ordinary life policy an easy, quick, and cheap source of loan money? It's easy compared to other methods of obtaining loans and it may be quick. Although the insurance company may legally hold your money for six months before sending it to you, they rarely do. The interest rates—for example, 8 percent—may be phenomenally low by today's standards, but keep these points in mind: (1) You are paying 8 percent to borrow your own money—which you have accumulated at a pitifully slow rate. (2) In the event of your death the amount you "owe" plus interest is deducted from the amount paid your beneficiary.

Most of us don't need much (if any) life insurance after age 65 if our home is paid for and we've done some investing. Assume you are 45 years old and your cost for $25,000 ordinary life is $700 per year, and your cost for the same amount of decreasing term (per year) is $200. If you are going to get a fair price comparison, you must invest the $500 difference. Now, $500 per year compounded at 9 percent will be worth over $55,000 in 20 years. What will the money in the ordinary life policy be worth? You may have that $25,000 of coverage, but you paid $14,000 into it. If you borrowed $10,000 of your own money, you'd have to pay interest on the loan. And the money sitting there in the policy isn't really growing as it should be.

In a recent discussion, a military retiree's wife said, "The main reason I'd want life insurance on John would be to pay off heavy debts for a nursing home or similar costs if they should arise during his final years." This is a valid concern. Even with the most conservative investment program, if you buy term insurance and invest the difference between that price and what you would pay for ordinary life insurance your investment will almost surely be worth much more than the insurance policy when you are 65.

You can choose from a dozen or more options on life insurance. Essentially they are all some modification of term or ordinary life insurance.

The important thing for you to do periodically—not just once in a lifetime—is to review your insurance to consider:

1. Am I adequately insured to provide for the loss of my earned income in the event of my death?
2. Am I overinsured?
3. Do I have money pouring into ordinary life insurance when I should be paying less for term and investing the difference?
4. If I select term coverage and plan to invest the difference, have I set up a method to accomplish this as a "forced saving" (such as payroll deduction)?

How Much is Enough?

If life insurance is used to replace the breadwinner's income for the family but it is not the best method of accumulating savings, then it stands to reason that the amount of life insurance held should be no more than required. Just how much is required is an individual choice, and no standardized computation is perfect for everyone. Your special needs must be included, and, as mentioned earlier, revised every time there is a change.

Some items apply to most of us. For example, funeral and burial expenses will be paid immediately. There will probably also be some legal fees to get everything in order. Your home mortgage may be the largest expense facing your widow(er); this can be handled nicely with a declining term policy selected for that purpose. As you consider your life insurance program, include Social Security benefits that may be due to your survivors. And, probably most important of all, look at your Survivor Benefit Plan coverage.

In most cases, the family will require about 80 percent of the breadwinner's income to maintain its standard of living. Once the above mentioned factors are figured in, you may discover you have plenty of insurance now. Several military retirees with whom we spoke said they needed additional insurance to fill gaps—such as the time between the youngest child reaching 18 years of age and the spouse becoming eligible for Social Security—but only during that time. This is another example of the importance of periodic review of insurance needs.

The Bottom Line

Life insurance is an individual matter. Keep it that way. Every discussion of life insurance needs won't apply to you. What applies to you won't apply to the next person. A chart might portray the exact situation for a young working couple with young children but not even come close to your situation. If it doesn't fit, don't try to force it.

The most important approach to life insurance protection is simply to determine what your family will need, figure what you have already provided (and are providing, for example with investments), and then decide how you'll make up the difference. Life insurance needs changing at each of life's milestones—birth, graduation, marriage, divorce, adoption, dependent parents, inheritance, retirement, handicaps, major debts, changes in inheritance tax laws, and so on. Each of these changes demands a review of your insurance status. You may need more—either permanently or temporarily—or less. As times change, so will your needs.

Transition from military to civilian life is a major event for insurance-planning purposes. It is every bit as important as the others mentioned above. We discuss Veterans Administration insurance in chapter 18. Even without the VA insurance possibilities, the fact remains that your status and needs are changing. The change could well be to your advantage.

One caution: We discussed the advantages and disadvantages of term versus ordinary life insurance. As we did so, we stressed advantages of term over ordinary life insurance in today's society. Most insurance firms and financial advisors agree with that approach. However, solely as a result of this comparison, do not run out and terminate ordinary life policies you've held for twenty or thirty years. In some cases, they are best kept as they are. In the event you do decide to cash in such a policy, it should be only after careful consideration and comparison. We are comparing *new* policies at about the time for transition to civilian life. In the case of an old ordinary life policy, there is a good chance you are now paying your premium for much less insurance than in the beginning. Let our discussion here alert you to that possibility, but check it out before acting.

There aren't nearly as many insurance agents who will try to push you into cashing in an old policy and taking out a new one as there once were, but they are still around. There are plenty of reliable insurance firms. Go to your library and check *Best's Life Insurance Reports* for the ratings, or have your agent show you his company's *Best's* rating. Consider what we've said above, do some figuring, form your objectives and questions, and get the opinion of several of them before making a commitment.

16

Money Matters

Career military families have experiences that cannot be equaled in any other walk of life. Financial situations are no exception to this rule. Each of us can recall personal events such as being stuck in Hong Kong with no cash; purchasing an automobile in Germany for shipment to the United States a month ahead of our own arrival; or buying a home (or leasing a condo) by long-distance telephone—including banking arrangements. During fast-paced military careers, we frequently discovered that our financial management had become crisis management. When one crisis was solved, another surfaced.

As a result of coping with untold financial crunches, we became expert at handling those situations. We adopted an attitude of, "Nothing surprises me," and we managed to stay cool under some unbelievable situations. At the same time, it seemed difficult to plan our financial matters very far in advance. When we reenter civilian life, most of us find that we are strong in some areas of financial planning and weak in others.

In this chapter, we are going to review some of the basics and highlight some items that deserve your attention as you make the transition to civilian life. In most part, these comments are based upon the experiences of other military retirees. We aren't trying to write a financial planning manual—there are plenty of excellent ones (see Bibliography). If you get only one good point from this chapter, it will be worthwhile. Remember, we've written it for everyone who is planning for military retirement; although a point may not apply to your situation, it could be just what someone else needs.

Emergency Funds

An emergency fund should be established at the start of adult life and reviewed periodically. If you don't have one now, as you prepare for civilian life, you should consider it first. You should be able to establish it with a lot less effort than you realize. But get it out of the way, so you can get on with your planning.

Most references will tell you to put aside between two and six months' salary for emergency funds. Remember, they base these figures on the loss of the breadwinner's income. Your ability to meet your emergency fund requirement is greatly assisted by the fact that you will have a military retirement check coming in each month. Your emergency fund should be precisely that—a minimum amount you have identified for an emergency. It should be kept to a minimum because it must be relatively "liquid"—easy to get on short notice. Normally, the more liquid the investment the lower the rate of return. The ultimate in liquidity is of course cash, but cash in a cookie jar is not earning anything.

What emergency situations could cause you to need money so quickly that you couldn't get it when you needed it? We mentioned loss of income. As a military retiree, you have an excellent hospitalization plan (CHAMPUS), and you may have a better one in your new career. If you lose your civilian job, you still have CHAMPUS.

But we must be aware that sudden medical emergencies can create staggering expenses that even the very best medical insurance won't cover. Legal expenses or accidents can create emergency needs for funds. Some of us may feel an obligation to keep some emergency funds available for young adult children who are on their own but living from hand to mouth. Granted, such requirements are personal and will probably differ between any two persons or families. A good rule of thumb is to have about six months' living expenses set aside in "safe dollars" that you can use in an emergency.

Your main consideration may well be an airline ticket home, major automobile repair job, or cash for an emergency trip. Certainly you don't want to tie up six months' pay in a low-paying passbook account. Even with emergency funds, get your money working for you.

Saving

It would be wonderful if we all saved a little each week or month, as our parents tried to convince us we should. Now we are old enough to realize (or admit) that they were right. That's not enough. There is never as much time as there was, but there is still time, and most of us can save. Discipline is the key. It is a lot easier to live for today, but if you stick with that philosophy what will your "todays" be like when you're 65 or 70?

Of all the time-worn cliches about how to save, our favorite is the most used, possibly because it is a key to success: *Pay yourself first!* When you sit down to write the checks or add your paycheck to your account, make the first payment to you. Transfer it to savings, bonds, stocks, funds, whatever you are doing with it—but save it. Most research indicates that a middle-income family should be able to put away 5 percent of its gross pay without feeling the pinch. One of the best retirement planning books says we can save 15 percent. At least we should plan to do that, though in exceptional cases we might have to hold out a little. It's too easy to say, "I can't afford it now."

If your pay was 5 percent less would your world end? A retiring master sergeant would save about $60 per month. If he retired at 45 and saved that $60 per month at 8 percent until he was 65, he'd have over $40,000. At age 65 he can draw about $400 per month from this account for fourteen years (his approximate life expectancy—today's tables). Not bad. But he's got to save it first.

The best way to save is to have your savings taken out of your pay. Save it before you see it, and you will never miss it. If you aren't doing it, start. If you are having savings taken out of your military pay, keep it up, even after you retire from the service—*especially* after you retire from military service. After you are a civilian, you aren't allowed to start a new military allotment for savings. That isn't necessarily a big problem. Since you can, and probably will, have your retirement pay sent to your bank, have the bank allocate a certain amount to savings.

Don't just think in terms of your military retirement pay. Once you are into your next career you should be able to save even more. Your employer may have a payroll deduction plan. If so, be sure to use it. If you have your money placed directly into passbook savings, be sure you manage it and transfer most of it into higher-yielding investments as soon as you can.

Speaking of investments, one of the best ways to look at your military retirement check is to consider it a return on your investment. We discuss this attitude regarding job interviews; try it also with finances: You are in your peak earning years. As you start your new career, consider your pay for that job as though the military retirement check weren't coming. Consider the military check as if it were an investment that's paying off, and only draw on it when you need it.

Maybe you won't always be able to make it work, but think how terrific it will be to save even a year's retirement pay and have it drawing interest. If that 45-year-old master sergeant we mentioned did that, his first year's retirement, invested at 8 percent (you can beat that!) would be worth over $100,000 at age 65 (see Table C in appendix 2). Meanwhile, you are living on the pay from your current job like everyone else. If you've painted yourself into a corner and you need to draw on your retirement pay, try to live on half of it (or some other percentage) plus your pay. As we said elsewhere, the sad fact is that most military retirees are underemployed after their service. And even more serious is the fact that almost all rely upon military retirement pay during their second career. Do what you can. Think of the possibilities. Save.

Credit

Wise use of credit can make fantastic improvements in your life-style; unwise use of credit can destroy you.

There are several kinds of credit. Chances are you've used them all, or at least have some knowledge of them. Any time we obtain goods or services and pay later, we are using credit. Utilities, the telephone bill, credit cards, and charge accounts all fit that category. Credit is a convenience, and in today's society some credit is a necessity. For our purposes here, we'll consider the main categories of credit, which are charge accounts, credit cards, and installment contracts.

Charge Accounts

Charge accounts are the type our parents and grandparents had at the general or company store. Each month they were billed for a month's purchases with no interest or service charge. Many stores today allow personal charge accounts of this type. Normally, if you pay within thirty days there is no additional charge for the credit (there are those who maintain it is built into the price). If payment is late, the store may add a small late payment charge. The number of stores offering this convenience is decreasing as major credit cards become almost universally accepted. It's been said that even credit cards will be ob-solete in ten years, but for now. . .

Credit Cards

Credit cards represent both the blessings and the evils of credit. Without them many families would need to make major changes in their way of doing things; with them many buyers go haywire.

Bank Cards

These cards may be used for many purposes. VISA and MasterCard are the most well known of these, although there are many others. Normally, you have a limit on the amount you may charge on the card, say $900 or $1,200 total. The cards are relatively simple to obtain through banks, and there is usually no charge for obtaining them. The banks bring in their profit by charging interest on the unpaid balance.

Travel and Entertainment Cards ("T&E")

T&E cards are a little tougher to get than bank cards, and you pay for the card itself. The American Express and Diner's Club cards are examples of T&E cards. With them you are expected to pay in full each month unless you have made specific arrangements for major items. There is a degree of prestige with T&E cards, and it is safe to say they are more readily accepted than other cards at hotels, motels, and restaurants. The reason, of course, is the implied fact that the bearer is a good credit risk, capable of paying up each month.

On the other hand, a greater variety of stores and small shops will accept bank cards (except in tourist areas, where a higher percentage of customers are likely to be using T&E cards). T&E cards have some added benefits at low or no additional cost. Possibilities include insurance, traveler's checks, shopping specials, special travel packages, emergency funds without any hassle, and others. Competition among T&E companies has spawned many new benefits, some of which are rather dubious. Before selecting a card, it pays to review just what it offers and how it fits your needs.

Single-Purpose Cards

Most Americans have one or more of these in their wallet or purse. Gasoline and most department store revolving charge accounts are the main cards in this category. Within this category, there are two main payment methods.

With most department stores, you pay interest on the unpaid balance. You are normally billed each month and the statement will show the minimum payment due. By paying only the minimum each month, you will end up paying more for your purchase because interest on the unpaid balance is added each month. It is wise to pay it off as soon as possible.

The other method of payment is the one most oil companies use. You use your credit card for the purchase and are billed at the end of the month. If you don't pay in full by a given date (e.g., the middle of the billing month) you are assessed an additional charge. Some stores also use this system.

Installment Contracts

Installment contracts usually are used to purchase major items such as appliances. You pay the down payment and agree to a certain number of payments. Although most installment contracts are on the level, be certain you know all the terms and can afford payments before entering into the deal. If you can get a bank loan, it probably will be less expensive than an installment contract through the dealer from which you purchased the item.

Think About Your Credit Status—In Advance

So much for those basic points on credit. We've no intention of insulting you. Surely you have some credit experience. But before going on with the following discussion, we need to be on the same sheet of music. We've just shown that credit is convenient, but it usually costs you money. In fact, convenience is the main reason higher-income families use credit cards. For others, credit is a way of postponing payment until after the holidays, payday, the new job pays off, or the "ship comes in." Credit is also a convenient way to slip into debt. Know exactly what you're doing, and use credit judiciously.

We are going to assume that we all know what a credit rating is, in general terms. Actually there isn't one universal grading system whereby you might be an 82 and your neighbor an 85. One lender may disapprove credit for you, and another may approve without question. They simply check the record and make their decision, much as you would if someone hit you up for a hundred-dollar loan.

After all those years of "duty, honor, and country," you probably believe you will be able to get credit anywhere, any time. Grit your teeth and read the following. Where do you fit?

YOUR OCCUPATION AND YOUR CREDIT RATING

There are factors other than occupation that count toward determination of your ability to obtain credit. Examples might be time in a given occupation, position in that occupation (owner, full time employee, etc.,), or how well known you are in the town (particularly true in small towns). But occupation remains one of the key elements.

The following is a typical listing by occupation.* You can get some idea where you stack up from it:

---

*From *Everyone's Money Book* by Jane Bryant Quinn. Copyright © 1980 by Jane Bryant Quinn. Reprinted by permission of Delacorte Press. Italics added.

Top Group: Business executives, teachers, engineers, scientists, accountants.

Group 2: Dentists, doctors, factory foremen, draftsmen, office supervisors, female office workers.

Group 3: Commercial aviators, civil service workers, clergymen, credit specialists, farm owners, lab and medical technicians, milkmen, journalists, news pressmen, registered nurses, railroad trainmen, male office workers, pharmacists, post office employees.

Group 4: Firemen, *commissioned military officers,* heavy equipment operators, policemen, skilled factory workers, railroad shopmen.

Group 5: Bus drivers, union janitors, sales clerks, salesmen, truck drivers, warehousemen, nonregistered nurses.

Group 6: Auto mechanics, building tradesmen, contractors, insurance salesmen, nonunion janitors, tenant farmers, lawyers.

Group 7: Self-employed businessmen, cooks, bankers, butchers, miners, *noncommissioned military officers,* gas station personnel, liquor manufacturers and salesmen, painters, *retirees,* union officials, unskilled factory workers.

Group 8: Barbers, beauticians, cab drivers, common laborers, domestics, housewives, longshoremen, musicians, restaurant and hotel employees, amusement park employees, merchant seamen, *lower-level military personnel,* nurse's aides, oil field workers, students.

Bottom Group: Farmhands, people on welfare, bartenders.

Note that commissioned officers are in Group 4, noncoms are in Group 7, retirees are in Group 7, and lower grade military personnel are in Group 8.

If, at the start, military personnel are that low in the pecking order, it stands to reason that a good credit record is important. Job listings as shown above are only one part of the entire picture. You can make it look a lot better with good credentials. But if you start with that job listing, then go to a very shaky credit record, you're out of luck.

There is another important point. Without that second career, credit is harder to obtain. The listing above is for active-duty persons who are drawing full pay and allowances. What would it be for a retiree with less than half that income . . . especially one with a flawed credit record? This is another strong reason to get that job set up before you leave the service.

As we have just discussed, establishment of credit in a new location frequently depends upon your current job or income. Therefore, a valid issue might be whether or not you should set up accounts before retiring from the service. Perhaps you should, particularly if you are new in town. You want everything in your favor, and already set up, before making the big switch to civilian life in a new community.

Investments

As with our experiences with credit, events during our military careers also influence our attitudes toward investments.

Early in our careers, most of us were single for a short time and used most of our income doing what young singles do. Then we married and started a family. After the immediate needs (i.e., furniture, baby clothes, and a car) were purchased and paid for, we began thinking about some type of savings plan. It took planning, but we decided we would save X number of dollars in the bank. These efforts at saving became frustrating because some unexpected event—like a PCS or car breakdown—would make us dip into those savings. But, somehow we continued our efforts to save. With each promotion we resolved to save the pay increase, but we rarely succeeded. We were rewarded for our persistence as we finally saved enough to meet emergencies and unexpected needs without totally depleting the savings.

Few service families can afford to gamble their savings on high-risk investments, but most of us have either done just that or known someone who has. The scenario frequently went something like this:

Once we reached the station in life at which our emergency needs were covered, we began thinking about investing for the future. As with most families, we thought of emergencies first, then solid investments, then a little "gambling money" or risk dollars. Anyone on a military payroll knows there is little available in that last category.

We heard how one of our friends just made a killing in the stock market, commodities, oil wells, or real estate. Then came the personal guilt trip. We had planned to have more money in the bank. Now the urge to "make up" for the shortfall made us a prime target for risky ventures. In our hearts, we actually believed our emergency and investment money, for which we had no immediate requirement, was risk capital. It was not. This was a dangerous trap back then in mid-career, and it's even more so now.

Risk-type investments absolutely require certain qualifications and criteria be met before you can reasonably expect a profit. Most basic of them is the rule that you must know what you are doing! Most professionals in risk investments expect to lose on some of their investments. To minimize losses, they diversify their investments into several areas. It follows that they also have relatively large sums of money in order to diversify. As they are fully trained and knowledgeable, they can evaluate the investment and its risk. They then have reasonable expectations concerning just what type of return they will achieve. Their returns are much more modest than we'd expect.

After retirement from the service, we may need greater reserves than we anticipate during active duty, and we must protect our savings. How do we develop our family investment portfolio? After working hard and saving (possibly less than we had hoped) we want to invest wisely.

In our view, a family's investment should be distributed something

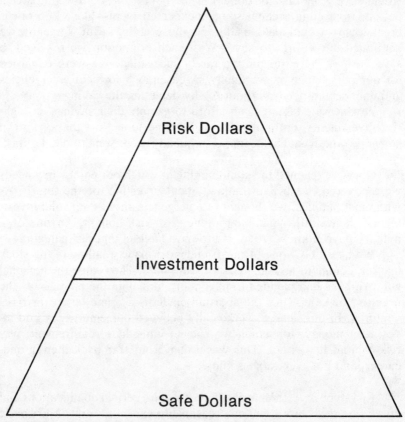

Safe dollar savings form the base for investments. Investment dollars, then, are a base for risk dollar investments. Safe dollars should represent a much larger part of the total picture than investment or risk dollars.

like in the accompanying diagram. Note that many more dollars are shown as "safe" than as "investment" or "risk." Also, each provides a firm base for the next, riskier, category.

Consider each category and the type of investment vehicles that would fit into each investment objective.

"Safe Dollars"

"Safe dollars" are funds that are put aside for permanent retirement, major emergencies, or some future expense you feel you must cover. We should have an idea what is needed for retirement. Most of us will need more than our military pensions. The greater the portion of our retirement check that's needed for daily expenses, the higher the safe dollar requirement.

As the name implies, safe dollars should be placed in relatively risk-free investments. These include money market funds, certificates of deposit, and credit unions (where one is certain of receiving at least the original investment upon demand) and of course, Individual Retirement Accounts (IRAs) and Keogh plans invested in these types of financial instruments.

Many military retirees, with several years remaining until actual retirement, prefer low-risk investments such as high-grade (AAA) municipal bonds, dividend-paying stock (preferred), or highly rated corporate bonds. By highly rated we mean bonds that are rated at least "AAA" (or equivalent) from a bond-rating agency such as Standard and Poor's.

One reason for the concession of accepting some risk, albeit very low, with safe dollars is that inflation can wreak havoc upon savings with conservative returns. First, subtract the annual inflation rate from the interest rate to determine actual savings. Then consider your personal income tax level as an item against the accrued interest.

Assume, for example, you have $10,000 in personal savings, receive $1,000 in interest, and are in the 25 percent tax bracket. You should realize you are paying out to the government $250 of the $1,000 gain.

The final equation might then look like this:

Interest income	$1,000
Income tax	−250
Inflation reduces investment's buying power by 7%	−700
Actual gain for the year:	$50

Note from this example that it is absolutely essential to reinvest your interest to keep pace with inflation. The example points out exactly what happens when one withdraws interest for living expenses. Inflation gradually erodes away the spending power of the investment.

The example also helps show why we recommend an IRA and Keogh plans as a high savings priority. IRAs and Keoghs defer taxes until you withdraw your money. Inflation, then, becomes the only negative force as your savings dollars grow.

Investment Dollars

There seems to be a tendency for military families to minimize their requirement for safe dollars and launch into a program of risk-type investments to achieve greater returns. It's common knowledge that the greater the risk, the greater the potential return. But another way to express the same equation is the greater the risk, the greater the potential loss. If you accurately evaluate the investment, then your risk taking is rewarded. If not, your savings might go right down the tubes. Consider this (exaggerated) parallel:

While on active duty, you have a chance to work for a general with a "tough" reputation. In fact, seventy-five out of the last hundred who worked for him were thrown out of the service. The other twenty-five were promoted after six months and reassigned. Now, you have the opportunity for the job. With sixteen years' service, and under the "up-or-out" policy, you must be promoted or get out—losing your retirement. Would you take the assignment, or would you opt for another job where you know that in eighteen instead of six months, you will get the same promotion? Our guess is that most of us would choose the safe job. Yet, it's amazing how many military people actually risk their entire life savings on an investment they know little about, all for an extra 5 or 10 percent return.

For investment dollars, select investments where there is little risk of losing the dollars you place into the investment. An excellent first objective of a plan for an investment fund is to have from $7,000–10,000 laid aside as an opportunity fund. Occasionally, there is an opportunity to invest in a safe, sound, low-risk but solid venture. Many fail to capitalize because they don't have access to the necessary funds.

Many families place their investment dollars in conservative real estate, rental property, highly rated bonds, long-term stock, certificates of deposit, or money market funds. These investments are for the purpose of making money without high risk.

Risk Dollars

These are dollars you can afford but of course don't want to lose. This must be a small portion of your total investment portfolio. Don't take chances just because high returns are promised. You might accept a little more risk than with your safe or investment dollars, but don't get carried away. Simply because high returns are possible in commodities, for example, does not mean that everyone should move into commodities. Over 90 percent of those—professional or not—who invest in commodities lose money. We wouldn't encourage anyone to invest in commodities. Growth stocks or commercial real estate are more reasonable areas for risk dollars.

Taxes

Successful financial planning must include tax considerations.

When you consider the value of saving on your taxes (or elsewhere) don't forget the magic of compound interest. If a 45-year-old cuts his annual taxes $500 and invests the money each year at 10 percent, when he is 65 he'll have over $30,000. There are a lot of tradeoffs, and changes in the economy can make yesterday's top investments today's disasters; but there are several tax breaks that should stand the test of time. Assuming you are launching a second career, you probably have around twenty years to go until you retire. Start with an IRA.

Individual Retirement Account (IRA)

The Indivdiual Retirement Account lets you save up to $2,000 a year toward retirement. If you make less than $2,000 in a year, you may contribute the entire amount of your pay to an IRA. The money you contribute to the IRA is tax deductible even if you don't itemize. You just subtract it from your income (tax forms will have a block for this). Obviously, the higher your tax bracket, the more you save with this provision, but everyone gains by it. Earnings on IRAs are permitted to accumulate without being taxed. The result is compounding at a phenomenal rate (see Table D in appendix 2).

The $2,000 limit is for individual taxpayers. If your spouse has no income for the year, a couple may open separate accounts up to a total of $2,250, divided in any way so long as no more than $2,000 goes into either account. Congress is considering allowing $2,000 per person without regard to employment. This would mean a great deal, for example, to homemakers. Although there are some arguments against it, based upon loss of tax revenue, this change will probably be approved. In the case of a working spouse, both husband and wife may now invest $2,000 for a total of $4,000 per year (see Table E in appendix 2).

You can open an IRA at most banks and at savings and loans. In addition, mutual funds and insurance companies and some stock brokers are welcoming IRAs. You just identify the funds as IRA money and invest much as you would otherwise.

If you withdraw IRA funds before you are 59½ years old, you will have to pay a penalty of 10 percent of the amount withdrawn. After all, it is supposed to be a retirement fund. If, in an emergency, you withdraw from an IRA account, you may find that, even with the 10 percent penalty, you can still gain as a result of the fantastic compounding effect. You may contribute to an IRA until age 70½, at which time you must begin your withdrawal.

When you start withdrawing funds from an IRA, that money is taxed as regular income. Presumably most of us will be in a lower tax bracket at that time. At any rate, it is much better to pay tax on income than to have no income.

Since banks and other savings institutions are competing for IRA dollars, select your investment carefully, with inflation in mind. IRAs are excellent opportunities, but select yours with cold, methodical analysis—not because the bank offers a set of bookends if you open your account by Friday.

Keogh Plans

Keogh plans are similar to IRAs except they are for self-employed persons, where IRAs are for wage earners. With a Keogh plan you can reduce your taxable income by 15 percent and invest up to $15,000. There are three additional advantages to a Keogh. First, you can also contribute $2,000 of your earnings to an IRA for a total of $17,000. Second, you can contribute as long as you are self-employed. Third, since you are self-employed, you can withdraw your Keogh savings in a lump sum and pay taxes, using a ten-year averaging method.

Shifting the Load

If you still have dependents at home, you might consider transferring some of your income-producing property into his or her name. Simply put, you establish an account in the name of the dependent, and the interest from that account is taxed to the dependent. Both you and your spouse may give a gift of $10,000 (total of $20,000) per year without paying gift or estate taxes. The accounts may be set up as either temporary trust or custodian accounts.

Temporary trusts permit you to name your children or other dependents as beneficiaries for at least ten years. During that time taxes on the assets placed in trust are taxed to the dependent. At the end of ten years, or in the event of the dependents' death, the asset reverts to you.

A custodian account is simple to set up. You merely transfer assets to a minor, and taxes on those assets come to that minor. The transfer is permanent, and the child may use the assets as he sees fit upon reaching legal age.

Tax Shelters

Much has been said concerning tax shelters. In the past, tax shelters were of interest only to those whose income was in the highest tax brackets or to other individuals with relatively high income. Normally this is still true, but the Tax Reform Act of 1981 has done a great deal to put tax shelters into the hands of the average taxpayer. But it still stands to reason that if you are in a low tax bracket, you have little need for tax shelters.

If you have an Individual Retirement Account or a Keogh plan, you already have a tax shelter that is readily available and encouraged by the government.

Investing only for tax breaks can actually lead to losses. If an investment is a good one *with or without* the tax break—and there is a large tax saving as well—then it could indeed be a smart move.

Most tax shelters do not really exempt you from taxes. Instead, they defer taxes until some later date. This deferral can hit you or your heirs when you can least afford it.

There are solid investments that also provide some very real tax breaks—tax-exempt bonds, real estate, and company deferred pay plans, for example. But do not select an investment solely because it is touted as a tax shelter.

State Tax Considerations

State tax requirements vary widely between states, and local tax laws vary within states. When a military family is seeking its civilian home, these tax burdens must be considered individually. Taxes have been defined as the price we pay for civilization, but the price isn't always the same.

A local area with outstanding schools will probably have higher school taxes than one in which the schools are marginal. If they aren't financed by direct school taxes, there must be other taxes that pay the bill. Sales taxes also differ greatly between states. There are minor taxes, some of which are really just sharing of the expenses (street lighting taxes, for example); and some of which are archaic, such as "head taxes" and "occupation taxes."

As is the case with federal taxes, the state tax that attracts the most retiree interest is individual income tax. Several retirees told us that they consider other state and local taxes as necessary, minor problems, but that the state income tax actually was one of many factors that determined their home selection. With some of them, it was more a matter of principle than of tax rates. Military retirees are subject to the tax laws of the state in which they claim residency. In most cases, there is some tax on military retired pay. In isolation, state income taxes usually aren't significant enough to deter someone who loves a certain state from living there. But, when combined with a heavy local tax load, some families decide they'll just move a couple of miles down the road—across the state line.

The following states have no income taxes: Alaska, Florida, Nevada, South Dakota, Texas, Washington, and Wyoming.

These states exempt all military retired pay: Hawaii, Illinois, Michigan, Pennsylvania, and West Virginia.

The other states have income taxes in some form. Many have special allowances for disability or survivor's insurance.

Since the federal income tax reductions between 1980 and 1984, state and local governments have found a need to come up with more revenue on their own. With decreasing assistance from federal funds, they have little option but to tax at their level. Consequently, the state and local tax picture is a constantly changing one.

A military retiree should check out the tax picture for the state and local jurisdiction in which he or she will live. Although it may not be the deciding factor (it probably won't be), it may well be an added expense that should not come as a surprise.

17

Government or the Private Sector?

A key decision, which influences much of your transition planning, is the sector in which you intend to spend the next third of your working life. For our discussion, we consider four major sectors: government, large corporations, small companies, and self-employment.

Government Service

Government work has great appeal for many as they move into civilian life. It certainly has advantages that make the transition more comfortable. Preferences for veterans are still in effect, although threatened in some states. The veteran is accustomed to working within the government bureaucracy, and most are comfortable in a large organization. Job security enjoyed by civil service workers looks a lot better now, as you consider joining their ranks.

Job Security

Job security is not the only consideration for the veteran. Even if it were, government service is no longer necessarily the perfect place to be. In recent years, the federal government has been cutting programs and people at a record rate. Most Americans felt it was long overdue, but when the cuts actually started, it was still a shock. And federal government cuts roll downhill. State and local government programs and jobs are reduced as they follow the federal lead to trim the budget. Government employment is relatively secure but not nearly as much so as it was a few years back. It probably won't ever be that secure gain.

Dual Compensation

For Regular officers, there is a big disadvantage to working for the federal government: The Dual Compensation Act limits their military retirement so long as they are also drawing checks for federal employment. This law was passed to silence those who were constantly harping about "double dipping"—drawing two government salaries. Most former military personnel argue that they have fulfilled their part of the deal by serving twenty or more years, and now they should have their retirement from the military. They feel they should be paid the going rate for their government job, to which they bring years of experience and training. The "Dual Comp Law" may be unfair, but it is also a fact of life. As a result, the government loses a lot of experienced talent for which it has paid a fortune. Regular officers go elsewhere, reorient themselves, and apply their talents to new endeavors.

State and Local Governments

State and local governments appeal to many military retirees. In addition to the same reasons for going with the federal government, there are some added advantages. The Dual Compensation Law doesn't hit the Regular officers if they are working at state or local government. They can draw full pay for their work—just like everyone else, plus their retirement they've earned from the military. And veteran's preference counts here at state and local levels too.

Location becomes a major consideration when you consider state and local government jobs. You're probably more likely to get a job in your hometown with state or local governments than with the federal government, simply because in most hometowns there aren't any federal jobs.

Knowing the Routine Helps

One more plus for seeking government employment: It takes a lot less effort, and you already know how "the system" works. Former military personnel are accustomed to government forms, few government jobs require resumes, and the application procedure is similar for most levels.

Certain skills (police work, most public administration, and some environmental and welfare work, for example) lean heavily toward government employment. If you specialize in such a field, the government—at some level—is probably a good place to start. But don't limit yourself!

Government Experience Shouldn't Restrict You

We interviewed a sharp lady who had been looking for a job as a stenographer with the state government. She had worked for a federal agency in Washington and was sure she stood a better chance of getting a government job than one in business. Since it appeared she would have to wait a couple of months before starting a state job, she decided to look around. She now works with a consulting firm and makes over twice what she would have made with the state. The point, of course, is that even though past experience was with a government agency (military included), future jobs need not be. Branch out if you want to, and do it when you want to. If you decide to work for the government, be sure it is your choice. Don't do it just because you gave up on something you'd rather have done.

Large Corporations

The appeal of large corporations to military retirees is strikingly similar to the lure of government work. Most large corporations are highly structured, and that structure bears a strong resemblance to military organization. Since we're all used to working in that environment, it's comfortable to head there for a second career. There are some excellent jobs with large companies.

Large firms with government contracts are the most likely to hire military retirees. If you specialize in their field, you have a good place to start your job search (or, at least your research).

When you consider one of these firms, remember there are two sides to the contract business. You already may know someone with the firm as a result of your military experience ("technical representative" with your unit, etc.). If so, start working that contact now, before you are out of uniform. Gather what information you can. Ask your military friends. If you don't have a contact, one of them might.

Another Restriction Against Regular Officers

Once again, there is a restriction against Regular officers, but this one isn't nearly as bad as the Dual Compensation Law is with government employment. The main clause reads, "A retired Regular officer is prohibited, at all times, from representing any person in the sale of anything to the Government through the Military Department in whose service he or she holds a retired status (see 18, U.S.C., 281)." Check this one out, but don't let it keep you from pursuing a good lead. The regulation is Department of Defense Directive 5500.7, and it's one you should know about now, rather than when you are processing out of the service.

DOD Regulation 5500.7 is an unwieldy one; but it is of little concern, as you can still work for just about any outfit as long as you aren't directly involved in the activities specified. The purpose of the regulation is to keep someone from setting himself up with a contract just prior to retirement. We feel that's an honorable purpose.

What's in a Title?

One of the major appeals by which large firms attract military retirees has nothing to do with real benefits or pay. It's strictly an ego-satisfying appeal, but it certainly works for some. Since large corporation structures so closely resemble the military's, they have all sorts of titles (one per job) that sound impressive. As with the military headquarters jobs in Washington, if you look at the job titles, you'll be impressed; but the jobs themselves aren't necessarily impressive.

A former Air Force Major General was offered a fine job with a small business in Texas. The questions he asked were:

"What will my office look like?"

"What will be the size of my staff?"

"What will my title be?"

The man never asked what the job was, what would be expected of him, what the pay was, or about future opportunities with the company! Can you believe that? Believe it. His main concerns were image and frills.

If image was the most important thing for the general, he should be happy. He decided against working for the small business; rather he chose to go with a large aircraft company, at a salary of about $30,000. He has a "title" (director of something or other), and he has an office with all the frills.

The young (in his thirties) guy who took the same job the general turned down (with the small business) made right at $100,000 in his second year. For the first year, his office was in a warehouse, his typing was done by the secretarial pool, and his staff was practically non-existent. He is extremely grateful to that general, as are his subordinates, who are fond of him but not so favorably impressed with the general.

Small Companies

At first, small companies just don't appeal to the majority of service families. This probably isn't a quirk of military people alone, but it's the military we are interested in. If a retiring aviation NCO is offered a job with Bell Helicopter, he can immediately relate to that firm. There are dozens, if not hundreds, of such large firms that ring a bell to most Americans: IBM, Xerox, the aircraft companies, petroleum companies, electronics firms, and so on. But if a small company he's never heard of offers him a job, it has less appeal—at least until he checks it out.

Great Hidden Potential

The appeal we discussed above is not likely to materialize with the small company; that is, the titles, physical surroundings, support machinery, and staff may not appear to be much. But a real ego boost may be just around the corner. There is a strong possibility that small businesses are the most overlooked hunting grounds for retiring military personnel. They need talent as much as (more than!) the large companies. The talent doesn't always come knocking, and their pool of resources is not as deep. The opportunity for advancement may be greater, and chances are that, as the firm grows, you have a much greater opportunity to be part of it. One thing is certain: You'll be more your own person in a small firm than in a large, highly structured, rigidly controlled one.

Familiar Ground or New Horizons?

It seems there are two definite camps of military retirees: Those who want to retain some familiar surroundings or routines, and those who don't. The small business world is about as far from military operations as you can get. For some that's great. They enjoy the flexibility and freedom of small business. For others, it's frightening. No matter which camp is yours, don't overlook small businesses when you begin your job search. In fact, you should start a separate file on them.

"I'd think twice before submitting your retirement papers, Clayton. It's a jungle out there."

Remember: The vast majority of employment is with small businesses. If you limit your search to large corporations, you cut your employment opportunities greatly.

Experience is Always Needed

Small businesses are less likely to have formal training programs than larger businesses. Some major corporations run complete "cradle-to-grave" programs, which include thorough training and apprenticeship, additional training, and professional grooming at each level of the corporate ladder. Because small businesses simply can't handle these types of programs, they're more eager to accept outside experience—including military experience and training.

A corollary to the training programs is the tendency of large corporations to develop their own staff and to promote from within. It's looked upon as a return on investment. As the smaller companies can't invest as much, it's smart business for them to gain on someone else's investment. One way they do this is by capitalizing on large corporation (or military) training and experience.

Flame of Hope or a Flash in the Pan?

With a large *or* small company, it pays to familiarize yourself with personnel policies. Some companies are highly dependent upon large, defense-type contracts. They sometimes get into a "boom or bust" situation. When there is a big contract, there is plenty of work. But the reverse is true; no contract, no job. Perhaps the entire company won't be hit; but if you are in a department that is, you just may be out of a job. This is a tough situation after you've put six or seven years into the company and are now around age 50.

Self-Employment

There are many advantages to being your own boss. The opportunity for income is greater than you could expect from most employers. There is a feeling of independence and creativity. A business of your own is a genuine part of the American free enterprise system. Once created, the entire business represents the personality of its owner.

There are disadvantages as well. Over 80 percent of new businesses fail in the first year of operation. Of the 20 percent that survive, a large percentage fail when the organization begins to grow past the "one-man operation" stage. The most common reason for the failures is undercapitalization. So if you consider going into business for yourself, keep the odds in mind.

There's more. If you own the company, count upon many more hours of hard work than meets the eye. Remember when you first went into the military and you thought everyone senior to you had it made? That feeling stayed with you at each level throughout your career. Similar to the burdens of seniority in the military are the added pressures and problems the employer alone must bear.

Begin with You

Anyone considering self-employment should start with a detailed self-analysis. Then study the risks involved. Take your time, and make a sound, deliberate decision.

How can you go about cutting the risks of self-ownership? The self-assessment is a good place to begin. Compare yourself to personal characteristics that have been identified with successful entrepreneurs:

1. Self-confidence. You must believe in yourself. You must believe in your own ability to achieve your goals and believe that events in your life are self-determined.
2. Long-term involvement. You must be able to commit four to ten years toward achieving your goals. This certainly implies full and complete dedication toward that end.
3. Drive and energy. Running your own business requires the ability to work long hours and still maintain a healthy, aggressive attitude.
4. Problem solving. The problems for the owner are difficult ones and take long and intense concentration.
5. Ability and willingness to learn from failure. Not every activity within the business will succeed. You must learn from the experience and move on.
6. Risk taking. Every business activity involves calculated risks. The successful entrepreneur must evaluate the up and down sides of each risk, make the decision, and live with it.
7. Money as a scorekeeper. The implication here is that money from the business cannot be an end in itself because the entrepreneur must maintain an objective view of the business operation—not make emotional decisions based upon a desire for high or improved return.
8. Acceptance of criticism. Criticism of the business activity is essential as a means of improvement. It must be accepted, objectively evaluated, then acted upon as needed.
9. Use of resources. Losing businesses are frequently turned into profitable ventures by the simple reduction of waste. A successful entrepreneur must keep a constant vigil on the use of company resources.
10. Self-imposed standards. Standards for the business are set by the boss. How well you set realistic standards, and work to achieve them, is an important consideration.
11. Initiative. Working in your own business is entirely different from being employed elsewhere. There is no one to make you come to

work on time. You set your own schedule, goals, and work ethic. You accept a leadership role in all tasks. There are no regulations or central regulation file for guidance. You are responsible for all organizational guidelines.

It is not likely you'll look good in all of the above categories. But in a review, if you find you're weak in several of them, self-employment may not be for you.

How Do Your Management Skills Measure Up?

Since you're going to be pretty much on your own as an entrepreneur, it's a good idea to consider management skills as normally applied to business. We've broken them into seven areas:

1. Marketing and sales. Every business enterprise must market a product. Even the best product, with the best price, will go nowhere without a sound marketing program. This is an area where the entrepreneur should assume the responsibility himself. Strong marketing help is difficult to hire because talented, experienced salesmen require large salaries. If you hire untried salespeople, you must realize it's nearly impossible to predict sales ability. It's been estimated that only about 3 percent of those who try their hand at sales are truly successful. This high failure rate is worth keeping in mind when a marketing program is considered.
2. Operations. This general category includes inventory control, quality control, purchasing, production, and overall operations. Normally, former military personnel will have some experience in these areas. But in business, cost effectiveness is much more important than in the military. The budget in the military is a routine matter, and effectiveness of the operation rather than expense dominates. In business you must consider whether or not you can afford the effectiveness of the operation. Purchasing is totally different in a civilian business environment, and you'll need expertise in this area for success.
3. Research, development, and engineering. No business activity is static. Changes will affect the way business is conducted. One must be ready to respond to those changes. Research, development, and engineering efforts vary among businesses. This activity is geared toward ensuring a future position in the market.
4. Financial management. This is absolutely essential for the entrepreneur. No one could or should have the financial interest of the

organization closer to his heart than the one who owns the organization.

One must prepare to raise capital and communicate with lenders. This requirement begins when you seek "start-up" capital and continues as you seek growth capital.

Another critical financial area is that of cash flow analysis. Income statements reflect only earned income. A business must react to the rate at which income comes in as compared to expenditures. Planning centers on cash flow.

5. Personnel management. Most former career military personnel will have some personnel management experience but will have to adjust for a civilian atmosphere and the civilian way of doing things. The major functions here will include leadership, listening, helping, conflict resolution, teamwork, selecting and developing subordinates, climate building, and general interpersonal skills. Since these skills are most commonly the ones that receive heavy emphasis in the military, most of us have a head start here.

A former career military person will probably discover that civilians have quite a few preconceived ideas of what someone from the military will employ as management techniques. Their preconceived ideas are usually wrong, but the new boss should anticipate those expectations and adjust his approach to management accordingly.

6. General administration and management. You've got experience here, but mostly in a military environment. We could include communications, planning, negotiating, personnel administration, problem solving, decision making, and project management. Suffice it to say you'll need those skills here, and you should plan to shift your techniques to fit the civilian business environment.

7. Legal and tax aspects. Most of us have some knowledge of taxes and law. But within the business environment, there are many specialized areas of law and taxes. The government continues to impose additional reports and taxes upon businesses, with the effect of complicating the operation. It's absolutely essential for a business to have an attorney and an accountant as advisors.

Although lawyers and accountants have expertise in their own fields, you should never expect the accountant to look over an operation and point out innovative ideas for saving money on taxes. This is something only the individuals directly concerned with the business undertake. Accountants will look at the financial reports and figure how to report your taxes. They'll also assist in completion of other government reports relating to taxes. So it's critical that you have a full understanding of the tax structure and laws. Taxes are a major expense and should be looked at in that light.

Attorneys cannot devote the time to educate an entrepreneur on legal complexities of the business. But they can, and do, handle some of the more involved processes of a business. But for day-to-day events it's up to the management to operate the business and to know when an attorney should be consulted. As with taxes and accounting fees, the legal costs can also be a major expense of running your business.

Capital

We mentioned earlier that most businesses fail because of lack of capital. True, you need management skills to succeed in business, but only to a degree. That is, a weakness in one management area can sometimes be compensated for by strength in another. Capital, on the other hand, is an absolute. There is no substitute for adequate capital. And most businesses fail for that very reason.

Businesses can become undercapitalized for several reasons. When one starts a business, he's normally enthusiastic about it. Typically, he'll study the venture carefully and develop a business plan. Then, he'll make an assumption concerning the revenue to be realized and anticipated expenses. The result of this assumption is estimated income. The required capital is usually a mixture of equity and financing. The bottom line is then the expected profits.

To raise the financing, most businesses turn to a bank or an investor. Investors and bankers, however, have a completely different view of a business venture than do entrepreneurs. The banker will listen to the story of huge profit potential. But his primary interest is spotting what is wrong with the plan and what could happen to make the venture fail, then what could be recovered in the worse-case situation. Naturally, the enterpreneur is absolutely certain nothing like that could possibly happen.

A good professional investor is similarly cautious. One professional investor told us how he would take the entrepreneur's projection and then double anticipated expenses and halve the anticipated profits. If the proposed venture still showed a profit, he'd be interested.

The banker and professional investor know that no one can truly anticipate all the expenses of a new business. And they also know many factors cause problems with the rate and volume of business income. Both rate and volume have a direct impact upon the amount of money required for a successful venture.

Because investors and bankers have a naturally cautious approach, you should select yours with great care. Since a banker is actually responsible for other people's money, he must take a cautious approach toward loaning it. He'll have little difficulty finding people who wish to borrow. But the main purpose of the banking business is to make money. So naturally, the banker is more interested in bringing money in.

It's essential to locate a banking source with experience in commercial loans, particularly in your chosen area. That bank should also have a reputation of being willing to work with a growing business. One of the ways the entrepreneur can help himself is to do whatever is possible to let a banker become acquainted with him personally and with the business operation. The longer and better a banker knows you, the more willing he will be to trust your judgment. Of course, you must be completely honest with him. He then becomes a valuable member of the organizational team. He's trained to spot problems and trends that can be unhealthy. This skill will balance the entrepreneur's natural optimism.

The banker is an excellent sounding board who frequently can spot problems before projects are begun. If one associates with an overly cautious banker—or an inexperienced one—this valuable free expertise is lost. Perhaps even worse, when the organization requires an extension of a healthy growth, the entrepreneur may face a rejection of credit at a critical time.

Approaches to Owning a Business

Approaches to owning a business commonly fit four categories: (1) turning a hobby into a business, (2) purchasing a franchise or distributorship, (3) purchasing an existing business, and (4) starting a new venture.

The Hobby

One of the most popular ways to begin self-employment is by turning a hobby into a business. The advantages, provided you are already established in the hobby, are rather obvious. You already have a knowledge of the product. And, from the business end of the venture, you have some contacts with similar interests, and you know what resources are needed. You know who the reliable suppliers are and what competition is out there.

If you intend to rely entirely upon a personal skill (such as art, writing, or crafts), *do not* wait until you're out of the service to give it a try. Just about any such activity can be done part time, and in fact that is how most get started. By the time you leave the service, you should have a good idea of the talent, expenses, facilities, and equipment required. Above all, you should know if you really want to pursue this thing full time. You may find that a fascinating hobby should stay just that. By far, the best way to go into business for yourself is gradually, learning as you go.

You should have some idea about the appeal of the product; what the appeal is, and to whom it appeals. But there's a real hazard here. When you consider a hobby, it's easy to assume others share your enthusiasm. With that assumption, you could grossly overestimate the market and be stuck with a product or service, but no demand.

A prime example of overestimation of the market is the abundance of karate and self-defense schools that have sprung up around the nation. Simply by the nature of the endeavor, anyone who is good enough to start a school must be totally disciplined and dedicated. To one who is that involved, it seems everyone should share that involvement and benefit from it.

Unfortuantely, although there are many successful self-defense schools, numerous smaller, individual efforts fail within the first year. The students' enthusiasm dwindles, and they drop out.

Some model builders experience this same disappointment. Based upon years of enthusiastic work on complex and detailed models, a person might decide to open a model shop. To his disappointment, he may find that most of the customers come to look at his exhibits, and only a few buy models—and the ones they buy are usually the small, simple, inexpensive ones.

As with the self-defense schools, model shops are sometimes highly successful. We offer the two as examples. You can apply the same theory to just about any other business.

Franchises and Distributorships

One of the quickest ways you can lose your life's savings is to enter the franchise field without doing your homework. You probably know several military retirees who are (or claim to be) doing great with a franchise. They're all over the country, and you can find plenty of them on the strip just outside the gates of most military installations. You can be sure that for every one of them there are several who have failed. Talk with them—both successes and failures. Study. Listen. And move very slowly. If you are just ready to get out of the service and have done no planning, have no franchise experience, and have limited funds, and your entire knowledge on the subject of franchising comes from a representative of a franchising firm—don't do it! You must know what you're doing before you tackle a franchise.

Franchises and distributorships appeal to many who feel they have the ambition and ability but lack business experience and know-how to get rolling. They figure they've got a sure thing if they get advice from the company experts. Since the experts work for the franchise company, who gets the short end when it comes to dealing with the company? Uh huh. . .

Ask These Questions

Even companies offering franchises and distributorships encourage thorough preparation and analysis before entering into a commitment with them. They want you to succeed, of course. But they must convince you to invest in their operations rather than go with the competition. For this reason, you dare not limit your preparation to materials furnished by the firm you are considering. During your analysis, satisfy yourself that you have clear, documented answers to the following:

1. What percent of those who purchase one of these franchises fail?
2. What percent are still in business after one year? Five years?
3. What percent of those in business today are earning the advertised amount? If the representative gets evasive about any of the answers, back away.

A good deal today normally will be a good deal tomorrow. There are a few investment opportunities that require quick action, but franchises and distributorships usually aren't among them. Don't rush into anything that costs you money. Instead, take another, closer look. Ask, for example:

1. Will the person who's pushing this deal make money even when I don't? If so, does that seem right to you?
2. Will I be required to purchase a large inventory? You may have all your money tied up in inventory. If you can't move it, you could be in big trouble.
3. Does the deal require that I obtain my supplies from a certain

individual or firm? You could severely limit your inventory and capability for expansion, and you'll probably pay retail prices.

Franchises and distributorships have made some individuals *very* wealthy. But the risk is great.

Purchase of an Existing Business

When it comes to buying a business, most potential buyers are apprehensive.

"If the business is any good," they might reasonably ask, "why is it for sale?"

Actually, that is probably the first question most of us would ask. If you begin with that question, you might find sufficient reason to pursue the deal further, or to get out of it. When you ask the question, naturally you must ask it of others in addition to the seller.

You should be suspicious—at least cautious—as you investigate the purchase of a business. But don't forget there are plenty of good, valid, honest reasons for successful businesses to be on sale. One of the most common is retirement of the owner.

An owner who is retiring from a business has spent many years building it, will be proud of his accomplishment, and will probably be of considerable help to the buyer. He may be willing to stay on for a while to train the new owner, at least enough for a smooth transition. He certainly knows the business better than most new owners, and a brief overlap could prove invaluable for years to come.

In many cases, the seller is willing to finance all or part of the purchase. This can be a godsend for the purchaser since his credit probably will be stretched to the limits.

There are also those whose *business* is starting new businesses, realizing appreciation, then moving on to new ventures. They may be either individuals or larger companies. Since their goal is appreciation, they have a sincere interest in making the company as successful as possible in a short time. But, in contrast to most retiring owners, a major part of their operation is *selling* the business. So you can expect a slicker, more polished, highly convincing presentation of the package.

Purchase of an existing business requires a great deal of time and planning. Time might well be more important than detailed planning because your investigation might lead you down unexpected paths for which you could never have planned. Use the time wisely, and look down each of those paths.

Once you determine that the existing business seems viable, you must determine its value. This is tricky. Certainly, you must go far beyond what the present owner says. Areas for immediate investigation include:

1. Accounts receivable. Are they all payable? Without an expensive and time-consuming collection effort?
2. Inventory. Is everything accounted for? Is it valued realistically?
3. Accounts payable. Are they current? Does the company have a good rating with supply sources?
4. Location. Is it assured? Are changes coming up in cost (e.g., a new lease coming due)? How about possible zoning changes? If this is now a good location, will it be in the future (how about that bypass they're building)?
5. How much value is assigned just for the "good will" of the business? Few are sold for simple cash value of assets. Normally, a thriving business will be valued at some multiple of net operating profit. In light of this probability, the prospective purchaser must evaluate the books and tax returns, and determine if profit is properly stated. Then he can determine if he thinks he can make a go of it.

Starting a New Business

Setting out on your own is probably the most difficult of all the choices. It is by far the most risky. If you succeed, it is certainly the most rewarding.

The Big Gamble

If you're actually starting "at the beginning," with no record in the business or industry, you must realize that the odds are against you. That challenge may be just what you like most about it. If so, you may need that positive attitude again and again as you start your business.

Forming your own business takes much more effort than working for someone else or purchasing an existing business. Expect plenty of stress and effort. It may take a heavy toll on your health, family life, and social activities. Unlike when you work for others, everything you do or fail to do has a serious effect upon your business. You are taking the risks, and they are considerable.

At the start, you'll have nothing on the balance sheet, so sources of capital will be difficult to locate. The earlier you start working on this angle, the better.

Plan to have money for operating capital on hand for the startup. Bankers are more willing to lend money for inventory than for operating capital. As we mentioned earlier, undercapitalization can ruin a business, usually when all the money goes for inventory, leaving little for operation.

If You Get It—Manage It!

Just as undercapitalization can destroy a business, poor management of working capital can have the same effect.

We talked with a young entrepreneur, George P., who wanted his own medical supply company. He started small, as most do, with borrowed money. His business progressed beyond his dreams.

After four or five years of success, George dealt himself a huge salary and benefits package. In doing so, he took a severe cut into reserves.

The next year a new company came into the area. It was much larger than George's firm and had the expertise to size up the market. The new outfit recognized a need for competition. Once they spotted George's vulnerability, they invaded his territory with new equipment and better pricing.

George needed working capital but had taken it up in personal living. He had no choice: He had to reduce his income or lose the whole works. He chose the former.

There are many ways you can cut into working capital. As an entrepreneur, one of the most common is simply paying yourself too much, destroying necessary reserves.

Many capital and management problems are caused by a lack of thorough preparation. That lack stems from understanding the difficulty of the task at hand. Anything done well looks easy, and a business is no exception.

The Restaurant: The Most Common Example

The restaurant industry is an excellent example. We all can recall a new restaurant that seemed to have everything going for it, then vanished overnight. There is certainly a high failure rate in this field, and the reason is usually some form of underestimation of the problem. But why? Unlike with introduction of a new product, everyone is familiar with the restaurant's product: food. There must be more to the failures than meets the eye.

As with many other business enterprises, the restaurant field is deceptive in its complexity. There are many considerations, and each is essential to success. Any one can cause the bottom to drop out of the business. Consider:

1. Location is critical. There are firms that exist just for the purpose of studying potential business locations. But even locations that seem like a sure thing don't always work out. In fact, in most good locations, you can spot one restaurant with waiting lines while a nearby one sits nearly empty.

2. Access can determine whether you win or lose. Along with the general location of a restaurant, the customer must be able to get there with no hassle. If it is along a highway, but without an exit nearby, customers will normally stop where it's more convenient. The customer must be aware of the easy access; in other words, it must be visible. Successful "hard-to-get-to" restaurants are in a minority, despite their "quaintness" or "uniqueness." And, of course, the final element of access: parking. Unless the restaurant is in a downtown business building or something similar, the customers must have handy parking. Without it, they'll go elsewhere.

3. Portion and waste control can make or break the new restaurateur. Large, generous portions for the price might appeal to customers, but if the portions are too generous, there will soon be a need to decrease them or raise prices. Neither option will please regular customers who have been enjoying the good deal.

4. Appeal to the public is obtained through the product (food), service, price, and the decor. Word of failure in any one of these categories spreads quickly.

5. In this example, as in numerous other enterprises, the new business is competing with established ones in the area. In other words, most customers were going to local restaurants before the new one opened; the new kid on the block must somehow lure those customers into his establishment.

6. The inventory control system must be effective to prevent heavy losses. Practically everything from a restaurant can be used at home, and it will be if the system isn't a good one.

7. Labor problems and costs impact upon various businesses in different ways. In the restaurant field, for example, personnel turnovers have a direct effect upon food production, service quality, and management in general.

8. Proper advertising, in any business, is expensive. The market is saturated with restaurant advertisements; "getting their attention" is a challenge in itself.

These few considerations for a restaurant business certainly aren't all the new proprietor has on his or her mind, but they serve as a useful example. Different businesses will have vastly different problems. But whatever the business, the owner must anticipate problems and have contingency plans for coping with them. In addition, he must always realize the unforeseen will occur, and usually at the worst possible time.

Why Isn't Someone Else Doing It?

If you have a product or service to sell, you must decide how you are going to reach the public. The dream that customers will "beat a path to your door" is usually just that—a dream. Even if you come up with another Frisbee, Rubik's Cube, or Cabbage Patch doll, you still need marketing, advertising, packaging, and sales—each an area requiring considerable expertise.

There is an abundance of guides for planning a new business, and anyone willing to try should check as many of them as possible. The Small Business Administration provides materials and assistance for those who are interested. Among the most common questions you should address are the following:

1. Does the product or service respond to a perceived need (e.g., a laundromat on this side of town)?
2. Is the product or service one upon which people will spend their money? Occasionally, it appears the public wants something, but although they're glad to have it in the area, they spend elsewhere. An example is: "We need a good clothing store in this neighborhood." But when the classy store opens, the local folks love it for window shopping but continue their buying at malls.
3. Will the product or service require creation of a market? Revolutionary new products, for which there has been no market in the past, require time for educating the public—creating the idea of need. It is easy to underestimate the time and effort necessary to market the product. For example, racquetball became a raging success in California where new trends catch on and die overnight. But there were some big-time failures in other parts of the country

when the local people didn't rush to embrace racquetball as quickly as the Californians did.

4. If other businesses with smaller products or services have failed— why? You have to look at both sides of the coin. Frequent failures may point out opportunities. On the other hand, the well-known reasons for the failures may be only the tip of the iceberg. Certainly there's a need for taking a detailed look at the situation. Caution: Other failures may influence the public's expectation of your business. ("Oh, there's another store opened where Charlie's used to be. They probably won't last either.")

5. Will there be a continuing need for the product or service? In the late 1970s, Citizen's Band radios were the nation's leading fad. Shops and dealerships sprung up everywhere. Today few of them are still around.

6. What type of location do you need? This is a critical consideration. High visibility and easy access (as mentioned in our restaurant example above) cost money. And the appropriateness of the real estate plays a major part in your success. There are, for example, few large warehouses in bustling downtown areas. The cost would be prohibitive. On the other hand, although space in an industrial area might be less expensive, it would make little sense to open a small gift shop there.

7. How much professional consulting is needed? What will it cost? As a minimum you need legal, accounting, and bookkeeping services. Consider these costs up front.

8. Is the marketing plan a proven approach? The best product won't sell unless it is made known to users. There are many ways to market a product; some work, some don't.

9. What type of return may I expect on the initial risk investment, and how much will expansion cost? Risk capital must bring high returns; otherwise why bother? For example, if the return will be around 15 percent, it is easier to invest the money with much less risk.

10. Do you really know the business or must you learn as you go? Learning as you go can be a costly deal. The inexperience may cause significant errors in determining expenses and revenues.

As with any business enterprise, detailed planning and research usually pay great dividends. Suppose you spend your valuable time and some of your money, only to find your idea isn't really a good one. What better time to find out than before you start? Now you can get that bad idea out of your head, and move on to a good one. In the end you have saved time and money.

18

Veterans Administration Benefits

Prepare! Plan! Study! Research! Inquire! . . . This business of transition doesn't sound like half the fun it once did. It is work, but it isn't bad if done in advance. This is doubly true with regard to benefits. Although you have already earned your benefits, you must keep well informed to gain the maximum from them.

During our school days many of us waited until the night before a test, then tried to cram a semester's knowledge into one evening of study. The next morning we would squeak by the exam, and a month later we had forgotten it all. Making the conversion from military to civilian is no math exam. Cramming won't work, even if you're the best "crammer" on the block.

For a little while after you announce your military retirement, there is usually a calm period. You begin to wonder if anyone heard about it. Then you wonder if anyone cares. But as the big day nears, you start getting busier. And busier. The last few days before you "get out" are straight out of *Future Shock*. Events occur so fast you can't comprehend them. The worst part is that everything seems to be speeding up. More and more questions are spinning in your mind, and each answer appears to contradict the one just before it. And when questions come to mind, you're in the car or in bed. You wonder, "Why didn't I think of that while I was in the finance office where I could get the answer?" While the movers are at your door, you are trying to get your medical records copied and pay allotments finalized. You have a great job interview but it is three hundred miles away. You need to close the deal on your home, and you discover that clearing military bases is as big a nuisance as it was twenty years ago. With your jaw pounding from the last-minute dental work you felt lucky to get, you realize that this is no time for cramming.

There is another reason not to hold off until the last minute: It may then be too late. Some critical decisions must be made long before the big day. Discovering a valuable benefit the morning you load the car will cause you only a lot of regret. A one-time chance may be gone after retirement (Survivor Benefit Plan, for example). Or, you may still have an option but be unable to take advantage of it because you are committed to other plans. Even if your civilian home is near a government installation or a Veterans Administration Center, it is tough to catch up on those things you should have done while on active duty—but didn't know about then—after you are out of uniform.

Don't expect the retirement services folks to brief you on everything. The best of them can't do that, and the worst ones wouldn't know where to start. If you start your own planning early enough and make some notes, it will be easy going. Read the Veterans Administration publications and your own service's material. Understand CHAMPUS and SBP. Above all, get all your questions answered before you check out.

You will find about thirty publications pertaining to various aspects of military retirement that you should read before firming up your retirement plans. They come from several sources, and each has a different shape or an odd size. One of the greatest retirement services would be to have all this printed on loose-leaf paper. You could organize it, make changes, file it, learn it, and compile it in advance. But that is not the way it is, so we still must accumulate a rather cumbersome package of material. No matter how it is packaged, we all still need to know the highlights of our benefits, at least enough to decide whether to pursue or drop an item.

Your benefits provide a broad range of possibilities. Many require that you take specific actions to receive them. Others require your personal touch to ensure that they fit your situation. You must take the time to digest and understand the different possibilities and select your own best course of action.

Military retirement benefits come from several sources, including the Veterans Administration (VA), the military services themselves, and state and local governments. In this chapter, we will consider the major VA benefits. The next chapter discusses some other benefits, which come from other than VA sources.

The Veterans Administration

Straight from *Title 38, US Code* comes this word on exactly who—or what—the VA is:

> The VA is an independent establishment in the executive branch of the Government, especially created for or concerned in the administration of laws relating to the relief and other benefits provided by law for veterans, their dependents, and their beneficiaries.

In other words, when you have questions or problems regarding GI loans, GI Bill education, disability, insurance, medical care, employment assistance, burial, rehabilitation training, or other items under these general headings, you will turn to the VA.

As with most federal agencies, dealing with the VA can be a frustrating process. Sheer numbers are certainly part of the problem. There are over eight million Vietnam-era veterans alone, plus those from other periods, including a few from the Spanish-American War. Most of those veterans are not into the bureaucratic process, and with any attempt to obtain VA help they lose valuable time. If you do your homework, and know precisely what you want (and how to go about it), the VA representative will be happy to deal with you, particularly since you've taken the trouble to prepare. You'll probably be pleased to discover that the VA, even though big, is quite human.

It's amazing that those who spend a career in the military service know so little about the VA. We can blame our services (education on the VA isn't their problem) and ourselves when we spend twenty or more years without even inquiring about benefits until we collect the gold watch (or $10 plaque) and are out in the street.

For purposes of VA administration, military retirees are considered "veterans" in the same sense as other veterans. Most reference material discusses service during all wars, back to and including the Spanish-American War. Although some of that may prove interesting, it doesn't make sense for us to dwell upon those programs. You could also be a Korean Conflict veteran, or even have served in World War II, but if you are making the transition from military to civilian life, you are either a Vietnam-era veteran (5 August 1964–7 May 1975) or a post-Vietnam-era veteran. Let's take a practical look at your VA benefits.

VA Disability Compensation

Don't confuse VA disability with disability retired pay. VA disability is determined by the VA and is separate from military retired pay. It is based on disabilities "incurred in or aggravated by active military service in the line of duty." The VA may not agree at all with the service when it comes to evaluating your disability.

Be certain you understand the meaning of the disability percentages. If the VA grants you a 20 percent disability, that does not mean you get 20 percent of your total retired pay tax free. It means that the VA, after an examination, determined that you're 20 percent disabled. What does that mean? With pay tables changing constantly, we don't want to get too specific or the information will be obsolete in a month. For a ballpark figure, think of it this way: 10 percent = about $60; 20 percent = about $75; 30 percent = about $105.

Using the figures from the example above, let's take a quick look at how the system works. Suppose the VA awards you the minimum disability: 10 percent. Each month, you will receive a VA check for about $60. There's no federal tax on that $60. But you don't get the $60 in addition to your retirement check. To get the VA check, you give an equal amount (in this example, $60) from your retirement. It's a simple process: The VA notifies the service, the VA check starts, and the military retirement check is decreased by the same amount. So why bother? There are several good reasons, the most obvious being the tax break. In a year, $60 per month would amount to $720 tax-free income. And remember, this example is based on minimum disability.

There's another important reason why you should file for VA disability before leaving the service. For many who know about it, this is the *main* reason. You can get Service-Disabled Veteran's Insurance (SDVI) only if you have a VA disability. We're going to talk about SDVI shortly, but for now remember it as a good deal, if you need it.

You can file for VA disability at any time, but it makes sense to do it during your pre-retirement processing. You have access to your medical records (incidentally, make a copy of those records before you get out since the service isn't required to do it for you), and someone at your personnel section can point you in the right direction and help with the forms. If not, call the VA.

In rare cases, VA disability compensation can be more than retirement pay. In such cases, which occur when retirement is relatively low and disability is high, the thing to do is forfeit the entire military retirement pay and draw the VA payment.

If there's any injury or ailment that you can trace to military service, file the claim and get the physical. After a military career, where physical conditioning and good health are required, you don't even want to think about disability. But you'll stand a lot taller if you know you've taken care of the future to the best of your ability. No

"You say you were run over by a tank, wounded by a hand grenade, and stabbed with a bayonet . . . Are you sure these were service connected?"

one is going to stand up at your retirement and embarrass you with an announcement that you are awarded disability. You'll be long gone from the service before the VA settles your claim.

Actually, odds are good that no one will tell you about VA disability compensation, and in particular about SDVI. That's why we're doing it. It will be in that stack of references we mentioned. First you might overlook it. (We hope not, after you've read this!) Second, if you find it, you'll probably get the impression it doesn't apply to you. It may, and *you* have to start the ball rolling.

The Army's *Handbook on Retirement Services* gives some additional points to ponder about applying for VA disability compensation:

1. Application is a separate action, which has no effect on retirement or other benefits unless you choose to accept the VA check. In that case, it's to your advantage. You forfeit none of your rights.
2. The VA percentage of disability is based upon your condition at the time of the exam. It may be increased, decreased, or discontinued later.
3. VA disability checks cannot be seized or garnisheed except to pay federal taxes.
4. In the event a claim is disallowed, it may be reopened later.

There are several variations of VA disability payments. We've been talking about obtaining the basic qualification. If you've lost a hand, foot, or eye in wartime, or if the VA determines that you're 60 percent or more disabled, or that you're permanently housebound, there are special adjustments. If your disability is over 50 percent, there will probably be a special compensation for dependents.

Suppose ten years from now your ailment or injury really brings you down. You knew about it but didn't mention it when you retired although the trouble started years before. When retirement time came, you didn't bother (or weren't advised) to file for VA disability compensation. At that time, the local medics were familiar with your medical history and could have helped you. Now you're going to file. But, because you've waited ten years, the burden of proof is now entirely upon you, and it may not be an easy task.

If, in the same example, you filed for VA disability as you left active duty, your case would have been easier to substantiate and certainly would have been more convincing. Even if the VA granted only the 10 percent minimum, they agreed to award it because it's service-connected. Ten years down the line, you need to discuss only the degree of disability. You have already proved it was service-connected.

We are not advocating going out and faking some nonexistent ailment. We are saying get a thorough physical before leaving active duty. VA disability compensation is one of your primary benefits. Some other benefits are based upon it. The VA is there for you. If you think you might have a valid case, file the claim. The VA will instruct you to get a physical exam to confirm the problem. You've been through physicals before.

VA Insurance

If anything is more confusing than everyday explanations of VA insurance programs, we haven't found it. Maybe it is because most of us aren't interested until the pressure is on. As we said earlier, we're going to concern ourselves with "now" benefits. So we will discuss VA insurance that is now open and consider it from the point of view of one who is about to become a civilian after about a quarter of a century in uniform.

The most confusing part of the entire insurance picture is the abbreviation mess. Here's a quick and clean primer on the subject.

SGLI

Servicemen's Group Life Insurance is the government insurance you have while on active duty or in the Ready Reserve. It's simply group term insurance. As of the most recent change (1981), active-duty members are automatically covered for the maximum ($35,000) amount unless a lower coverage is elected or the service member cancels coverage. Coverage is in effect until 120 days after separation from active duty. If you want to continue this low-cost VA insurance beyond that 120 days, you convert it to VGLI.

VGLI

If you want it, Veterans Group Life Insurance (VGLI) becomes effective on the 121st day after separation from active duty. It is a five-year, non-renewable term policy, limited to the amount of SGLI you have while you're on active duty. (Did anyone ever tell you that?) You may elect coverage that is less than your SLGI, but not more.

Consider VGLI as a five-year coverage between your Serviceman's Insurance (SGLI) and a civilian policy. At the end of the five years, you can convert your VGLI to a permanent insurance plan *without* proof of health condition. Just be certain to set it up in advance; if the VGLI expires before you've got other coverage, it will then be too late. There is no grace period.

Think about this benefit. You come out of the service at age 45, convert your SGLI to VGLI, which to you means the same as continuing your service insurance, and in five years you get up to $35,000 civilian insurance without a physical examination requirement. At age twenty, that's no big deal because most of us think we'll live forever. At fifty, in the prime earning years, paying tuition, nursing an ulcer, and serious about estate planning, this can be a godsend.

If back there at Minot, San Diego, Benning, Yuma, or wherever you were, you signed the paper canceling your SGLI coverage, that decision will be with you now. With no SGLI, there can be no VGLI and no conversion to a civilian policy without proof of health. Fortunately, the services start with the maximum, and most of us leave it alone.

SDVI

Service-Disabled Veteran's Insurance is the insurance we mentioned in the discussion of VA disability compensation. If the VA awards you any disabilty—even the 10 percent minimum—you're eligible for SDVI. You may obtain this insurance in amounts from $1,000 to $10,000 in multiples of $500. You're required to be in good general health with the exception of your service-connected disability. There are a variety of permanent plans from which to choose, or you may apply for the five-year level term plan. SDVI insurance is commonly referred to as "RH" insurance, simply because RH is the prefix used for these policies. You must apply for SDVI within one year of the date you were awarded VA disability. If you have $35,000 in VGLI, you may still purchase $10,000 of SDVI if you have a VA disability.

The Others

In any discussion of VA insurance programs, some familiar names crop up and cloud the issue. We haven't forgotten them. As they are no longer open, we'll mention them here and show the cut-off dates.

USGLI: United States Government Life Insurance. Available until 24 April 1951 for World War I veterans and those who entered service prior to 8 October 1940.

NSLI: National Service Life Insurance. Began the day USGLI

cut off (8 October 1940) and was available to World War II veterans until 24 April 1951.

VSLI: Veterans Special Life Insurance. Began the day after NSLI ended (25 April 1951), for Korean War veterans. Ended 31 December 1956.

VRI: Veterans Reopened Insurance. This was reopened NSLI coverage for World War II and Korean veterans with service-connected disabilities (or serious non-service-connected disabilities). It was open only from 1 May 1965 through 2 May 1966.

OSGLI

This is not insurance. It is the *Office* of Servicemen's Group Life Insurance. This office is the administrator for VA life insurance and handles SGLI and VGLI matters. The title might throw you if you're applying for *V*GLI, but this is the right office.

Key VA Insurance Points

1. You must have SGLI while in the service to get VGLI when you get out.
2. You must obtain VGLI within 120 days after release from active duty so that it becomes effective on the 121st day.
3. VGLI cannot exceed the amount of SGLI you had on active duty.
4. SDVI—Service-Disabled Veteran's Insurance ("RH") is available to veterans who are awarded VA disability.
5. You must apply for SDVI within a year from the award of disability.
6. Insurance can be a major benefit, and the rates for VGLI and NSLI are good.

The above information should be enough for you to determine whether or not you want to pursue the VA insurance possibilities. If you believe you meet the requirements, you'll want more information. Contact OSGLI at 212 Washington Street, Newark, NJ 07102 or any VA office.

Educational Assistance

Somewhere in your thoughts of returning to civilian life, you may consider returning to school. Maybe you want a teaching certificate or your master's degree. Or you'd like to get a college degree, now that it appears you will be in one place long enough. Perhaps you've been working in a specialized field that doesn't easily transfer to civilian life. The GI Bill might be ideal for you.

Since WWII, many Americans have taken advantage of GI Bill educational training programs. There have been some modifications— actually there have been different "GI Bills"—but the principle has remained the same: Eligibility is based upon service. You served, you are probably eligible, and the GI Bill is one of your benefits. So if you decide you want to take advantage of it, do it.

There are two active programs, one for those who served before 1 January 1977 and one for those whose service was after that date. We'll refer to the former by its traditional title, the GI Bill, and to the post-1977 program by its official title, Veterans Educational Assistance Program.

The GI Bill

We'll start with the end—for emphasis: You have ten years from date of release from active duty to enroll in school or training under the GI Bill. No matter when you get out, all eligibility expires 31 December 1989. Congress is giving serious consideration to extending this cutoff date, so check the current status before applying.

If your service was between 31 January 1955 and 1 January 1977 and was for more than 181 days of continuous active duty, you're eligible for GI Bill benefits. Reservists who joined the reserves before 1 January 1977, then began their 181 days' service during 1977 are also eligible. Anyone discharged with service-connected disabilities, even though service was for less than 181 days, is probably eligible and should check with the VA.

If you served on active duty for eighteen continuous months, you're entitled to receive forty-five months of full-time educational benefits. If you have less than eighteen continuous months, you get a month and a half of full-time benefits for each month served. If you choose part-time attendance, you get the equivalent coverage.

Post-Vietnam Veterans Educational Assistance Program

Those who entered military service after 31 December 1976 may participate in this voluntary contributory matching program. For each dollar the active-duty service member puts up, the VA will contribute $2. The service member's contribution must be between $25 and $100 per month and is limited to $2,700.

The maximum entitlement under this program is thirty-six months or the number of months of participation, whichever is less. The cutoff date for this program is ten years from release from active duty.

If more education is part of your life plan, be sure to contact the VA and take full advantage of your educational benefits. Again, you've already earned them.

Vocational Rehabilitation

Remember when we were talking about the importance of getting that physical and filing a claim for VA disability? It's important here also. If you have a service-connected disability rated 10 percent disabling or more, you may be eligible for vocational rehabilitation. In this program, the VA pays the full cost of tuition, books, and supplies, plus a subsistence allowance. With three dependents, you get $375 per month. But your school expenses are paid!

Even with a disability you might not be eligible for or interested in this program. The key point here is that you must have a disability rating before being considered.

GI Loans

If you have 180 days recent service or are being released for a service-connected disability, the VA may guarantee a home loan up to $27,500 or 60 percent of the principal amount, whichever is less. In some rural and farm areas, designated by the VA as "housing credit shortage areas," the veteran may be eligible for a direct VA loan up to $33,000. For purchase of a mobile home, the VA guarantee limit is $20,000 or 50 percent of the principal amount, whichever is less. VA mortgage terms may be up to thirty years. This information changes periodically, so it is important to have current figures before you begin your planning. The VA will send you the appropriate forms and guidance, and they will answer your questions by phone.

The VA has its own guidelines for interest rates. Before you consider a VA loan, call and check on the current maximum rate. They also must appraise a new home, which may cause a delay. Further, the VA usually limits the number of "points" the lender may charge. (Due to limits on the amount of interest lenders may charge, they charge points—each equal to 1 percent of the loan amount.) Required down payments on VA loans are usually lower than for other types, and you may pay off your loan early without penalty. All of these characteristics, combined with today's high prices and interest rates, tend to turn lenders off. But with some searching, you should be able to locate one, provided you meet other income and credit requirements.

Whether you use your VA loan now or later isn't the most important item. What is important is that you're ready when and if you want one. Normally, the VA will send you a Certificate of Eligiblity just after you're discharged. You can wait, and if you don't get it within a couple of months, apply. Since you're eligible while in the service, why not get it out of the way? Call the VA and ask for a Form 26-1880, complete it, and it's done, with no pressure on you or the VA.

Other VA Benefits

Even with budget and program cuts the Veterans Administration still offers a variety of benefits for those who served. True, veteran's benefits are a frequent target for government savings, but they're still a fair deal. We've talked about the heavy items already—education, insurance, loans, and disability compensation. There are other, smaller but important benefits.

Burial Flag

An American flag may be issued to drape the casket of a veteran. Flags are issued at VA offices, VA national cemeteries, and most post offices.

Burial Allowance

A change made in 1983 limits the $300 burial allowance (previously available to all vets) to those on VA pensions or disability compensation and those who die in a VA medical facility—another small reason for getting that disability recorded. In addition to this payment, the VA will pay a $150 plot or interment allowance if the requirements just stated are met, except for those buried in a national cemetery.

Headstones or Markers

The VA will furnish a headstone or marker upon request for veterans buried in other than national cemeteries. No request is necessary for national cemeteries.

National Cemetery Burial

You, your spouse, and your minor children may be buried in any national cemetery that is administered by the VA. Arlington National Cemetery, the exception, is administered by the Department of the Army. Although Arlington Cemetery burials are becoming increasingly restricted, space is still available for active-duty and retired military personnel. Burial in any national cemetery is, of course, subject to available space.

Employment Assistance

The VA has local employment representatives who assist with job counseling, testing, and placement services. If you don't have one in your area, contact the nearest VA office for information. We feel that you may hit upon a job anywhere. Launching a new career will take more than a visit to the VA, but you may get valuable leads there.

You may get more than a lead if you are interested in working for the federal government. As a result of your military service, you get special consideration for federal jobs. This advantage, plus the familiar territory of government work, draws many veterans to federal employment. Regular officers: Don't forget the dual compensation law, which restricts your earnings if you work for the federal government.

Summary

The Veterans Administration administers the bulk of programs for all United States veterans, of all wars. For most veterans, including military retirees, the primary programs are those discussed above. In addition, there are programs for dealing with alcoholism and drug dependency; survivors assistance; special equipment and clothing allowances for the handicapped; specially adapted housing; and VA medical treatment for the disabled or those veterans who are unable to pay for their treatment. Special education programs also include farm cooperative training, apprenticeships, loans, counseling, and tutorial assistance.

VA programs are comprehensive and cover many specific areas. If you feel you may qualify, or you want to inquire about a program, the best advice remains: Contact the VA. They are there for you, and they'll help you.

19

Non-VA Benefits

Veterans Administration benefits are well known, because generally they are available to all veterans. For military retirees, however, there are other benefits, which are as familiar—if not more so—as VA benefits. These include installation craft shops, chapels, Recreation Services' facilities and equipment, exchanges, commissaries, legal assistance, libraries, and other facilities that are usually taken for granted by those on active duty.

The most reasonable way to consider these benefits is to remember they may be used by retirees and their families on a "space available" basis. In other words, the active-duty force gets first priority. If retiree use of the facility, service, or equipment does not interfere with services to those on active duty, it is generally made available.

By the time we are ready to retire from the service and begin a second career, most of us are highly knowledgeable about these benefits, the majority of which are administered by the services themselves. So we won't attempt to explain how commissaries or exchanges are funded or what they are. As we talked with military retirees, we picked up many pointers we believe are worth passing on. We'll do that now, with hopes we can save you some money or heartache later on.

Exchanges and Commissaries

Within the United States, retirees rarely have problems obtaining permission to use exchanges and commissaries. It's almost taken for granted that they are all available for both active-duty personnel and retirees. But on rare occasions, use of certain facilities is limited to active-duty personnel. In a stateside situation, this may occur as a result of limited supplies, a restricted area, or a situation such as the small troop exchanges on basic training installations. Most retirees never face these situations.

Overseas, the exact opposite may be true. If you are planning a trip, and in particular if you plan to live overseas, check what privileges are available. In many cases, host nation agreements allow use of exchanges and commissaries by active-duty personnel only. In addition, the installation commander may also temporarily deny facilities to retirees if there is a problem meeting the needs of his or her troops. Inquire ahead of time to avoid embarrassment and financial hardship. Above all, do not show up at some isolated station and demand use of facilities. Remember your active-duty days, and don't put those young people in a bad situation. Retirees are rarely in a position to demand, especially when the problem is a result of poor planning.

Speaking of planning, for many retirees, availability of exchanges and commissaries is an important consideration in the process of retirement home selection. If you are considering retirement near a major installation, it is reasonably safe to figure on availability of most privileges. You do need to find out what's there and what isn't before you settle. Some retirees discover after the final move that the nearby installation doesn't fit the family needs. The importance of this consideration spills over into your own special interests that don't necessarily apply to everyone, such as crafts, base theaters, and clubs. Although access to these benefits can be important from a recreational point of view, discovering they are inadequate probably won't be catastrophic. But if you are counting on exchanges or commissary privileges, you simply can't afford *not* to check in advance. If you move near an installation that closes, or if your privileges are denied for other reasons, it's like having the spending power of your retirement reduced.

Clubs

Retiree membership in officer or noncommissioned officer clubs is the option of the board of governors for the particular club involved. Retiree privileges vary dramatically, even within the same geographical area. For example, in one area with an Army installation and a Navy base nine miles apart, retiree membership in the Army club is $12 per month and the Navy club costs $48 per year. As in most such situations, there is a reciprocal agreement (club card from one is accepted by the other). For a savings of almost a hundred dollars a year, the smart retiree would pay the $48. This isn't to say Navy clubs are less expensive than Army ones or Air Force ones. There are cases where the

Army club is the best deal by far. Just compare before you commit yourself. In this example, at age 45 you could join the club for $48 per year and invest the difference once a year at 9 percent. When you're 65, you'd have a painless $5,300 with no sacrifice. There will be plenty of uses for it, you can be sure.

"Space A"

Remember leaving for overseas—hustling to get to the departure base by Monday morning and waiting until Thursday for takeoff? Three whole days that you could have been with the family, shot. Wasted. Three days of living out of a duffle bag, sick from all the shots, homesick, and heartsick. Most of us swore we never wanted to lay eyes on another military terminal. And meant it.

Then there is our vow, repeated every day of boot camp: If I ever get away from here, wild horses couldn't drag me back!

Ten or twenty years later, as you are driving through on the interstate, you might decide to stop and have one nostalgic look at hell on earth. You discover it's a regular garden spot. They're still pushing recruits all over the place, but it seems so . . . different. What has changed? Perspective, friend, just your perspective.

There is one benefit we can appreciate fully only if we're willing to look at it from a new perspective: space available travel. Military Airlift Command (MAC) flies to just about everywhere in the free world. If there is a space available, a military retiree can fly free. The importance of a good attitude surfaces when you recognize the fact that you are now last priority. After all active-duty personnel and their dependents, and after that last box of aircraft parts, or socks, or radios, is loaded, you can board if there's room.

"Space A" travel is a benefit that can be worth a lot in many ways. You can save enough in air fares alone to pay for a vacation. You can see parts of the world you missed while on active duty. You meet a lot of interesting people, including the natives where you visit, other retirees, and the troops who are now running the show. On the other hand, you can end up not leaving the ground and spending several frustrating days waiting for a ride that never materializes.

As with other benefits, you get the most out of Space A travel by careful, thorough planning. Even with the best of planning, things can—and do—go wrong. Remember, MAC is not running an airline. They have a mission to accomplish. If they can accomplish that mission *and* accommodate a traveling former service family, everyone will be happy.

But just as it was when we were in their shoes, the mission must come first. The flight may be cancelled or rescheduled, or it may divert to another airport. Be ready to accept these irritants in good spirits or forget about Space A.

If you're planning to use Space A travel, remember:

1. The former service member may travel Space A within the continental United States and overseas. Dependents may travel only on overseas flights.
2. You need a passport with appropriate visas. (You didn't need them before because you were traveling on official military orders.)
3. There is a $10 processing charge for each Space A passenger. This charge is from base of origin to destination (which you specify prior to departure). No matter how many stops you make along the way, this one-time charge is good unless you fail to show up for a scheduled flight, or change destination en route.
4. Call the Space A counter at your departure point and get some idea what's available. Several terminals have recordings that answer most questions on outbound flights and procedures. You can get the big picture from the recordings, then call with specific questions.
5. Remember, do not plan to get off the plane and head straight to the exchange (unless you know it's authorized). Many overseas bases extend exchange privileges only to active-duty military personnel and some civilians who work with them on their mission.
6. The same rules apply to guest houses and visitors' quarters. Active-duty personnel get first priority, and in some cases they are the only ones who can use the facility. So the next item must be:
7. Take enough money to cover your expenses. Don't make the mistake of counting 100 percent on Space A, exchanges, commissaries, government quarters, etc. Plan to cover the worst situation, and hope for the best. Be sure to have enough for a commercial ticket home if you should get stranded.
8. Allow time, and relax. If you can't do this, or if you simply can't accept being last priority after all those years of coming first—go commercial, and pay accordingly.
9. Dress properly. You might end up on a cargo plane or a transport that combines cargo and passenger capability, such as the C5. There will be ladders to climb, and the aircraft heater might not keep you comfortable once you are en route. You might also end up sleeping in a terminal or two.

If you can do it, take full advantage of your Space A privilege. Although the terminals sometimes look like everyone is doing it, you might be pleasantly surprised if you give it a try.

State and Local Benefits

Before deciding where to settle after leaving the service, be sure to compare state and local benefits for veterans and military retirees. These benefits come in many forms and can make a big difference for you.

Five states (Hawaii, Michigan, Illinois, Pennsylvania, and West Virginia) exempt military retired pay from state income taxes. If you are eligible for VA disability compensation, it is tax exempt in twenty-six other states. Most of the remaining states give you some sort of break, usually geared to age or earnings. Just make a note to consider tax structures with other factors, and know the tax setup in your new home state. The state tax situation changes constantly. It's doubtful that many military retirees would select a state just because of the tax structure; but when it is combined with other considerations, it can make the difference.

Check state and county veterans programs carefully. Even though there are variations, most offer some benefits. Employment preferences and retirement credit toward state employment are the most common. Others include education assistance, emergency assistance, burial allowances, grave markers, veterans' homes, and special programs for those with VA-recognized, service-connected disability. Many counties furnish free copies of veteran's marriage and birth records and will record discharge papers free. NOTE: Be sure to check with the courthouse wherever you retire, and record your discharge. This record can be important later as you seek benefits or your survivors attempt to prove your dates of service. If for no other reason, record it there for the sake of that one person in every family who will someday be trying to piece together the family tree.

20

CHAMPUS

The benefit most of us will use sooner or later is the one that seems to cause the most consternation among military retirees: medical care. Most of the frustration stems from unavailability of military medical facilities, long waiting periods to obtain treatment, and failure to understand CHAMPUS.

As a military retiree, you and your dependents are entitled to medical treatment and care at military medical facilities on a "space available" basis. If there is no space because it is needed for active-duty personnel and their dependents, you must make other arrangements.

Another consideration is the capability of the military facility to meet your needs. Many small military bases have clinics with pharmacies, laboratories, and other essential services. If you need specialized treatment, hospitalization, or surgery, you'll be referred to a military or civilian hospital. The availability and capability of medical facilities, then, become increasingly important when you decide where you'll settle.

Unless you have a large military hospital nearby, you'll probably need to use CHAMPUS (Civilian Health and Medical Program of the

"Look on the bright side, Elmo. You're covered by CHAMPUS."

Uniformed Services). Almost everyone knows about it, but few know how to use it until the need arises.

There has been a great deal of confusing information written about CHAMPUS, but in truth we must say the most recent guides are written in clear, understandable language. The American Forces Information Service fact sheets tell what you need to know clearly and concisely. These are available at military medical facilities or from any CHAMPUS representative. If you really want the details, you can obtain a copy of the complete CHAMPUS regulation (DOD 6010.8R) from: Superintendent of Documents, Government Printing Office, Washington, DC 20402. (Refer to Stock Number 008-001-00102-9.)

Following are some highlights that should allow you to ask the right questions and to know what you should expect from CHAMPUS.

What CHAMPUS Is

Technically, CHAMPUS is not a health insurance program since no premium payments are involved. It is actually a medical benefits program with funds allocated by Congress for sharing medical expenses.

Who Is Eligible for CHAMPUS?

You are eligible if you are retired from the uniformed services or a dependent of an active or retired service member. Benefits for dependents continue after the sponsor's death until the dependent's status changes (marriage, over 21, adopted, becomes an active-duty service member, etc.).

Active-duty members are not eligible for CHAMPUS; medical care for active-duty personnel is the responsibility of their service.

Required Identification

Retirees, spouses, and children must present a current and valid Uniformed Services Identification and Privilege Card (the ID card) in order to be accepted for treatment under CHAMPUS. Children under ten are registered through parent's ID cards.

Starting in 1980, the armed forces registered families under the Defense Enrollment Eligibility Reporting System, better known as DEERS. This computer system contains information pertaining to those who are eligible for military benefits—including medical treatment under CHAMPUS—and is designed to cut waste and fraud regarding claims. Those who apply for treatment should be registered under the DEERS system, or expect delays or possible denial of treatment. Those retiring from the service should be certain they are registered under DEERS before completing out-processing at the military personnel office.

"Participating" or "Nonparticipating"?

To really understand the workings of CHAMPUS, we need to understand the two categories of physicians, suppliers, and services. Simply, there are those who accept CHAMPUS and those who don't. But we need to look at them in CHAMPUS terms so that we can communicate with CHAMPUS.

The term *provider* refers not only to doctors, but also to those who provide other related services such as laboratory work, X rays, ambulance service, and medical supplies.

Participating Provider

One who *agrees* to accept CHAMPUS-determined allowable charge as payment in full is a *participating provider.*

Nonparticipating Provider

One who *does not agree* to accept CHAMPUS payments is known as a *nonparticipating provider.*

Champus periodically updates its allowable charges based on prevailing fees and percentages allowed by Congress.

When you get medical treatment or service from a participating provider, you satisfy the deductible, then the provider bills CHAMPUS for the remainder.

In the case of a nonparticipating provider, you pay the bill, then file a claim with CHAMPUS, who then pays you the allowable amount. If the bill exceeds the CHAMPUS allowable, it's your responsibility to pay it.

Use Military Facilities First

CHAMPUS is designed for use when care is not available in a military medical facility. If you live within 40 miles of a military hospital, you must obtain a statement of nonavailability before CHAMPUS will pay for any nonemergency inpatient care. Some military installations require a nonavailability statement for outpatient care also.

The Statement of Nonavailability (DD Form 1251) indicates only that the appropriate care is not available. It has nothing to do with whether or not CHAMPUS will pay the bill. For example, if an individual needs a physical for a civilian pilot license and the military facility has no flight surgeon, that facility might issue a nonavailability statement. CHAMPUS would not pay the bill, however, because physicals for licensing, schools, and so on are not approved for CHAMPUS.

What You Pay

As mentioned earlier, CHAMPUS is not really a health insurance program. But for all practical purposes, we can think of it as one. And, as with other health insurance programs, there are inpatient costs, outpatient costs, and deductibles. We are discussing only retirees and their families. There are different rates for active-duty families.

Outpatient

Deductible: You pay the first $50 of CHAMPUS-determined reasonable charges during any fiscal year. In the event more than one member of your family is treated, the total outpatient deductible for one family during any fiscal year will not exceed $100.

Copayment: After the deductible is satisfied, CHAMPUS pays 75 percent of the CHAMPUS-determined reasonable charges. You pay the rest.

Inpatient

Deductible: There is none for inpatient care.

Copayment: CHAMPUS pays 75 percent of the CHAMPUS-determined reasonable charges. You pay the remaining 25 percent.

The above illustrates an important fact. Even with CHAMPUS paying three-fourths of the bill, a major illness or serious accident could be financially devastating. It makes good sense to fill the gap with insurance. Good policies are offered through most major military-related organizations and are worth considering.

After CHAMPUS

CHAMPUS coverage for the military retiree and his or her family continues until they either become ineligible (as in the case of children growing up) or become eligible for Medicare at age 65 (usually the retiree and spouse). Our book is for those in a mid-life career change.

For them, Medicare is about twenty years away. Be assured, you're covered until then.

Each military installation has a Health Benefits Advisor. Before using CHAMPUS, you should contact that person's office and obtain current information regarding CHAMPUS assistance.

21

This Is Not the End

You've now taken a general look at what you have to accomplish in your pre-retirement planning, and, we hope, have determined about how long you have in which to do it.

You may have noticed we return to certain themes again and again. This is especially true with regard to planning ahead and providing for the family beyond what military retirement provides. Our reasoning is that most of us have been lulled into a false sense of security about "the system" taking care of us.

One Hand Feedeth . . .

Take, for example, the action by Congress while we were working on this book. Mainly because they didn't understand it, too few military members signed up for the Survivor Benefit Plan before retirement. The services convinced Congress that many more would opt for SBP if given another chance. Since the decision must be made before retirement, special legislation was needed to give retirees another opportunity to choose SBP. President Reagan signed the Omnibus Budget

Everything can work out for you, also . . . with the proper planning.

Reconciliation Act of 1981 in August of that year. That law allowed a one-year "open season," which ended 30 September 1982. During that period, tens of thousands of retirees applied for SBP—and were thankful for the opportunity.

Why did so many apply? One reason was lack of preparation prior to retirement. Another was change of circumstances since retirement. But a major drawing card for SBP was, and is, the fact that it's adjusted for inflation. If retirement pay increases 6 percent, so does the deduction for SBP, and so does SBP coverage. It's all "automatic," and as we mentioned in an earlier chapter, that characteristic alone makes it worth a lot. But there's more: Once you are gone, your spouse still gets the cost of living allowances as military retired pay increases.

We argue, in favor of SBP, that these appealing aspects of the program can't be ignored. A lot of retirees agreed, according to the results of the open enrollment period.

While the Other Taketh Away

But during the last month of the open enrollment period, Congress made another change. In this one, military retirees under age 62 will receive only half the annual cost of living increase for three years, with a strong possibility that the provision will be extended, probably permanently. Congress' sudden shift to basing retired pay on age—when nothing else in the system is—proves a point: The power of the purse string is in Congress. And when political pressures lean against the military retiree, so will Congress.

The Social Security System is in serious trouble. "Fixes" abound, but none show much lasting promise. Somewhere down the line, Congress will be forced into something more drastic than we have seen in the past. We all have a stake in Social Security. We have paid into it, but by the time most of us are ready to draw on it, will it even be there? Probably. But it will be more expensive for those who are paying. And they're not going to like it. They will demand that Congress change the system.

There will be some changes in Social Security in the near future. But, suppose in the year 2000 (that is not far away), there's renewed outcry about the cost of the system. Then, suppose someone surfaces the fact that $34 *billion* (the projection for the year 2000) is going to military retirement. What do you think will happen?

Even the most pro-military senator or representative will find it tough defending the military retirement system when it's bucked up against the old, the poor, and the infirm. The military retirees' case isn't helped by their relative youth at the time they become civilians "And," the argument might go, "just about all of them under 65 are employed in second careers." It will make little difference that the retirement came after twenty or thirty years of devoted service, for which retirement is partial pay.

Expect a change in the military retirement system during your lifetime. It might not come about as we've described, but we believe it's going to come.

Too often we assume, "Any change will affect only those just beginning their careers. We've already completed our contract, so it won't hurt us." What contract? We have no contract guaranteeing our retirement income. It can be changed or modified any time the votes are there. Believe it. It's been done in the past.

United We Stand . . .

There's not much chance military retirement will be eliminated. But it will be changed. Retirement organizations like The Retired Officers Association, the Noncommissioned Officers Association, the Marine Corps League, and others are trying to look out for us. But they are limited in what they can accomplish.

The key to success for these organizations is membership. You might not be a "joiner," but if you don't support them, don't expect them to work miracles for you. Military retirees, like any other group, must be organized to be effective. Consider for a moment the simple fact that there are over 25,000 military retirees in the Washington, D.C., area. The potential for some political representation is certainly there, particularly when we think about the over 1.4 million of us elsewhere in the country.

We Cannot Forget . . .

When we leave active duty, we still have obligations to ourselves, our families, and the widows and children of our comrades. Those obligations include keeping well informed and making our voices heard. How you feel about a certain issue isn't as important as the fact that you have feelings on it, and those feelings are represented.

So, when you leave the service, become a civilian. Don't try to live in the past. Know what's going on with those military retirement benefits—the benefits you earned—just as you would if they were a quarter of a million in stock or bonds. Make your voice heard if you feel you have a good case. The most effective way for you to do that is through one or more of the major organizations for that purpose. You choose yours.

Keep in Touch

Joining one or two carefully selected military retiree organizations will keep you informed about what "they" are doing with your hard-earned benefits. But there are several other parts of the retirement picture, and you've got to remain current in each.

Communication, in just about every sense of the word, is essential during your transition. Keep in touch and keep informed.

Read It All

There are dozens of good books on retirement planning. We're going to list a few of the current best for you. Each of them will give you additional references on specific subjects. Don't get discouraged when, after reading an entire book, you find only a chapter or a few pages that apply to your situation. Most of the material was written either for civilian job changers or for *real* retirement, at between 60 or 70 years of age, so it takes some sorting. But if you get one good pointer, the book is worthwhile.

Your research doesn't spot only your weak areas. It also highlights your strengths. This can give you a tremendous boost when you need it most. For example, if you discover your legal affairs are in order, you can concentrate on other aspects of your pre-retirement planning. Your research has relieved you of a heavy burden and also permitted you to orient your efforts where they are most needed.

Talk It Over—Openly

On any military installation in the world, there is one thing every career person has in common with every other. Each of them is going to retire (or die first). With that in mind, you would think installation libraries would devote entire sections to pre-retirement planning. You would expect classes, starting at about the ten- or fifteen-year service level, for everyone. We know it doesn't work that way. While we're on active duty, there's a sort of denial that *we* will retire.

The commercial sector realizes the importance of good pre-retirement planning. We hope the military will catch up someday. Everyone is going to leave the service, one way or another. Everyone.

Companies hoping to attract talent believe the best advertisement is a satisfied retiree. When someone who worked a lifetime for an outfit recommends it, most people listen. The military is no exception.

Somehow, service members must stop looking at "retirement" to civilian life as joining the competition. Those who plan their retirement ahead of time are the few who are doing it right. Why act as though retirement is some top-secret operation? If you're still on active duty, which is the ideal time to be reading this, you can do yourself and many others a great favor if you'll just get together and talk about pre-retirement planning.

Answer the Question!

What am I going to be?

The answer to that question can save you years of heartburn. Tape a slip of paper on your bathroom mirror with that question on it. Ask it any way you want, but ask it of yourself until you know the answer—the specific answer. Don't accept from yourself something like, "I'd like to work for the aircraft industry." You can fly in the aircraft industry, you can be a computer operator for the aircraft industry, you can drive a truck for the aircraft industry, you can be a lawyer for the

You were a success in the service, and you will be a success in civilian life.

aircraft industry, or you can clean toilets for the aircraft industry. All are jobs that must be done, and there are hundreds more.

Once you know the answer well enough that you can say you want to be a turbine mechanic, a waiter, an accountant, a law officer, or a teacher—or something equally specific—you'll be amazed at how much easier it will be to get on with your transition. Until you have the answer your job search will be random and embarrassing, your interviews (if you get any) will be humiliating, and your resume won't have a specific goal. But even worse, you won't be sure what you want. If you stumble onto a job, you'll always wonder if it's really right for you.

The commonly stated goal of ". . . an opportunity for upward mobility within the company, and to apply my rare leadership, managerial, and administrative talents . . ." just doesn't get it. Remember that. Be specific with yourself first, then with your job search.

Just answer the question, "What am I going to be?"

Remember Those Closest to You

Above all, communicate with your spouse. All these years, she's come along with you wherever the orders sent you. The service always had the final say. If she tried to establish a career of her own, she was uprooted and had to start anew. How many homes has she established for you, in how many places? Now, this move is *the one* where the two of you have the final word. You decide where you're going, what house you'll live in, and what you'll do for a living. She's going to be part of it, probably the most important part. Talk each step over, right from the start. No more blaming the military, so don't blow your big chance to do it right.

Continue Your Education

Suppose after you talk it all over with your spouse, decide what you want to do, and settle on where you're going to do it, you realize you're going to need some more schooling. Don't worry about it. At least you know where you're heading, so you know what schooling you need. We talked with military retirees who went to school and became lawyers, dentists, craftsmen, teachers, managers, and just about anything else you can imagine. Get as much schooling as possible while on active duty, then finish as soon as you are out of uniform. If you're sure what you want, there is no sense in fooling around for a year or two.

Money, Money, Money

Start your financial planning now. Ideally, you have plenty of time for accumulating a nice nest egg. Even with kids to raise and all the expenses of everyday life, it's possible to save some. Compounding is a wonderful thing. You will be glad you saved, no matter how humble your effort may have seemed at the time. Do not plan to live on your military retirement alone. You may have to at some time or another, but don't plan on it. You can do better. Do it now. When those "golden years" that everyone talks about arrive, you'll be ready and they *will* be golden years.

Remember Yourself—You Deserve It!

So now you're ready to start the retirement process and do it right. After you've thought about your spouse, the children, finances, benefits, a job, a house, a new town, insurance, legal matters, and the mental stress of the whole thing, you might wonder if you'll ever have any time for yourself.

You *will* have it. Plan for it. Plan to relax, and grab that family time you have been waiting for. Plan to do all those nice things you have been promising yourself and your loved ones, like getting in shape, cutting out the smokes, or actually going on a vacation rather than sending the family while you work.

And When the Day Arrives . . .

Someday soon you'll look back and realize how short a military career is, and how time flies. On that day you will feel all the emotions that go with leaving the service. And in a private corner of your soul, you'll give thanks for the military years past, and for the civilian ones in your future.

Godspeed.

The Mortgage Money Guide

This information from the Federal Trade Commission is a guide to the new phenomenon called "creative home financing." It is intended to help you learn some of the basic concepts needed in shopping for a home loan. While you'll find many plans described in these pages, no attempt has been made to outline every new financing technique on the market. New financing alternatives are frequently being introduced, and we do not recommend any particular plan over the others. Shop and compare the options to decide which plan is best for you.

Getting Started

If you've been thinking about buying a home, you may wonder if it's still possible. Interest rates and purchase prices have become unpredictable. Traditional mortgages with fixed interest rates and long terms are more difficult to find.

As a result, new mortgage plans called "creative financing" are emerging. These plans represent a departure from traditional mortgages: They can involve more risk for the buyer and are frequently tied to changes in the market. But they also can make home buying possible and may offer lower interest rates.

So if you want to purchase a home, it may not be too late. But to get a mortgage that meets your needs, you should educate yourself first.

This guide will introduce you to the new plans. Other sources of information include your state, county, or city consumer affairs office; local realtors, home builders, and lenders; bookstores; and the real estate section of your newspaper. You may also want to buy a book of mortgage payment tables to help you calculate whether you can afford a specific loan.

Above all, shop carefully. And, as you read through this guide, keep in mind the following:

- Don't use yesterday's assumptions about today's real estate market.
- The key is affordability. Consider your total housing costs—including loan payments (now and in the future), maintenance, property taxes, and your anticipated income changes.
- Look into several sources of financing. You may be able to combine two or more mortgages.
- Ask questions. For example, an enthusiastic seller may not be familiar with the fine points of the financing arrangement.
- Negotiate with the seller or lender. Better terms may be available than those initially offered.
- Consider getting an attorney or a real estate broker to represent you. This could be the largest investment of your life.
- Study all available materials about your mortgage costs. With loans from institutional lenders, the creditor is required to give you a statement of your loan costs and terms before you sign the agreement. This information will include the *annual percentage rate* (APR) which measures your total credit costs, including interest, points, and mortgage insurance.

Defining Your Terms

To buy or sell a home today, it's important to know the new vocabulary. Don't let terms like "amortization" or "appreciation" scare you. Understanding the new concepts can save you time and money; it can also prevent you from obtaining a mortgage ill-suited to your needs.

Three important words are: "interest," "principal," and "equity." When you first buy a home you're likely to make a down payment

HIGHLIGHTING THE ESSENTIALS

Type	Description
Fixed Rate Mortgage	Fixed interest rate, usually long-term; equal monthly payments of principal and interest until debt is paid in full.
Flexible Rate Mortgage	Interest rate changes are based on a financial index, resulting in possible changes in your monthly payments, loan term, and/or principal. Some plans have rate or payment caps.
Renegotiable Rate Mortgage (Rollover)	Interest rate and monthly payments are constant for several years; changes possible thereafter. Long-term mortgage.
Balloon Mortgage	Monthly payments based on fixed interest rate; usually short-term; payments may cover interest only with principal due in full at term end.
Graduated Payment Mortgage	Lower monthly payments rise gradually (usually over 5–10 years), then level off for duration of term. With flexible interest rate, additional payment changes possible if index changes.
Shared Appreciation Mortgage	Below-market interest rate and lower monthly payments, in exchange for a share of profits when property is sold or on a specified date. Many variations.
Assumable Mortgage	Buyer takes over seller's original, below-market rate mortgage.
Seller Take-back	Seller provides all or part of financing with a first or second mortgage.
Wraparound	Seller keeps original low rate mortgage. Buyer makes payments to seller who forwards a portion to the lender holding original mortgage. Offers lower effective interest rate on total transaction.
Growing Equity Mortgage (Rapid Payoff Mortgage)	Fixed interest rate but monthly payments may vary according to agreed-upon schedule or index.

Considerations

Offers stability and long-term tax advantages; limited availability. Interest rate may be higher than other types of financing. New fixed rates are rarely assumable.

Readily available. Starting interest rate is slightly below market, but payments can increase sharply and frequently if index increases. Payment caps prevent wide fluctuations in payments but may cause negative amortization (see "Losing Ground" section). Rate caps, while rare, limit amount total debt can expand.

Less frequent changes in interest rate offer some stability.

Offers low monthly payments but possibly no equity until loan is fully paid. When due, loan must be paid off or refinanced. Refinancing poses high risk if rates climb.

Easier to qualify for. Buyer's income must be able to keep pace with scheduled payment increases. With a flexible rate, payment increases beyond the graduated payments can result in additional negative amortization (see "Losing Ground" section).

If home appreciates greatly, total cost of loan jumps. If home fails to appreciate, projected increase in value may still be due, requiring refinancing at possibly higher rates.

Lowers monthly payments. May be prohibited if "due on sale" clause is in original mortgage (see "Reading the Fine Print" section). Not permitted on most new fixed rate mortgages.

May offer a below-market interest rate; may have a balloon payment requiring full payment in a few years or refinancing at market rates, which could sharply increase debt.

Lender may call in old mortgage and require higher rate. If buyer defaults, seller must take legal action to collect debt.

Permits rapid payoff of debt because payment increases reduce principal. Buyer's income must be able to keep up with payment increases.

(continued)

HIGHLIGHTING THE ESSENTIALS (*continued*)

Type	Description
Land Contract	Seller retains original mortgage. No transfer of title until loan is fully paid. Equal monthly payments based on below-market interest rate with unpaid principal due at loan end.
Buy-down	Developer (or third party) provides an interest subsidy which lowers monthly payment during the first few years of the loan. Can have fixed or flexible interest rate.
Rent with Option	Renter pays "option fee" for right to purchase property at specified time and agreed-upon price. Rent may or may not be applied to sales price.
Reverse Annuity Mortgage (Equity Conversion)	Borrower owns mortgage-free property and needs income. Lender makes monthly payments to borrower, using property as collateral.
Zero Rate and Low Rate Mortgage	Appears to be completely or almost interest free. Large down payment and one-time finance charge, then loan is repaid in fixed monthly payments over short term.

on the property. But, because you financed the purchase, you are now in debt and the lender "owns" most of the property's value. In traditional mortgages, the monthly payments on the loan are weighted. During the first years, they are largely *interest;* in time, more of each payment is credited to the loan itself, or the *principal.* Gradually, as you pay off principal, you build up *equity,* or ownership. Your equity also increases if the value of the home increases. This process of gradually obtaining equity and reducing debt through payments of principal and interest is called *amortization.*

Until recently most mortgages had fixed monthly payments, a fixed interest rate, and full amortization (or transfer of equity) over a period of 20 to 30 years. These features worked in the buyer's favor. Inflation made your payments worth more. So, although the payments seemed hard to meet at first, over time, it became easier.

Creative financing plans are different from traditional mortgages. They may help you buy a home you otherwise couldn't, but they also may involve greater risks for buyers. For example, the interest rate

Considerations

May offer no equity until loan is fully paid. Buyer has few protections if conflict arises during loan.

Offers a break from higher payments during early years. Enables buyer with lower income to qualify. With flexible rate mortgage, payments may jump substantially at end of subsidy. Developer may increase selling price.

Enables renter to buy time to obtain down payment and decide whether to purchase. Locks in price during inflationary times. Failure to take option means loss of option fee and rental payments.

Can provide homeowners with needed cash. At end of term, borrower must have money available to avoid selling property or refinancing.

Permits quick ownership. May not lower total cost (because of possibly increased sales price). Doesn't offer long-term tax deductions.

and monthly payments may change during the loan to reflect what the market will bear. Or the interest rate may fluctuate while the payments stay the same, and the amount of principal paid off may vary. The latter approach allows the lender to credit a greater portion of the payment to interest when rates are high. Some plans also offer below-market interest rates, but they may not help you build up equity.

In shopping for financing sources today, keep in mind the terms which are keys to the affordability of the home:

- the *sales price minus your down payment,* or amount you finance;
- the length, or *maturity* of the loan;
- the size of the *monthly payments;*
- the *interest rate* or rates;
- whether the payments or rates may *change;*
- how *often* and how *much* the payments or rates may change; and,
- whether there is an *opportunity for refinancing* the loan when it matures, if necessary.

These concepts will be discussed in greater detail as we describe specific types of financing.*

Fixed Rate Mortgage

Fixed rate mortgages have an interest rate and monthly payments that remain constant over the life of the loan. This sets a maximum on the total amount of principal and interest you pay during the loan. Traditionally, these mortgages have been long-term. As the loan is repaid, ownership shifts gradually from lender to buyer.

For example, suppose you borrow $50,000 at 15 percent for 30 years. Your monthly payments on this loan would be $632.22. Over 30 years, your total obligation for principal and interest would never exceed a fixed, predetermined amount.

Fixed rate mortgages are not as readily available as in the past. Because the market is highly changeable, many lenders are reluctant to lock themselves in to rates that cannot adapt to new conditions.

Some lenders are still offering fixed rate mortgages at high rates. If you can afford the high monthly payments, inflation and tax deductions may still make a fixed rate mortgage a reasonable financing method, particularly if you are in a high tax bracket. Other lenders are exper-

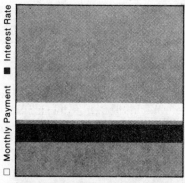

Year from the Date Loan Was Granted

Fixed Rate Mortgage. Traditionally both interest rate and monthly payments are fixed for the life of the loan.

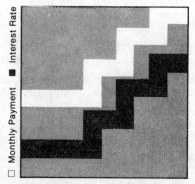

Year from the Date Loan Was Granted

Flexible Rate Mortgage. If there are no payment or rate caps, interest rate and monthly payments fluctuate according to an index.

---

*The charts contained in this guide are for illustrative purposes only. They are not intended to be precise representations of each type of mortgage.

imenting with new types of fixed rate mortgages which have, for example, shorter terms or balloon payments. For example, you might be able to find a 15-year mortgage with a fixed rate of interest that is 1 percent or 2 percent below market rates. In this type of plan, your down payment and monthly payments are higher but your debt is fully repaid at the end of the term.

Flexible Rate Mortgage

Flexible rate mortgages have an interest rate that increases or decreases over the life of the loan based upon market conditions. Some lenders refer to flexible rates as *adjustable* or *variable*. For example, Federal savings and loans offer "adjustable mortgage loans," and national banks offer "adjustable rate mortgages." Because flexible rate loans can have different provisions, you should evaluate each one carefully.

In most flexible rate loans, your starting rate, or "initial interest rate," will be lower than the rate offered on a standard fixed rate mortgage. This is because your long-term risk is higher—your rate can increase with the market—so the lender offers an inducement to take this plan.

Changes in the interest rate are usually governed by a financial index (see "Changing Rates" section). If the index rises, so may your interest rate. In some plans, if the index falls, so may your rate. Examples of these indexes are the Federal Home Loan Bank Board's national average mortgage rate and the U.S. Treasury bill rate. Generally, the more sensitive the index is to market changes, the more frequently your rate can increase or decrease.

Suppose your interest rate is tied to the Bank Board index. Your mortgage limits rate changes to one per year although it doesn't limit the amount of the change. For example, assume your starting interest rate is 14 percent on 1 September 1982. Based on these terms, if the Bank Board index rises 2 percentage points by 1 September 1983, your new rate for the next year will be 16 percent.

Rate Caps

To build predictability into your flexible rate loan, some lenders include provisions for "caps" that limit the amount your interest rate may change. These provisions limit the amount of your risk.

A *periodic cap* limits the amount the rate can increase at any one time. For example, your mortgage could provide that even if the index

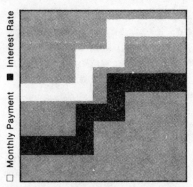

Flexible Rate Mortgage/Rate Cap. With a rate cap, even if the index rises, increases in the rate and monthly payment are limited.

Flexible Rate Mortgage/Payment Cap. If the index increases, so does the interest rate. However, monthly payment changes are limited (although the total amount owed may increase).

increases 2 percent in one year, your rate can only go up 1 percent. An *aggregate cap* limits the amount the rate can increase over the entire life of the loan. This means that, for example, even if the index increases 2 percent every year, your rate cannot increase more than 5 percent over the entire loan.

Many flexible rate mortgages offer the possibility of rates that may go down as well as up. In some loans, if the rate can only increase 5 percent, it may only decrease 5 percent. If no limit is placed on how high the rate can go, there may be a provision that also allows your rate to go down along with the index.

Because of inflation, and because they limit the lender's return, capped rates may be difficult to find.

Payment Caps

Although your interest rate may increase on a flexible rate loan, your monthly payments may not necessarily rise, or they may increase by less than changes in the index require. This may occur because *the payments themselves are capped.*

For example, assume your mortgage provides for unlimited changes in your interest rate but your loan has a $50 per year cap on payment increases. You started with a 14 percent rate on your $50,000 mortgage and a monthly payment of $592.44. Now assume that your index increases 2 percentage points in the first year of your loan. Because of this, your rate increases to 16 percent, and your payments in the second year should rise to $671.80. Because of the payment cap, however, you'll only pay $642.44 per month in the second year.

But remember: A payment-capped loan doesn't mean you don't have to pay the difference. Negative amortization (see "Changing Rates" section) usually takes place with payment-capped loans to ensure that the lender eventually receives the full amount. In most payment-capped mortgages, the amount of principal paid off changes when interest rates fluctuate. Suppose you are paying $500 a month with $393 going toward interest, with your rate at 15 percent. Then your rate increases by 17 percent. This means your monthly payment should increase to $539, but because of a cap, it increases to only $525. Because this change in interest rates increases your debt, the lender may now apply a larger portion of your payment to interest. When rates get very high, even the full amount of your monthly payment ($525) won't be enough to cover the interest owed; the additional amount of interest you owe is added to the principal. This means you now owe—and eventually will pay—interest on interest.

Variations

One variation of the flexible rate mortgage is to fix the interest rate for a period of time—3 to 5 years, for example—with the understanding that the interest rate will then be *renegotiated*. Loans with periodically renegotiated rates are also called *rollover mortgages*. Such loans make monthly payments more predictable because the interest rate is fixed for a longer time.

Another variation is the *pledged account buy-down mortgage with a flexible rate*. This plan was recently introduced by the Federal National Mortgage Association (Fannie Mae), which buys mortgages from lenders and provides a major source of money for future mortgage offerings.

In this plan, a large initial payment is made to the lender at the time the loan is made. The payment can be made by the buyer, the builder, or anyone else willing to subsidize the loan. The payment is placed in an account with the lender where it earns interest. This plan helps lower your interest rate for the first year.

In one plan, it could lower your rate, for example, by 4 percent in the first year. If you borrowed $50,000 at 17 percent, for example, this would reduce your rate to 13 percent, and your monthly payments to $553.10, a savings of approximately $160 monthly. Then, for the next 5 years, your interest rate would only increase, for example, by 1 point each year. After that, your mortgage becomes a flexible rate mortgage with interest rate and payment changes every 5 years, based upon an index.

This plan does not include any payment or rate caps other than those in the first years. But, there also can be no negative amortization, so possible increases in your total debt are limited. Because of the buy-down feature, some buyers may be able to qualify for this loan who otherwise would not be eligible for financing.

Summary

In shopping for any type of flexible rate loan, remember to look for the following:

- the initial interest rate;
- how often the rate may change;
- how much the rate may change;
- the initial monthly payments;
- how often payments may change;
- how much the payments may change;
- the mortgage term;
- how often the term may change;
- how much the term may change;
- the index that rate, payment, or term changes are tied to; and,
- the limits, if any, on negative amortization.

Balloon Mortgage

Balloon mortgages have a series of equal monthly payments and a large final payment. Although there usually is a fixed interest rate, the equal payments may be for interest only. The unpaid balance, frequently the principal or the original amount you borrowed, comes due in a short period, usually 3 to 5 years.

For example, suppose you borrow $30,000 for 5 years. The interest rate is 15 percent, and the monthly payments are only $375. But in this example, the payments cover interest only, and the entire principal is due at maturity—in 5 years. That means you'll have to make 59 equal monthly payments of $375 each and a final balloon payment of $30,375. If you can't make that final payment, you'll have to refinance (if refinancing is available) or sell the property.

Some lenders guarantee refinancing when the balloon payment is

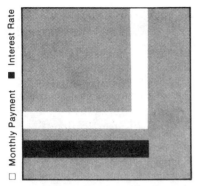

Year from the Date Loan Was Granted

Balloon Mortgage. Fixed interest rate; payments are also fixed but may apply only to interest. After short term, a final payment of principal is due.

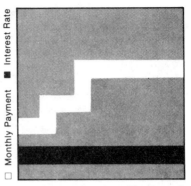

Year from the Date Loan Was Granted

Graduated Payment Mortgage. Fixed interest rate; payments rise gradually for first few years, then level off for duration of loan.

due although they do not guarantee a certain interest rate. The rate could be much higher than your current rate. Other lenders do not offer automatic refinancing. Without such a guarantee, you could be forced to start the whole business of shopping for housing money once again, as well as paying closing costs and front-end charges a second time.

A balloon note may also be offered by a private seller who is continuing to carry the mortgage he or she took out when purchasing the home. It can be used as a second mortgage where you also assume the seller's first mortgage.

Graduated Payment Mortgage

Graduated payment mortgages (GPM) are designed for home buyers who expect to be able to make larger monthly payments in the near future. During the early years of the loan, payments are relatively low. They are structured to rise at a set rate over a set period, say 5 or 10 years. Then they remain constant for the duration of the loan.

Even though the payments change, the interest rate is usually fixed. So during the early years, your payments are lower than the amount dictated by the interest rate. During the later years, the difference is made up by higher payments. At the end of the loan, you will have paid off your entire debt.

One variation of the GPM is the *graduated payment, flexible rate*

Growing Equity Mortgage. Fixed interest rate, but payments may rise according to agreed-upon schedule or an index. Increases are applied to principal, shortening term of loan.

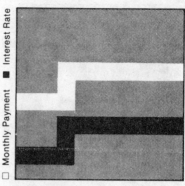

Fixed Rate Mortgage with Buy-down. Rate and payments are relatively low for first few years, then jump to reflect full rate in mortgage.

mortgage. This loan also has graduated payments early in the loan. But, like other flexible rate loans, it ties your interest rate to changes in an agreed-upon index. If interest rates climb quickly, greater negative amortization occurs during the period when payments are low. If rates continue to climb after that initial period, the payments will, too. This variation adds increased risk for the buyer. But if interest rates decline during the life of the loan, your payments may as well.

Growing Equity Mortgage (Rapid Payoff Mortgage)

The growing equity mortgage (GEM) and the rapid payoff mortgage are among the latest plans on the market. These mortgages combine a fixed interest rate with a changing monthly payment. The interest rate is usually a few percentage points below market. Although the mortgage term may run for 30 years, the loan will frequently be paid off in less than 15 years because payment increases are applied entirely to the principal.

Monthly payment changes are based on an agreed-upon schedule of increases or an index. For example, the plan might use the U.S. Commerce Department index that measures after-tax, per capita income, and your payments might increase at a specified portion of the change in this index, say 75 percent.

Suppose you're paying $500 per month. In this example, if the index increases by 8 percent, you will have to pay 75 percent of that, or 6 percent additional. Your payments will increase to $530, and the additional $30 you pay will be used to reduce your principal.

With this approach, your income must be able to keep pace with the increased payments. The plan does not offer long-term tax deductions. However, it can permit you to pay off your loan and acquire equity rapidly.

Shared Appreciation Mortgage

In the shared appreciation mortgage (SAM), you make monthly payments at a relatively low interest rate. You also agree to share with the lender a sizable percent (usually 30 percent to 50 percent) of the appreciation in your home's value when you sell or transfer the home, or after a specified number of years.

Because of the shared appreciation feature, monthly payments in this plan are lower than in many other plans. However, you may be liable for the dollar amount of the property's appreciation even if you do not wish to sell the property at the agreed-upon date. Unless you have the cash available, this could force an early sale of the property. Also, if property values do not increase as anticipated, you may still be liable for an additional amount of interest.

There are many variations of this idea, called *shared equity* plans. Some are offered by lending institutions and others by individuals. For example, suppose you've found a home for $100,000 in a neighborhood where property values are rising. The local savings and loan is charging 18 percent on home mortgages; assuming you paid $20,000 down and chose a 30-year term, your monthly payments would be $1,205.67, or about twice what you can afford. But a friend offers to help. Your friend will pay half of each monthly payment, or $600, for 5 years. At the end of that time, you both assume the house will be worth at least $125,000. You can sell it, and your friend can recover his or her share of the monthly payments to date plus half of the apprecation, or $12,500, for a total of $48,500. Or, you can pay your friend that same sum of money and gain increased equity in the house.

Another variation may give your partner tax advantages during the first years of the mortgage, after which the partnership is dissolved. (You can buy out your partner or find a new one.) Your partner helps make the purchase possible by putting up a sizable down payment and/or helping make the monthly payments. In return, your partner may be able to deduct a certain amount from his or her taxable income. Before proceeding with this type of plan, check with the Internal Revenue Service to determine the exact requirements.

Shared appreciation and shared equity mortgages were partly inspired by rising interest rates and partly by the notion that housing values would continue to grow over the years to come. If property values fall, these plans may not be available.

Assumable Mortgage

An assumable mortgage is a mortgage that can be passed on to a new owner at the previous owner's interest rate. For example, suppose you're interested in a $75,000 home. You make a down payment of $25,000, and you still owe $50,000. The owner of the home has paid off $20,000 of a $30,000, 10 percent mortgage. You assume the present owner's mortgage, which has $10,000 outstanding. You also make additional financing arrangements for the remaining $40,000, for example, by borrowing that amount from a mortgage company at the current market rate of 16 percent. Your overall interest rate is lower than the market rate because part of the money you owe is being repaid at 10 percent.

During periods of high rates, most lending institutions are reluctant to permit assumptions, preferring to write a new mortgage at the market rate. Some buyers and sellers are still using assumable mortgages, however. This has recently resulted in many lenders calling in the loans under "due on sale" clauses (see "Reading the Fine Print" section). Because these clauses have increasingly been upheld in court, many mortgages are no longer legally assumable. Be especially careful, therefore, if you are considering a mortgage represented as "assumable." Read the contract carefully and consider having an attorney or other expert check to determine if the lender has the right to raise your rate in these mortgages.

Seller Take-back

This mortgage, provided by the seller, is frequently a "second trust" and is combined with an assumed mortgage. The second trust (or "second mortgage") provides financing in addition to the first assumed mortgage, using the same property as collateral. (In the event of default, the second mortgage is satisfied after the first.) Seller take-backs frequently involve payments for interest only, with the principal due at maturity.

For example, suppose you want to buy a $150,000 home. The seller owes $70,000 on a 10 percent mortgage. You assume this mortgage and make a $30,000 down payment. You still need $50,000. So the seller gives you a second mortgage, or take-back, for $50,000 for 5 years at 14 percent (well below the market rate) with payments of $583.33. However, your payments are for interest only, and in 5 years you will have to pay $50,000. The seller take-back, in other words, may have enabled you to buy the home. But it may also have left you with a sizable balloon payment that must be paid off in the near future.

Some private sellers are also offering first trusts as take-backs. In this approach, the seller finances the major portion of the loan and takes back a mortgage on the property.

A new development may now enable private sellers to provide this type of financing more frequently. Previously, sellers offering take-backs were required to carry the loan to full term before obtaining their equity. However, now, if an institutional lender arranges the loan, uses standardized forms, and meets certain other requirements, the owner take-back can be sold immediately to Fannie Mae. This approach enables the seller to obtain equity promptly and avoid having to collect monthly payments.

Wraparound

Another variation on the second mortgage is the wraparound. Suppose you'd like to buy a $75,000 condominium and can make a $25,000 down payment, but can't afford the payments at the current rate (18 percent) on the remaining $50,000. The present owners have a $30,000, 10 percent mortgage. They offer you a $50,000 wraparound mortgage at 14 percent. The new loan *wraps around* the existing $30,000 mortgage, adding $20,000 to it. You make all your payments to the second lender or the seller, who then forwards payments for the first mortgage. You'll pay the equivalent of 10 percent on the $30,000 to the first lender, plus an additional 4 percent on this amount to the second lender, plus 14 percent on the remaining $20,000. Your total loan costs using this approach will be lower than if you obtained a loan for the full amount at the current rate (for example, 18 percent).

Wraparounds may cause problems if the original lender or the holder of the original mortgage is not aware of the new mortgage. Upon discovering this arrangement, some lenders or holders may have the right to insist that the old mortgage be paid off immediately.

Land Contract

Borrowed from commercial real estate, this plan enables you to pay below-market interest rates. The installment land contract permits the seller to hold onto his or her original below-market rate mortgage while "selling" the home on an installment basis. The installment payments are for a short term and may be for interest only. At the end of the contract the unpaid balance, frequently the full purchase price, must still be paid.

The seller continues to hold title to the property until all payments are made. Thus, you, the buyer, acquire no equity until the contract ends. If you fail to make a payment on time, you could lose a major investment.

These loans are popular because they offer lower payments than market rate loans. Land contracts are also being used to avoid the due on sale clause (see "Reading the Fine Print" section). The buyer and seller may assert to the lender who provided the original mortgage that the due on sale clause does not apply because the property will not be sold until the end of the contract. Therefore, the low interest rate continues. However, the lender may assert that the contract in fact represents a sale of the property. Consequently, the lender may have the right to accelerate the loan or call it due, and raise the interest rate to current market levels.

Buy-down

A buy-down is a subsidy of the mortgage interest rate that helps you meet the payments during the first few years of the loan. Suppose

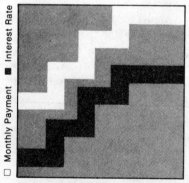

Year from the Date Loan Was Granted

Flexible Rate Mortgage with Buy-down. Rate and payments are initially low, then jump and may change throughout loan depending on changes in the index.

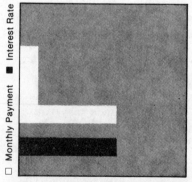

Year from the Date Loan Was Granted

Zero or Low Rate Mortgage. No interest or low fixed rate. Requires substantial down payment and rapid repayment in equal installments.

a new house sells for $150,000. After a down payment of $75,000, you still need to finance $75,000. A 30-year first mortgage is available for 17 percent which would make your monthly payments $1,069.26, or beyond your budget. However, a buy-down is available: For the first three years, the developer will subsidize your payments, bringing down the interest rate to 14 percent. This means your payments are only $888.65, which you can afford.

There are several things to think about in buy-downs. First, consider what your payments will be after the first few years. If this is a fixed rate loan, the payments in the above example will jump to the rate at which the loan was originally made—17 percent—and total more than $1,000. If this is a flexible rate loan, and the index to which your rate is tied has risen since you took out the loan, your payments could go up even higher.

Second, check, to see whether the subsidy is part of your contract with the lender or with the builder. If it's provided separately by the builder, the lender can still hold you liable for the full interest rate (17 percent in the above example), even if the builder backs out of the deal or goes out of business.

Finally, that $150,000 sales price may have been increased to cover the builder's interest subsidy. A comparable home may be selling around the corner for less. At the same time, competition may have encouraged the builder to offer you a genuine savings. It pays to check around.

There are also plans called consumer buy-downs. In these loans, the buyer makes a sizable down payment, and the interest rate granted is below market. In other words, in exchange for a large payment at the beginning of the loan, you may qualify for a lower rate on the amount borrowed. Frequently, this type of mortgage has a shorter term than those written at current market rates.

Rent with Option to Buy

In a climate of changing interest rates, some buyers and sellers are attracted to a rent-with-option arrangement. In this plan, you rent property and pay a premium for the right to purchase the property within a limited time period at a specific price. In some arrangements, you may apply part of the rental payments to the purchase price.

This approach enables you to lock in the purchase price. You can also use this method to "buy time" in the hope that interest rates will decrease. From the seller's perspective, this plan may provide the buyer time to obtain sufficient cash or acceptable financing to proceed with a purchase that may not be possible otherwise.

Zero Rate and Low Rate Mortgage

These mortgages are unique in that they appear to be completely or almost interest free. The buyer makes a large down payment, usually one-third of the sales price, and pays the remainder in installments over a short term.

Suppose you want to buy a $90,000 home but you find the market interest rate unacceptable. You opt to use your savings to make the down payment, say $30,000, on a zero rate (or no-interest) mortgage. Then you pay a front-end finance charge—for example, 12 percent of the money you need to borrow, or about $8,400. You then agree to repay the principal ($60,000) in 84 monthly installments of $714.29. In 7 years, the loan will be paid off.

In these mortgages, the sales price may be increased to reflect the loan costs. Thus, you could be exchanging lower interest costs for a higher purchase price. Partly because of this, you may be able to deduct the prepaid finance charge and a percentage (for example, 10 percent) of your payments from your taxes as if it were interest. Before going ahead with these plans, however, you or your attorney may want to check with the IRS to determine if your mortgage qualifies for this tax treatment.

Reverse Annuity Mortgage

If you already own your home and need to obtain cash, you might consider the reverse annuity mortgage (RAM) or "equity conversion." In this plan, you obtain a loan in the form of monthly payments over an extended period of time, using your property as collateral. When the loan comes due, you repay both the principal and interest.

A RAM is not a mortgage in the conventional sense. You can't obtain a RAM until you have paid off your original mortgage. Suppose you own your home and you need a source of money. You could draw up a contract with a lender that enables you to borrow a given amount each month until you've reached a maximum of, for example, $10,000. At the end of the term, you must repay the loan. But remember, if you do not have the cash available to repay the loan plus interest, you will have to sell the property or take out a new loan.

Changing Rates

Lenders use indexes to decide when to raise or lower the interest rate on a flexible rate mortgage. For example, when the financial index your lender uses rises, the interest rate on your mortgage may also increase—it depends on how the index is applied. Fluctuations in the interest rate can change your monthly payments, mortgage length, or principal balance.

Some of today's most frequently used indexes are:

- *the rate on 6-month Treasury bills,* or on *3-year Treasury notes* (or how much the U.S. Treasury is willing to pay on money it borrows);
- *the Federal Home Loan Bank Board's national average mortgage contract rate* charged by major lenders on the purchase of previously occupied homes (or how much people are paying on new mortgages nationwide); and,
- *the average costs of funds* for savings and loans insured by the Federal Savings and Loan Insurance Corporation (or how much lending institutions are paying on the money they borrow).

Some indexes reflect what the market will bear across the country; others reflect local trends. Also, some money indexes are controlled solely by individual lenders. The index you select should be one that can be verified easily; its past performance may give you an indication of how stable it is. Have someone with expertise translate past and potential changes into dollars and cents.

Also find out how the index is used. For example, if the index changes monthly, is the lender also changing the rate on your loan monthly? Or, are there limits on the number of times and/or the amount your rate can fluctuate?

Finally, check how much advance warning the lender will give you before your new rate and/or new payments go into effect.

Reading the Fine Print

Before going ahead with a creative home loan, you may want to have a lawyer or other expert help you interpret the fine print. You may also want to consider some of the situations you could face when paying off your loan or selling your property. Also, make sure you understand the terms in your agreement—such as *acceleration, due on sale* clauses, and *waivers.*

An *acceleration clause* allows the lender to speed up the rate at which your loan comes due. Suppose you've missed a payment, and your contract gives the lender the right to "accelerate" the loan when a payment is missed. This means that the lender now has the power to force you to repay the entire loan immediately.

Here, taken from a mortgage contract, is a sample acceleration clause: *"In the event any installment of this note is not paid when due, time being of the essence, and such installment remains unpaid for thirty (30) days, the Holder of this Note may, at its option, without notice or demand, declare the entire principal sum then unpaid, together with secured interest and late charges thereon, immediately due and payable. The lender may without further notice or demand invoke the power of sale and any other remedies permitted by applicable law."*

Note the use of the term "without notice" above. If this contract provision is legal in your state, you have *waived* your right to notice. In other words, you've given up the right to be notified of some occurrence—for example, a missed payment. If you've waived your right to notice of delinquency or default, and you've made a late payment, action may be initiated against you before you've been told; the lender may even start to foreclose.

Know whether your contract waives your right to notice. If so, obtain a clear understanding in advance of what you're giving up. And consider having your attorney check state law to determine if the waiver is legal.

A *due on sale* clause gives the lender the right to require immediate repayment of the balance you owe if the property changes hands. Here's an example of a due on sale clause: *"If all or any part of the Property or an interest therein is sold or transferred by Borrower without Lender's prior written consent . . . Lender may, at Lender's option, declare all the sums secured by this Mortgage to be immediately due and payable."*

Due on sale clauses have been included in many mortgage contracts for years. They are being enforced by lenders increasingly when buyers try to assume sellers' existing low rate mortgages. In these cases, the courts have frequently upheld the lender's right to raise the interest rate to the prevailing market level. So be especially careful when considering an "assumable mortgage." If your agreement has a due on sale provision, the assumption may not be legal, and you could be liable for thousands of additional dollars.

Losing Ground

Repaying debt gradually through payments of principal and interest is called amortization. Today's economic climate has given rise to a reverse process called negative amortization.

Negative amortization means that you are losing—not gaining—value, or equity. This is because your monthly payments may be too low to cover the interest rate agreed upon in the mortgage contract. Instead of paying the full interest costs now, you'll pay them later— either in larger payments or in more payments. You will also be paying interest on that interest.

In other words, the lender postpones collection of the money you owe by increasing the size of your debt. In extreme cases, you may even lose the equity you purchased with your down payment, leaving you in worse financial shape a few years after you purchase your home than when you bought it.

Suppose you signed a flexible rate mortgage for $50,000 in 1978. The index established your initial rate at 9.15 percent. It nearly doubled to 17.39 percent by 1981. If your monthly payments had kept pace with the index, they would have risen from $408 to $722. But because of a payment cap they stayed at $408. By 1981 your mortgage has swelled from $50,000 to $58,350, even though you've dutifully paid $408 every month for 48 months. In other words, you have paid out $20,000 but you are $8,000 more in debt than you were in 1978.

Certain loans, such as graduated payment mortgages, are structured so that you regain the lost ground with payments that eventually rise high enough to fully pay off your debt. And you may also be able to pay off the extra costs if your home is gaining rapidly in value or if your income is rising fast enough to meet the increased obligation. But if it isn't, you may realize a loss if, for example, you sign a below-market flexible rate mortgage in January and try to sell the home in August when interest rates are higher. You could end up owing more than you'd make on the sale.

Tables

Table A
DECLINE IN PURCHASING POWER OF THE DOLLAR

Using 1984 dollars, here is how the purchasing power of that dollar erodes at the inflation rates indicated. For example, at an annual inflation rate of 7 percent, one 1984 dollar will be worth 34 cents in 1999.

YEAR	INFLATION RATE				
	6%	7%	8%	9%	10%
1984	$1.00	$1.00	$1.00	$1.00	$1.00
1985	.94	.93	.92	.91	.90
1990	.69	.65	.61	.57	.53
1995	.51	.45	.40	.35	.31
1999	.37	.34	.29	.24	.21

Table B
INCOME GROWTH RATE REQUIRED TO KEEP PACE WITH INFLATION

In order to remain *even* with the inflation rates shown in the above table, you would have to maintain a growth of at least the following rates. For example, at a 10 percent inflation rate, it will take $415 in 1999 to purchase what $100 does in 1984.

YEAR	INFLATION RATE				
	6%	7%	8%	9%	10%
1984	$100	$100	$100	$100	$100
1985	106	107	108	109	110
1990	142	150	159	168	177
1995	190	210	233	258	285
1999	240	276	317	364	418

Table C
COMPOUND INTEREST—CUMULATIVE EFFECT

If you invest one dollar at the beginning of each year at the percent indicated, your money will compound as shown. For example, after ten years one dollar per year at 12 percent will have grown to $19.65.

End of Year	8%	10%	12%	14%	16%
5	6.34	6.72	7.11	7.53	7.98
10	15.65	17.53	19.65	22.04	24.73
15	29.32	34.94	41.75	49.97	59.92
20	49.42	62.99	80.69	103.75	133.83
25	78.95	108.17	149.32	207.32	289.08
30	122.35	180.93	270.27	406.72	615.15
35	186.10	298.11	483.44	790.65	1300.00

Table D
AVERAGE ANNUAL RETURN ON ORIGINAL INVESTMENT

When you consider the *average* annual return on untaxed interest, the result can be startling. For example, by compounding the return rate of 10 percent over a 20 year period, the return averages 28.6 percent per year. With IRA and Keogh plans, this is the type of result one may reasonably expect.

Rate of Return	5 Yrs.	10 Yrs.	15 Yrs.	20 Yrs.
8%	9.4%	11.6%	14.5%	18.3%
9%	10.8%	13.7%	17.6%	23.0%
10%	12.2%	15.9%	21.1%	28.6%
11%	13.7%	18.4%	25.2%	35.3%
12%	15.2%	21.0%	29.8%	43.2%

Table E
HOW YOUR IRA CAN GROW

Here are examples, using the current maximum annual investments, of how your IRA can grow over 10-, 20-, and 30-year periods at 8 and 12 percent.

Annual Interest Rate	Period Covered	$2,000 Individual Taxpayer	$2,250 Married, One Wage Earner	$4,000 Married, Two Wage Earners
8%	10 Years	$ 32,183	$ 36,113	$ 64,201
8%	20 Years	104,346	117,389	208,693
8%	30 Years	266,942	300,309	533,883
12%	10 Years	$ 41,174	$ 46,658	$ 82,849
12%	20 Years	181,460	204,142	392,920
12%	30 Years	653,941	735,683	1,307,882

(Based upon annual interest rates, compounded daily)

Some Key References

Below is a list of references that helped us to varying degrees as we prepared this book. As a result of the economic turmoil of recent years, some of the figures and examples stated within them are obsolete (a homeowner's loan for 8 percent, for instance); but the ideas within them are sound. On the other hand, we made a last-ditch effort to ensure that, where the changes were important, we based our book upon information from current popular references.

You may well place different values upon individual sources than we have. Perhaps that is because we used them for different purposes. But our common purpose is a smooth transition to civilian life. With that in mind, we suggest that you consider the following:

What Color Is Your Parachute? by Richard Nelson Bolles. This book has become the best-selling career changer's book, and deservedly so. Although it is a serious book about a serious business, for those who are accustomed to heavy military reading it may seem a little "flip" at first. Within it is most of the information you will need for establishing some orientation in your job search. The reference section is worth the price of the book. We also recommend Bolles' other books (see Bibliography), but this one is essential. Updated annually.

Everyone's Money Book by Jane Bryant Quinn. You probably already have one of these. It is about the handiest available reference, and it's written in plain English. Quinn's book is great for day-to-day situations and for long-range planning as well.

Dress for Success by John T. Molloy has become a classic in its own right. Pay attention.

If you're going to travel by "Space A," we recommend Connie Connor's book, *Space A* for the human side, combined with *Military Space-A Air Opportunities Around the World* for the "technical" side of the process. With the two of them, you can go anywhere.

The market abounds with references on how to invest your money and get rich. For some of the authors, their secret is selling books to those who will believe them. For basic financial guidance, we'll stay with the old standby: Benjamin Graham's *The Intelligent Investor*.

Those who want a retirement book that looks forward to *real* retirement should read Grace W. Weinstein's *Life Plans*. Not only is she an expert, but her discussion of some difficult decisions is brilliantly done. A good book for long-range planning.

The Retired Military Almanac is a valuable reference for military retirees. It is loaded with cold, hard facts and is updated annually. Every military retiree should have one handy. It's very impressive.

Resume writing is big business. Any two references will disagree on many points. We like Bostwick's *Resume Writing*.

The best source of information in the United States is the federal government. There are now several guides to the government on the commercial market. The information in those references is available free (or at a much lower price) from the government itself. Turn to your government first (Veterans Administration, Federal Trade Commission, etc.); you'll probably find the answer there.

Bibliography

Albert, Kenneth J. *How to Pick the Right Small Business Opportunity*. New York: McGraw-Hill Book Co., 1980. Associates in the Social Sciences.

Barnes, John. *More Money for Your Retirement*. New York: Barnes and Noble Books, 1980.

Bayless, Hugh. *The Best Towns in America*. Boston: Houghton Mifflin Co., 1983.

Biles, George E. *So . . . You're Hanging It Up!* Rutherford, N.J.: Alternate Choice, 1980.

Block, Julian. *Tax Saving: A Year-Round Guide*. Radnor, Pa.: Chilton Book Co., 1982.

Boll, Carl R. *Executive Jobs Unlimited*. New York: MacMillan Publishing Co., 1979.

Bolles, Richard Nelson. *What Color Is Your Parachute?* Berkeley, California: Ten Speed Press, 1983.

———. *Where Do I Go from Here with My Life?* New York: The Seabury Press, 1974.

———. *The Three Boxes of Life*. Berkeley, Calif.: Ten Speed Press, 1978.

Bostwick, Burdette E. *Resume Writing*. New York: John Wiley & Sons, 1982.

Boyer, Richard, and Savageau, David. *Places Rated Almanac*. Chicago: Rand McNally and Co., 1981.

———. *Places Rated Retirement Guide*. Chicago: Rand McNally and Co., 1983.

Brandt, Steven C. *Entrepreneuring*. New York: New American Library, 1982.

"Can You Afford to Retire" *Newsweek*, 1 June 1981, p. 24.

Carter, Malcolm N. "Getting Bargain Houses on the Auction Block." *Money*, March 1982, p. 14.

Casey, Douglas. *Crisis Investing*. New York: Pocket Books division of Simon & Schuster, 1980.

CHAMPUS Handbook. CHAMPUS publication 6010.46-H, Aurora, Colo., 1983.

Cohen, Jerome B. *Personal Finance*. Homewood, Ill.: Richard D. Irwin, 1979.

Connor, Connie Gibson Wehrman. *Space A*. Oakton, Va.: Military Travel News, 1980.

Crawford, William, and Crawford, Lela Ann. *Military Space-A Air Opportunities Around the World*. Arlington, Va., 1983.

Federal Benefits for Veterans and Dependents. Veterans Administration Fact Sheet IS-1. Washington: Government Printing Office, 1984.

"Get Into an I.R.A.!" *Consumers Digest*, May/June 1982, p. 14.

Golden, James R., and Taylor, William R., eds. *The Officer's Manual of Personal Finance and Insurance*. Harrisburg, Pa.: Stackpole Books, 1979.

Gordon, Sol, ed. *Retired Military Almanac*. Washington: Uniformed Services Almanac, 1984.

Gourgues, Harold W. *Financial Planning Handbook*. New York: Institute of Finance, 1983.

Graham, Benjamin. *The Intelligent Investor*. New York: Harper and Row, 1973.

Grisham, Roy A. Jr., and McConaughy, Paul D., eds. *Encyclopedia of U.S. Government Benefits*. New York: Everest House, 1981.

Hallman, G. Victor, and Rosenbloom, Jerry S. *Personal Financial Planning*. New York: McGraw-Hill Book Co., 1983.

Harris, Louis and Associates, Inc. *1979 Study of American Attitudes Toward Pensions and Retirement*. New York: Johnson and Higgins, 1979.

Hayman, Harry S. "Special Edition SBP Open Enrollment." *The Retired Officer*, December 1982, p. 35.

Hazard, John W. "Managing Your Money: How Investing Can Save Taxes." *U.S. News & World Report*, 15 February 1982, p. 73.

Information Please Almanac. New York: Simon & Schuster, 1981.

Kamoroff, Bernard. *Small-Time Operator*. Laytonville, Calif.: Bell Springs Publishing, 1983.

LeClair, Robert T. et al. *Money and Retirement—How to Plan for Lifetime Financial Security*. Reading, Mass.: Addison-Wesley Publishing Co., 1982.

Loeb, Marshall. *Marshall Loeb's Money Guide*. Boston: Little, Brown, and Co., 1983.

Looking Ahead—How to Plan Your Successful Retirement. Washington: Action for Independent Maturity, a dvision of the American Association of Retired Persons, 1981.

Mancuso, Joseph R. *How to Start, Finance, and Manage Your Own Small Business*. Englewood Cliffs, N.J.: Prentice-Hall, 1978.

McDonald, Thomas F. "Early Retirement:I. Few Are Ready for the 'Silver Bullet'." *Army Times,* 11 July 1977, p. 1.

———. "Early Retirement:II. 'An Absence of the Expected Role'." *Army Times,* 18 July 1977, p. 15.

Meyer, Dyke F., and Yohey, Walter A. Jr. *1982 Financial Planning Guide for Military Personnel*. San Antonio: AFTAC Enterprises, 1982.

Michelmore, Peter, "The New Investment Opportunity No One Should Miss." *Reader's Digest,* December 1981, p. 99.

Miller, Theodore J., ed. *Make Your Money Grow*. (A Kiplinger Changing Times Book.) Washington: Dell Publishing Co., 1983.

Molloy, John T. *Dress for Success*. New York: Warner Books, 1980.

Mortgage Money Guide, The. Federal Trade Commission, Division of Credit Practices. Washington: Government Printing Office, 1982.

Nelson, Paula. *Where to Get Money for Everything*. New York: William Morrow and Co., 1982.

Nyman, Keith O. *Re-Entry: Turning Military Experience into Civilian Success*. Harrisburg, Pa.: Stackpole Books, 1982.

Otte, Elmer. *Inherit Your Own Money*. New York: David McKay Co., 1978.

———. *Rehearse Before You Retire*. Appleton, Wis.: Retirement Research, 1977.

———. *Retirement Rehearsal Guidebook*. Indianapolis: Pictorial, 1976.

Payne, Richard A. *How to Get a Better Job Quicker*. New York: Mentor Books, 1980.

Porter, Sylvia. *Sylvia Porter's New Money Book for the 80's*. New York: Avon Books, 1980.

Prentice-Hall. *Concise Explanation of the Economic Recovery Tax Act of 1981*. Englewood Cliffs, N.J., 1981.

Quinn, Jane Bryant. *Everyone's Money Book*. New York: Dell Publishing Co., 1980.

"Real Estate Agents Who Work for *Buyers*." *Changing Times,* August 1982, p. 38.

Reed, Jean, ed. *Resumes That Get Jobs*. New York: Arco Publishing Co., 1983.

Research Institute of America. *The RIA Personal Inflation Guide*. New York, 1982.

Robbins, Paula I. *Successful Midlife Career Change*. New York: AMACOM, 1978.

Schwartz, Joseph. *Don't Ever Retire but Do It Early and Often*. New York: Farnsworth Publishing Co., 1979.

Sheehy, Gail. *Passages*. New York: Bantam Books, 1981.

———. *Pathfinders*. New York: Bantam Books, 1981.

Sumichrast, Michael, and Shafer, Ronald G. *The Complete Book of Home Buying*. New York: Bantam Books. Published by arrangement with Dow Jones-Irwin Co., 1982.

Tannenhauser, Robert, and Tannenhauser, Carol. *Tax Shelters—A Complete Guide*. New York: Signet, 1980.

"The Battle to Save Social Security." *U.S. News & World Report*, 20 July 1981, p. 41.

"The Condo Option." *Changing Times*, April 1982, p. 33.

Tobias, Andrew. *The Only Investment Guide You'll Ever Need*. New York: Bantam Books, 1980.

Toffler, Alvin. *Future Shock*. New York: Random House, 1970.

Tuhy, Carrie, "Bold Moves That Paid Off." *Money*, May 1982, p. 53.

U.S. Department of Defense. *Department of Defense Directive 5500.7*. Washington: 15 January 1977.

U.S. Department of Defense, Office of the Actuary, Defense Manpower Data Center. *DOD Statistical Report on the Military Retirement System, FY 1980*. Alexandria, Va.: Defense Manpower Data Center, 1981.

U.S. Laws, Statutes, etc., *United States Code. Vol. 1, Title 38. Veterans' Benefits*. Washington: Government Printing Office, 1981.

Weinstein, Grace W. *Life Plans*. New York: Holt, Rinehart and Winston, 1979.

Index